THE AFTERMATH OF WAR
World War I and U.S. Policy
Toward Latin America

THE AFTERMATH OF WAR

World War I and U.S. Policy
Toward Latin America

by

JOSEPH S. TULCHIN

1971

New York: New York University Press

Introduction

The basic features of the Latin American policy of the United States after 1918 were determined by American experiences during World War I. Dependence upon foreign powers for fuel, investment capital, and communications was considered tantamount to political dependence and a potential threat to the nation's security. The crusade to make the world "safe for democracy" disillusioned Americans with the protectorate solution to the problems of instability in the hemisphere. After the war, the government made ending America's dependence upon foreign powers for petroleum, capital, and cables a strategic objective of policy and, in crisis after crisis, sought to withdraw from the existing protectorates and to avoid any escalation of American involvement in the internal affairs of other nations. The absence of a threat from Europe, together with America's uncontested hegemony in the hemisphere, meant there was less cause than at any time since the war with Spain to commit the power and prestige of the United States to the resolution of hemispheric disputes. The problem for policymakers after the war was to strike a careful balance between pressure and influence; to protect America's expanded interests in the hemisphere without having to assume formal control over another sovereign state.

The strategic objectives in petroleum, loans, and cables

were achieved by 1925, the terminal year for this study. As American dependence declined, the State Department dulled the edge of its enthusiasm for protecting the rights of private interests abroad and insisted on no greater advantage for Americans than equal opportunity—the "open door." It violated this pattern only in the Caribbean, which it persisted in considering a sphere of special interest. Both the Democratic and Republican administrations tried to make the pattern of United States behavior in the Caribbean consistent with behavior in South America and in other areas of the world. Sometimes they succeeded, as in Cuba, Haiti, and the Dominican Republic, where the first steps were taken to end American intervention. Other times, as in Honduras and Nicaragua, the pull of habit and the fear of chaos were too strong, and overcame the State Department's reluctance to become entangled in hemispheric disputes.

One striking feature of Latin American policy during this period warrants mention by way of warning to the reader. With very few exceptions, the United States government formulated and executed foreign policy without reference to the demands or responses of the Latin American nations. Though the latter tried to use the League of Nations and the Pan American movement to undermine United States paramountcy in the hemisphere, the United States had no trouble neutralizing the effect of multilateral organizations in the hemisphere and seemed to ignore the reactions of other nations in making decisions. This insulation from outside forces gives the process of formulating policy an academic quality.

The research for this book was facilitated by the courtesy of the staffs of the Yale and Harvard University libraries, the staff of the Manuscript Division of the Library of Congress, and the staff of the National Archives, Washington, D.C. Special mention must be made of Ronald L. Heise, whose unfailing kindness and intelligence smoothed the path of everyone who entered the Diplomatic, Legal, and Fiscal Records Division of the National Archives. A grant from the Henry L. Stimson Fund, through the Concilium on International Studies of Yale University, made it possible for me to work in Washington. I owe a great deal to Ernest R. May, who first suggested this study and helped me through its various stages; to David F. Trask and Gaddis Smith, who read the manuscript and helped me improve it; and to Robin W. Winks, who gave me the benefit of his valuable counsel on innumerable occasions.

Contents

List of Abbreviations

LC	Library of Congress
WTB	War Trade Board
ONI	Office of Naval Intelligence
SS	Secretary of State
SecNav	Secretary of the Navy
SecTreas	Secretary of the Treasury
SecCom	Secretary of Commerce
DS	Department of State
HAHR	*Hispanic American Historical Review*

THE AFTERMATH OF WAR
World War I and U.S. Policy
Toward Latin America

CHAPTER 1

Adjusting to War

The Great War in Europe presented the United States with a golden opportunity to establish its hegemony in Latin America. Ever since the war with Spain, the United States had been concerned to protect its interests in what was known as the Caribbean Danger Zone. The Latin American policy of the United States had been predicated upon the assumption that South America and the Caribbean were fundamentally different areas and required distinct policies. Military strategists, diplomats, and Presidents Theodore Roosevelt, William Howard Taft, and Woodrow Wilson accepted the boundary of American strategic interests marked by Captain Alfred Thayer Mahan at the Amazon River. After 1914, the war in Europe left the United States virtually free from fear of outside intervention and opened the way to the expansion of American influence in the rest of the hemisphere. The focus of foreign-policy debate shifted from the proper way to eliminate the prime causes of intervention in the Caribbean—political instability and fiscal irresponsibility—to a consideration of how the government should help American business interests assume the paramount role once played by Europeans caught up in the mobilization efforts of their own nations. The sphere of United States interest now included the entire Western Hemisphere. The government realized that it was neither

3

willing nor able to enforce the same kind of rigid control in all of the hemisphere that it maintained in the Caribbean. The problem was to develop a policy which would protect the nation's influence without overcommitting its resources.[1]

Wilson never questioned the need to forestall European intervention near the Panama Canal. He accepted the responsibility of a special sphere of American influence. However, he doubted the efficacy of the Roosevelt Corollary and distrusted the business interests which were so important to dollar diplomacy. To emphasize his differences with Taft and the Republicans, Wilson announced publicly soon after his inauguration that he would not recognize the unconstitutional and unjust government of Victoriano Huerta in Mexico and that he would not lend the influence of his administration to the consortium of American bankers doing business with China. The United States would extend its influence around the world by its example; it would teach the world to be democratic. Wilson objected to the China loan because:

> The conditions of the loan seem to us to touch very nearly the administrative independence of China itself, and this administration does not feel that it ought, even by implication, to be a party to those conditions. . . . The responsibility on the part of our Government implied in the encouragement of a loan thus secured and administered is plain enough and is obnoxious to the principles upon which the government of our people rests.[2]

[1] Report of Adm. George Dewey to SecNav, "Power and Influence of the United States in the Caribbean and South America," June 25, 1901, "Records of the General Board," File No. 433, Serial No. 171; General Board memorandum, April 4, 1917, "Main and Advanced Bases in the Caribbean for use in War with Germany," File No. 408, Serial No. 696; J. A. S. Grenville, "Diplomacy and War Plans in the United States, 1890–1917," *Royal Historical Society Transactions,* ser. 5, vol. II (1961), 1–21.

[2] *Papers Relating to the Foreign Relations of the United States* (Washington, D. C., 1861–   ), 1913, 170–71 and 7. Hereafter this series of published documents is referred to simply as *Foreign Relations,* with the appropriate year. Samuel Flagg Bemis, "Woodrow Wilson and

Wilson and his first secretary of state, William Jennings
Bryan, soon discovered that it was not so easy to reverse the
policies of their predecessors. They tried to break a pattern
of increasing American intervention in the Caribbean. Instead, by 1917, the United States twice had gone to the brink
of war with Mexico, had taken complete control of Santo
Domingo and Haiti, and had reduced Nicaragua to protectorate status. So long as the United States took upon itself the
responsibility for order and stability in the Caribbean, the
government seemed powerless to avoid the escalation of
American involvement in the internal affairs of nations in
the Caribbean Danger Zone.

Very soon after he took up his duties, Bryan tried to apply
Wilson's general statements on democracy in Latin America
to a financial crisis in Nicaragua. He was convinced that if
something were not done quickly, the Nicaraguan government would sink into bankruptcy. His first proposal was to
negotiate a treaty with Nicaragua that would give the United
States an option on the old canal route through Lake Nicaragua and along the San Juan River. In return, the United
States would give Nicaragua sufficient funds to relieve her
financial difficulties. At the insistence of the Nicaraguans,
Bryan consented to include in the treaty the Platt Amendment provision by which the United States would guarantee
the political stability of Nicaragua. As an alternative to the
treaty, Bryan devised a scheme to relieve all Caribbean nations from extortionist bankers. He would give the United
States new influence in the hemisphere and yet avoid the
direct responsibilities of the Platt Amendment. He proposed
that the United States government lend money to the under-
developed nations at 4½ percent interest and then float its

Latin America," in *American Foreign Policy and the Blessings of
Liberty and Other Essays* (New Haven, 1962), 384; Wilfred H. Callcott,
The Caribbean Policy of the United States, 1890–1920 (Baltimore,
1942), 317–18; William S. Coker, "Dollar Diplomacy versus Constitutional Legitimacy," *Southern Quarterly,* 6 (1968), 428–37, for Wilson's
attitude toward revolutions and unconstitutional governments; Frank
Freidel, *Franklin D. Roosevelt,* 3 vols. (Boston, 1952   ), I. *The apprenticeship,* 237–38, for Bryan's willingness to dispatch boats to protect
American interests.

own bonds in the United States at 3 percent interest, using the difference in interest rates to amortize the Central American bonds. The president refused to accept the enormous financial responsibilities that went along with this scheme. He had already rejected the China Consortium, which implied much less government involvement.[3]

When the Senate rejected the proposed canal option treaty on August 2, 1913, Bryan had to permit Nicaragua to get money from private sources. He brought the project to the attention of several bankers because he believed Brown Brothers and Company, the firm that had handled Nicaragua's business in the past, had exacted onerous terms in their earlier dealings with the Nicaraguans. Negotiations to interest new bankers proved tedious, and conditions in Nicaragua were critical, so the government was forced to deal with Brown Brothers. A contract was signed on October 8, 1913, against Bryan's advice and in the face of State Department criticisms of specific provisions of the contract. Under the contract, the secretary of state agreed to appoint a director and an examiner for the Nicaraguan National Bank and the Nicaraguan Railroad, which were financed by the loan. In so doing, Bryan committed the United States government to greater responsibility for Nicaraguan affairs than it had ever assumed before, responsibility which his predecessors probably would have sought to avoid. Bryan continued the pattern of existing dollar diplomacy because he could see no other way to obtain the financial help which Nicaragua needed. He did not give up his own financial scheme and took every Latin American loan project as an opportunity to pester the president with it. Wilson rejected the plan, once and for all, on March 20, 1914.

When Wilson took office, Latin Americans did most of their trading and borrowing in Europe. American bankers and businessmen complained that this was so because their

[3] Selig Adler, "Bryan and Wilsonian Caribbean Penetration," *Hispanic American Historical Review*, XX, 2 (1940); Arthur S. Link, *Woodrow Wilson*, 5 vols. (Princeton, 1947–   ), II, 331–42; Dana G. Munro, *Intervention and Dollar Diplomacy in the Caribbean* (Princeton, 1964), 160–216 and 388–406.

government would not give them adequate support. By 1913, complaints from the business community were growing louder and more frequent, even though American economic interests in Latin America were greater than any other nation in the world, and the United States was increasing its share of the market faster than its competitors. The United States investment stake in the area increased from a negligible amount before 1900 to $1.6 billion in 1914. In this situation, more and more businessmen called upon the government to expand its special sphere of interest beyond the Caribbean and to end the governmental neglect which, they claimed, placed North American businessmen abroad at a marked disadvantage with their European competition. The government was not unwilling to extend American influence beyond the Caribbean. It proceeded with caution in order to establish a balance between influence and involvement.[4]

Requests for a more aggressive policy came in to the Department of the Treasury and the Department of Commerce as well as to the Department of State, and all three secretaries were sympathetic in their responses. Secretary of the Treasury William Gibbs McAdoo advocated extending Caribbean dollar diplomacy to the entire hemisphere. In January 1915, he asked the State Department to accept a Peruvian loan contract which would bind the Peruvian government, in the event of any default of payment, to request the secretary of state to designate a citizen of the United States to take control of the *Recaudadora,* or tax-collecting company. The president did not think it proper to take on this exercise of political power in behalf of private parties, any more than

[4] Report by W. H. Lough, commercial agent of the Bureau of Foreign and Domestic Commerce, Nov.–Dec., 1914, transmitted to the Department of State by SecCom Redfield, "General Records of the Department of State," National Archives Record Group 59, Decimal File 820.51/orig. Hereafter, State Department records are referred to by record group, decimal file number, and date. The complaint against lack of government support is discussed in Munro, *Intervention and Dollar Diplomacy,* 15; articles by J. A. Farrell, J. H. Hammond, and E. E. Pratt, *The Annals,* 60 (July 1915); *Babson's Report,* April 27, 1915, "Investment Opportunities in Latin America," the William Gibbs McAdoo papers, Box 544, LC.

he had in the Nicaraguan negotiations, and Secretary Bryan
agreed with him. Peru was not in the Caribbean.[5]

McAdoo raised the issue later in the year with Robert
Lansing, Bryan's successor. He pointed out that Americans
were afraid to invest in Latin American securities because
they thought the governments lacked political stability.
Those governments would become stable if they could be
financed and their internal development promoted. He said:

> I think it is essential, if we are to accomplish anything
> at all, that this Government shall give such assurances
> to the American bankers and investors as Great Britain
> gives the British bankers and investors, namely that the
> Government will see to it that the bonds and obliga-
> tions of foreign governments, bought in good faith by
> British investors, are protected.[6]

He suggested that the United States government tell bankers
that it would take "every reasonable step . . . short of armed
intervention" to compel payments on loans by Latin American governments. Unless the government were willing to
give such assurances to American bankers, he warned, the
United States would lose its opportunity in Latin America.
He asked Lansing to take the lead in formulating a policy
"which will encourage our people to go ahead with the development of South America, upon the assurance that our
Government will give every possible protection to their just
rights."

Lansing's response was equivocal. He acknowledged the
desirability of having Americans dominate the development
of Latin America and was sympathetic to McAdoo's plea. On
the other hand, he pointed out to his colleague that he had to
make Latin American policy consistent with the president's
position on Far Eastern loans, and he questioned how much
the State Department could guarantee to bankers in advance.
Even during the Taft administration, the department had
been cautious in its dealings with bankers. President Wilson

---

[5] Wilson to Bryan, Jan. 29, 1915, RG 59, 823.51/350.
[6] McAdoo to Lansing, Aug. 23, RG 59, 833.51/160.

continued to insist that private financial negotiations with any Latin American nation must not "guide and determine" United States policy.[7]

The president's firm stance was undermined by the actions and public statements by government officials encouraging trade and investment in Latin America. Assistant Secretary of the Navy Franklin Roosevelt intervened in a dispute between the Argentine Naval Commission and the Fore River Shipbuilding Corporation, which was finishing the battleship *Moreno.* The Argentine navy had sent two transports of sailors to take over the ship, but, because of a dispute over charges for alterations, could not obtain delivery. Within a few days, Roosevelt brought about an amicable settlement. In urging his case on the American interests, he bluntly stated his own and the navy's attitude toward foreign trade:

> You will, of course, recognize the interest that this Government has in the building of both the *Rivadavia* and the *Moreno,* not only because this Government took such an active part in obtaining the contracts, but also because of its desire to see that the Argentine Government shall receive the ships. . . . It is probably no secret to you that the Argentine Government has been thoroughly dissatisfied over the seizure of a number of its ships and munitions of war being constructed in Europe at the time of the outbreak of war last summer, and if the Argentine Government can be made to feel secure in this country, I have no doubt that there will be many opportunities given us for increased business.[8]

Spurred by the propitious circumstances, as much as by the government's encouragement, American entrepreneurs

[7] Lansing to McAdoo, Aug. 30, RG 59, 833.51/160; Lansing to Wilson, Sept. 6, 1915, RG 59, 811.55/2624a; SS to James Speyer, May 29, 1912; RG 59, 812.51/46a; Wilson to Lansing, Aug. 31, 1915, and F. A. Vanderlip of National City Bank to Lansing, Sept. 2, 1915, quoted in Callcott, *Caribbean Policy of the United States,* 366.

[8] Freidel, *Apprenticeship,* 272–73; Lamont to SS, June 30, 1921, RG 59, 820.51/1; F. C. Schwedtman, "Lending Our Financial Machinery to Latin America," *The American Political Science Review,* XI, 2 (May 1917), 239–51.

did take advantage of the opportunity which the Great War in Europe offered them. Bankers took the initiative. With European money markets closed for the duration of the war, Latin America had to borrow in the United States. To handle this new business, New York banking houses under the leadership of J. P. Morgan and Company set up a South American "group" which was "to act as a unit in handling the governmental or semi-governmental securities offered from the leading South American countries." Thomas W. Lamont was the head of this committee. Its member firms were: Morgan's; Kuhn, Loeb and Company; National City Company; Guaranty Trust; Harris, Forbes and Company; Lee, Higginson & Company; and the First National Bank of Boston.

Moneylending was only one facet of expanding economic contact. Direct investment and trade generally went along with it. Enterprising salesmen could win new contracts because they were able to guarantee financing from New York banking houses. By the end of the war, United States businessmen were dealing directly with South America and no longer using European intermediaries. In the years immediately after the war American businessmen fairly poured into Latin America. When asked to report on "new arrivals" in his district in 1919, the ambassador to Argentina complained that there had been too many to mention in his monthly dispatch. Earlier in the year he had reported that the country was "unquestionably awakening to the importance of interesting American investors and directors of commercial enterprises in Argentine opportunities." In another dispatch he stated explicitly that the remarkable development of American enterprise was due to the closing of European markets to Argentina during the war.[9]

The problem for the State Department of adopting the proper posture toward financial and commercial activity in Latin America was intimately bound up with the larger, more

[9] Interview with Ralf Chandler, former representative of the Baldwin Locomotive Corporation, Oct. 17, 1962; Ambassador F. J. Stimson to SS, Sept. 29, Mar. 24, and Mar. 21, 1919, RG 59, 810.00/a-35; James W. Angell, *Financial Foreign Policy of the United States* (New York, 1933), 79–80.

pressing question of loans to belligerents in the war raging in Europe. At the outset, on August 15, 1914, Bryan had told the press that "loans by American bankers to any foreign nation which is at war are inconsistent with the true spirit of neutrality." Wilson was sensitive to the situation because he realized there was no precedent for such a prohibition; by October of the same year, he admitted that it was impossible to cut off the United States from general world trade and let it be known that the government did not consider it unneutral to grant trade credits to both sides. When trade credits proved insufficient to keep the American industrial machine going, and the business and banking communities continued to press the government for greater freedom of action, the Department of Commerce and the Treasury Department took up the argument for unfettered commercial intercourse with European governments. In the face of this pressure, Wilson withdrew his objections, and on March 31, 1915, the Department of State issued a statement declaring its entire neutrality in the matter.[10]

This action was popular within the Department of State, since most of the professional diplomats were ardent supporters of the Allied cause. They were aware that the neutrality of the United States government would have the effect of buttressing the credit of the Allies at a crucial time and would help to imbue the American people with the consciousness that their material interests were bound up with the Allied cause. It had the further effect of diverting the vast bulk of American investment funds to Europe, away from Latin America, despite the growing need for such funds in the hemisphere. There would not be a surplus of investment capital available for the Latin American market until the middle of 1918, so that the issue of "reasonable" support for American interests would not recur until after the war.[11]

[10] New York Times, Aug. 16, 1914, 1:1; Link, Wilson, III, 62–64; and R. W. Van Alstyne, "Private American Loans to the Allies," Pacific Historical Review, II, 2 (June 1933), 182; Foreign Relations, 1915, Supplement, 820.

[11] Van Alstyne, "Private American Loans," 193; G. Gaddis Smith, Britain's Clandestine Submarines, 1914–1915 (New Haven, 1964); Freidel, Apprenticeship, 236 ff.; Gordon Levin, Woodrow Wilson and World Politics (New York, 1968), 37–42.

Although Wilson had been unable to accept responsibility for the economic development of the entire Western Hemisphere, he did make some attempt to improve relations with Latin America. One such attempt, which set him apart from his Republican predecessors and successors, was his interpretation of the Monroe Doctrine. He wanted to share the doctrine with the other nations of the hemisphere and avoided using it as an instrument of policy even when he was acting to protect the United States sphere of special interest in the Caribbean. He told Secretary of State Robert Lansing that he did not consider European intervention in the Western Hemisphere to be a violation of the Monroe Doctrine so long as it involved no attempt at political control. Wilson thought the Monroe Doctrine should serve as a basis for hemispheric cooperation through a Pan American pact, with mutual guarantees of political sovereignty and territorial integrity and strict control over munitions traffic in the hemisphere. He hoped to make the pact the basis of a Pan American society of nations which would serve as an example for the rest of the world. The idea for the pact had been presented by Representative James L. Slayden of Texas to President Taft, who rejected it. Slayden presented it to Wilson through Colonel House. The Latin American nations responded enthusiastically to the plan, at least in principle. Such a pact suited their concept of international law and offered them a way to restrict United States power in the hemisphere. Though the pact did not get beyond the stage of preliminary discussions, Wilson never gave up the idea of a league of American nations. Mutual guarantees of political sovereignty and territorial integrity were written into the Covenant of the League of Nations, and his idea of a Monroe Doctrine which would serve the entire hemisphere found a place in Article 21 of the Covenant as a "regional understanding." After the United States Senate rejected the Covenant, Wilson returned to a league of the Western Hemisphere nations as the "only available offset to the follies of Europe." [12]

[12] Wilson to Lansing, Apr. 11 and 19, 1917, RG 59, 710.11/319 1/6 and 2/6; *New York Times,* Dec. 2, 1918, quoted in C. H. Carlisle,

After 1914, the military, strategic, and commercial importance of Latin America became a function of United States
involvement in Europe, and the government reevaluated its
policy toward Latin America in the light of the lessons
learned during the conflict. When the United States entered
the Great War, it complicated the conduct of foreign relations immeasurably. The agencies, boards, commissions, committees, and councils created to organize the war effort pene-
trated every area of the American life. The sheer number of
these organizations and the lack of coordination among them
led to confused lines of authority and embarrassing break-
downs in communication and operation. Nearly five thousand wartime governmental agencies were set up at one time
or another, and many of them had dealings with other nations, including those of Latin America.

The Council of National Defense was created by the
National Defense Act of June 3, 1916, for the purpose of
laying the foundation of interdepartmental cooperation. By
July 1917, the loosely organized council was dissolved, and
its functions were taken over by the War Industries Board.
As the months wore on and the administrative chaos that
engulfed Washington did not appreciably improve, the heads
of major boards and departments had to fend for themselves
to carve out spheres of responsibility based upon their
executive skills and their influence with the president. The
president tried to control as much of the war effort as he
could. As one official confided to his diary,

> Washington is distinctly depressed. Everyone complains
> against the lack of coordination in the Government.
> There is no War Council, no one body of men making
> war, no Secretary of Munitions. Everything great and
> small must be referred to the President, who receives no

"Woodrow Wilson's Pan American Pact," *The Proceedings of the South
Carolina Historical Association*, XIX (1949), 14; C. Castro-Ruiz, "The
Monroe Doctrine and the Government of Chile," and F. Alonso Pezet,
"Pan American Cooperation in Pan American Affairs," *The American
Political Science Review*, XI (1917), 217–38; J. Barrett, "What the War
Has Done to the Monroe Doctrine," *Current Opinion*, 65 (1918), 291–
93; Wilson to Colby, Oct. 4, 1920, the Bainbridge Colby papers, LC.

one, listens to no one, seems to take no one's advice;
consequently, there are many delays and precious time
is lost because of the necessity of referring everything
to the White House.[13]

Jealousies and antagonisms on the highest levels inhibited
the efficient operation of the government machinery. Even
on the most theoretical plane of organization, the operations
of the major established departments overlapped, so that as
the war went on outright competition between units of government only served to exacerbate existing problems.

The Department of State tried to eliminate competition
and confusion by asserting its control over all aspects of the
nation's foreign relations, if only to have all foreign business
of the government pass through the department's cable
facilities. Establishing that control proved a herculean task.
Nearly every important wartime agency had international
functions which they tried to exercise independently. Officers
of the department complained vigorously to the president
whenever they felt their conduct of foreign relations compromised by the activities of other government organizations.
After months of inconclusive wrangling, a committee within
the department established the Interdepartmental Exchange,
which provided for the designation of liaison officers for the
several departments and the concentration of all international work in the State Department. As liaison committees
proliferated, the exchange became increasingly cumbersome
and soon fell into disuse. Department officials insisted that
all foreigners negotiate with the United States through the
department rather than directly with the individual boards.
The latter were never happy with what they considered the
State Department's interference in their affairs, and quite

[13] The diary of William Phillips, Jan. 1, 1918, Houghton Library,
Harvard University. For further comments on the lack of organization
in the government, see G. S. Gibb and E. H. Knowlton, *The Resurgent
Years, 1911–1927* (New York, 1956), 226–27; Willard Straight to Henry
P. Fletcher, Nov. 10, 1917, the Henry P. Fletcher papers, LC; Phillips
diary, Mar. 28 and Dec. 14, 1917; and the diary of Chandler P. Anderson, LC, June 26, June 27, and July 26, 1918.

often they did not conduct their international business through proper channels.[14]

The office of Undersecretary Frank L. Polk was the center for the department's efforts to follow all phases of United States foreign relations. Before the War Trade Board was created, and before Title Seven of the Espionage Act of 1917 gave the president authority to control exports, one of Polk's assistants, Gordon Auchincloss, had called together an informal committee of New York bankers to exercise that control. The committee was composed of representatives from the Guaranty Trust, the National Bank of Commerce, the National City Bank, and the Equitable Trust. Even before the declaration of war, banks in New York had begun reporting their foreign transactions and, on their own initiative, had often refused to take questionable business.[15]

The president had to intervene in direct confrontations between the department and other agencies. In 1917 and 1918 a crisis arose with Mexico over the price of sisal from Yucatán province; sisal was essential for binder twine used in agricultural harvesting. A local Mexican *comisión,* which controlled the marketing of sisal, had inflated the price from the prewar level of 4½ cents per pound to 19 cents per pound in 1917 and was threatening to drive it even higher if the United States did not agree to provide the province with whatever products it wanted to import. Mark Requa, an assistant to Food Administrator Herbert Hoover, negotiated directly with the Mexicans. His plan was to demand a lower price on sisal in exchange for supplying Mexico with the corn it desperately needed. The State Department did not want the United States to use corn as a weapon. When Requa asked for troops to force acceptance of a fair price, the State Department urged patience and caution. Intervention would disrupt the production of sisal instead of guaran-

[14] Phillips diary, Dec. 14 and 20, 1917; T. A. Bailey, *The Policy of the United States Toward the Neutrals, 1917–1918* (Baltimore, 1942), 92, n. 60.

[15] Memorandum by Gordon Auchincloss, Apr. 6, 1917, the Papers of Frank L. Polk, House Collection, Yale University; *Foreign Relations, 1917, Supplement 2,* II, 918–19.

teeing an adequate supply at a fair price, and it would disrupt trade in other necessary Mexican products such as oil.
Requa and Hoover had to bow to the Department of State,
because the president would not run the risk of war with
Mexico.[16]

Within the Department of State the pressures of war led
to a sharp increase in the reporting and intelligence work
of the diplomatic and consular officers. A series of general
instructions from December 1917 to July 1918 called for
periodic reports on political, economic, financial, and commercial conditions abroad and for comment on trade possibilities after the cessation of hostilities. In June 1917, the
department was sending and receiving more cables a day
than it had during any week before March of the same year.
This sudden increase in activity upset the transmission of
messages to other governmental organizations. On one occasion it took more than a week for the State Department to
deliver an ordinary communication to the Navy Department,
which was situated in another wing of the old State Department Building. Chandler P. Anderson, Bernard Baruch's
legal aide in the War Industries Board, complained that he
had to go personally to the Department of State or to the
War Trade Board to demand copies of cables, which, he said,
were intended for the War Industries Board and were vital
for carrying on its business. Even within individual agencies,
lines of communication and authority remained uncertain
for the duration of the war.[17]

The War Trade Board is a particularly good example of
uncontrolled bureaucratic growth. It was still working out
the details of its organization only scant months before the

[16] Bailey, *Policy of the United States Toward the Neutrals*, 328–29;
memorandum, dated Feb. 6, 1918, Fletcher papers; Herman Oliphant,
assistant director of the WTB, to Hoover, Nov. 27, 1917, "Records of
the War Trade Board," National Archives Record Group 182, Entry
192, Box 26, Bureau of Research and Statistics—Mexico; and Consul
General Philip Hanna to SS, Jan. 10, 1918, RG 59, 812.50/61. Hereafter
WTB records are referred to by record group, entry, and box numbers.
The division name will be added for clarity, if necessary.
[17] Anderson diary, May 18 and June 13, 1918; Phillips diary, June
29, 1917; assistant to the secretary of the WTB to G. T. Kirby, chief of
the Bureau of Foreign Agents, July 10, 1918, RG 182, Entry 151, Box 6.

Armistice. As one division chief admitted at the end of August 1918, "Unfortunately, as yet the machinery for carrying into orderly operation foreign service for the War Trade Board has not been set up and turned to its job." Latin America was badly served in this regard. In the four months after January 1918, the Bureau of War Trade Intelligence sent out more than one thousand cables of inquiry to Latin America, more than 75 percent of the total number of such cables sent in that period, and over 10 percent were not even answered. The head of War Trade Intelligence was kind enough to blame this on the lack of staff.[18]

The lack of coordination among government representatives in the field was an obstacle to carrying out policy in Latin America. The various boards and agencies grew so fast that they hardly ever had time to hire and train their own agents for foreign posts. Wherever possible, they took advantage of existing government personnel in the field, generally the representatives of the Department of State or the Department of Commerce. Since these departments were themselves woefully understaffed, the newly created agencies then turned to United States citizens overseas and, in some cases, to foreign nationals. For vital positions close to home, in which coordination was an obvious requirement, individuals were selected with care and given charge of all the war work in their bailiwick, as in Cuba; or, as in Mexico, where all war work was assigned directly to the ambassador, whose staff was increased to cope with the new responsibilities.

In Havana, Consul General Henry H. Morgan represented the Shipping Board, the War Trade Board, and the Food Administration in addition to the Department of Commerce.

[18] Shelton Hale, assistant secretary of the WTB to Kirby, July 2, 1918, RG 182, Entry 151, Box 6; Kirby to Burnett, special WTB representative in Buenos Aires, Aug. 30, 1918, Entry 151, Box 6, Bureau of Foreign Agents; B. S. Cutler, Department of Commerce, to Vance McCormick, Mar. 21, 1918, Entry 11, Box 1, Executive Country Files— Argentina; Richard Ely, assistant director, Bureau of War Trade Intelligence, to McCormick, May 2, 1918, Entry 13, Box 33, Records of the Executive Office Relating to the Organization of the WTB— South America, Foreign Offices.

He bickered constantly with the United States minister, William Gonzales. Gonzales felt that Morgan was assuming the prerogatives of the United States diplomatic representative in Cuba. Wherever in Latin America there was sufficient war work to call for additions to the peacetime staff of the United States legation or embassy, there was some difficulty over the responsibility for that work and over the hierarchy of authority at the post. How this was resolved depended upon the personality of the chief of the diplomatic mission and upon the war work that was to be done. If there was ambiguity in the organization, a department might resort to informal communication with another department's representative to secure information, as the Department of Commerce did with the State Department's special representative in Brazil throughout the war. Where the chief of mission asserted his authority, as Ambassador F. J. Stimson did in Argentina, the State Department backed him up.[19]

While the War Trade Board was willing to defer to the Department of State, the other agencies of the government were not as self-effacing, and they often undercut one another. In Chile and Bolivia, a secret agent assigned to purchase tin for the United States Navy discovered that the commercial attaché in Lima was not only engaged in the same work but that he was outbidding him, so that he was unable to fill his order. That same Navy agent managed to embarrass the efforts of the American ambassador to Chile to stabilize the nitrate market and was recalled. The need incessantly to be asserting the control of the Department of State over all political aspects of the nation's foreign relations was tiresome and wasteful of the department's energy, and it only served to underline the vulnerability of the de-

[19] Gonzales to SS, Aug. 14, 1918, RG 182, Entry 11, Box 164, Executive Country Files—Cuba; Julius Klein, Bureau of Foreign and Domestic Commerce, to Henry Amory, special representative of the Department of State in Rio de Janeiro, Sept. 9, 1918, "Records of the Department of Commerce, Bureau of Foreign and Domestic Commerce," National Archives Record Group 151, Box 2232, File 432—Brazil (Hereafter these records are referred to by record group, box, and file numbers.). On the Argentine case, see Lansing to Stimson, July 2, 1918, RG 182, Entry 39, Box 36, Secretary's Office, cables outgoing—Argentina.

partment's authority. The president did nothing to correct the situation.[20]

The dominant figures in the Department of State after Bryan left were Secretary Robert Lansing, Counselor Frank L. Polk, Assistant Secretary William Phillips, and Solicitor Lester H. Woolsey. Phillips was a career diplomat; the others were lawyers. When the increased wartime work load forced an expansion of the department staff, vital positions were taken by professional diplomats, such as Leland Harrison and G. Howland Shaw, and by lawyers, such as Gordon Auchincloss and Carlyle Barton. Wilson was prejudiced against both lawyers and diplomats. He considered diplomatic officers members of an aristocracy who could not understand his policies and purposes. His attitude toward lawyers was remarkable, considering his dependence upon them in government. Robert Lansing commented:

[The President] does not like lawyers or want their advice. He frankly says so. He seems to resent their logical methods of thought. He may use them to an extent as to the form of a document, but their views as to its substance are not desired. Why he feels this way I cannot conceive unless he thinks that they are slaves to precedent and are therefore narrow and conservative in thought. . . .[21]

Lansing may have overstated the case in general, but he was perceptive with regard to the president's attitude toward him. Wilson never trusted Lansing's mental processes and once remarked that Lansing "was stupid." With or without the president's blessing, the Department of State grew enor-

[20] Ely to McCormick, May 2, 1918, RG 182, Entry 13, Box 33, Records of the Executive Office Relating to the Organization of the WTB —South America, Foreign Offices; S. J. Marks, chief, Nonferrous Metals, Navy Department to C. P. Carter, Bureau of Foreign and Domestic Commerce, Aug. 27, 1918, RG 151, Box 3197, File 813.1—Bolivian Ores; Anderson diary, May 29, 1918; Phillips diary, Feb. 16, 1917; Willard Straight to Henry P. Fletcher, May 4, 1917, Fletcher papers; and the diary of Wilbur J. Carr, LC, Aug. 13, 1918.

[21] The Papers of Robert Lansing, LC, Private Memoranda, Mar. 20, 1919; Link, *Wilson the Diplomatist*, 26–27.

mously during the war, both in size and in influence, and
this growth affected the formulation and the execution of
foreign policy after the war.

When the United States entered the war against Germany
in April 1917, it was concerned that the nations of Latin
America either follow its lead or, at least, remain neutral
and provide no aid to its enemies. There was a strong sense
within the Department of State that past relations between
the United States and Latin America were not an ideal
prologue to close cooperation in wartime. Officials gave considerable thought to winning the sympathy and friendship
of the nations in the hemisphere. They were sensitive to the
fact that the nations in South America objected to the subor-
nation of the sovereignty of independent nations in the
Caribbean. They pointed out that, to be successful, American policy would have to be consistent throughout the hemisphere: the issues which concerned the United States and
Latin America—defense, trade, communications—were hemispheric; hence the policy governing American behavior
should be conceived in hemispheric terms. John Barrett,
director of the Pan American Union, attempted to marshal
the forces of his organization behind the United States war
effort. On his own authority, Barrett issued a series of statements to the press designed to allay the fears of the American people that Latin America was pro-German. He so
overstated his case that the representatives of the neutral
nations in the hemisphere objected. They insisted that he
had no right to separate his personal opinion from his official
opinion as director general on matters concerning hemispheric relations. At the end of 1917, Barrett turned his
attention to convincing the officials of the United States government that it was necessary to create a committee of experts
to promote inter-American cooperation and to insure that
the products vital to the American war effort continued to
flow from South America to the United States and Europe.
He circulated his views in a memorandum and covering
letter.[22]

[22] Memorandum by Boaz Long, "Constructive Steps which should be
taken in Central America before the Close of the European War," Feb.
15, 1918, RG 59, 711.13/55; unsigned memorandum, "The Pros and

This was typical of Barrett's conception of the role of the Pan American Union as an instrument of United States foreign policy. He would often inflate his own importance and would infuriate the members of the Pan American Union by pretending to speak for them without their consent. In calling for a committee of experts, he went too far and embarrassed the United States government. Not content with sending copies of his letter and memorandum to influential men within the government, he gave a shortened version of it to the press, in the form of an interview in the *Washington Post* of November 23, 1917. Wilson was appalled. He never would approve of such abuse of the Pan American Union and realized immediately that this action would destroy the director's usefulness as a go-between for Latin America and the United States. The president ordered Lansing to put an end to Barrett's activities and to publish a denial of the government's connection with them. Under pressure from the Department of State and from the members of the Pan American Union, Barrett apologized for his actions and published a retraction of his memorandum. This incident marked the end of Barrett's usefulness at the Pan American Union, and he was eased out of office as soon as a suitable successor was found.[23]

Barrett's parting shot for Pan American cooperation was to beg George Creel to set up a special Latin American di-

Cons Regarding the Establishment of a School in Central America," n.d., in the Leland Harrison papers, LC; memorandum by J. H. Stabler, chief of the Latin American Division, Apr. 18, 1917, RG 59, 711.25/25; unsigned memorandum, "The Political Situation in Latin America," Jan. 12, 1918, RG 182, Entry 192, Box 8, Bureau of Research and Statistics; and a Latin American Division memorandum, May 1, 1918, RG 59, 710.11/368; John Barrett to his mother, Mar. 24, the press release, "Latin America and the War," Apr. 10, and Assistant Director Yanez to Barrett, Nov. 26, 1917, all in the papers of John Barrett, LC, General Correspondence, Boxes 16 and 17; Barrett to George Creel, Nov. 19, 1917, "Records of the Committee on Public Information," Executive Division Correspondence, National Archives Record Group 63, CPI 1-AI.

[23] Lansing to Barrett, Nov. 30; Barrett's letter to the members of the Governing Board of the Pan American Union, Nov. 30; his public denial, Nov. 28; and his apology to Lansing, Dec. 1, 1917, Barrett papers, Box 17.

vision within the Committee on Public Information to carry
on the work Barrett had been trying to do within the Pan
American Union. Here, he showed better judgment. The
job of the Committee on Public Information was to convince everyone that the United States could never be beaten;
that the United States was a land of freedom and democracy
and, therefore, could be trusted; that, thanks to President
Wilson's vision of a new world and his power to achieve it,
victory for the Allied armies would usher in a new era of
peace and hope.

Whatever success the committee enjoyed in Latin America
was due mainly to the fact that President Wilson's vision of
a new world order struck a responsive chord throughout the
hemisphere. Latin Americans were willing to base a new
Pan Americanism upon the principles of international justice which Wilson made central to United States participation in the war. Even *La Nación* of Buenos Aires, a conservative paper traditionally suspicious of any movement for
hemispheric cooperation, waxed eloquent in its praise of
Wilson's war aims:

> During many years the term Pan Americanism was the
> cause of anxiety and caviling on the part of Latin
> America. What does Pan Americanism mean? Political
> hegemony, territorial expansion, North American com-
> mercial domination? His nation has entered the war,
> impelled by an ideal—the only means of moving human
> beings. If that ideal is Pan Americanism we are all Pan
> Americans.[24]

People all over the hemisphere were moved by Wilson's
sentiments. They heralded the dawn of a new Pan Ameri-

[24] Latin American press comments on Wilson's war aims enclosed in
dispatches from Handley (Lima), Sept. 1, 1917; Debellier (Santiago),
June 14; Stimson, June 17; Leavell (Guatemala City), June 15; and
Goding (Guayaquil), June 15, 1918, RG 59, 710.11/339, 362, 364, 367,
371. See also O. N. Brito, *O Monroismo e a Sua nova phase* (Rio de
Janeiro, 1918). On the committee, see Barrett to Creel, Dec. 17, 1917,
Barrett papers, Box 17; James R. Mock, "The Creel Committee in Latin
America," *HAHR* XXII, 2 (May 1942).

canism; they matched Wilsonian rhetoric. If their governments were slow to fall in line with the American war effort, it was because they feared their growing economic dependence upon the United States, a dependence which seemed to be a part of close hemispheric cooperation. They did not want to become protectorates of the United States.

The outbreak of hostilities in Europe brought economic dislocation to Latin America. As the war proceeded, Latin America's troubles increased. When the United States entered the war, it was a further shock to the economic system of the hemisphere. The trade pattern of the entire hemisphere was subjected to great pressure. The secretary of state called a meeting with Latin American representatives to discuss ways of coping with the problems created by the war. Countries which had exported most of their money crops to the Central Powers, such as Guatemala with its coffee, had to develop new markets or face economic collapse. Guatemala consigned the greatest part of its 1917 and 1918 coffee crop to San Francisco, where American commercial interests already involved in Guatemala were able to unload it at depressed prices. Commodities like newsprint, which German merchants had marketed all over South America before the war, now came from the United States or from Scandinavian sources through North American merchants. Very much the same happened in iron and steel. Latin America either had to turn to the United States to supply vital necessities or simply cut consumption. In either case, Latin American importers were at the mercy of United States credit terms, trade regulations, and licensing restrictions. The figures for total trade with individual countries present the changing pattern of economic relationships with stark simplicity, as in these two examples:

United States exports to Argentina for the eleven months ending May 1915 were $27 million. A year later, they had more than doubled to $59 million; and at the end of May 1917 were $76 million. Imports from Argentina, for the same three years, increased from $66 million to $101 million and then to $139.5 million. United States trade with Bolivia during this period shows even more dramatic expansion, although it was never so important as trade with Argentina. Exports to Bolivia for the eleven months ending May 1915 were $460,000, increasing to $1.1 million in 1916, and $2.5 million in 1917.

Latin Americans were unhappy with their economic role in the war on two grounds. First, they were sensitive to the fact that they were completely dependent upon the United States for vital supplies. Second, they resented what they considered the wanton disregard of their legitimate interests and demands in Allied planning.[25]

The United States was not prepared to be economic guardian for the entire hemisphere, however much it had coveted the role. Inter-American trade was embarrassed by a severe lack of shipping. The Shipping Board established broad priorities for the use of the available tonnage; what the various agencies chose to do with their quotas was their business. Claims on tonnage were met in this order: first, things needed for the Allies; second, things so important to the economic welfare of the neutral nation that it was politically important to send it there; and third, things the United States did not need that were necessary for support of American-owned companies abroad. The war gave hemispheric trade strategic importance. The navy was convinced that lack of adequate shipping facilities in the Western

[25] Unsigned and undated memorandum in "Records of the Department of the Treasury," Bureau of Accounts, Country File—South America, National Archives Record Group 39, Box 203. Hereafter these records are cited by record group and box numbers. Figures for Bolivia's exports are not available because they were considered part of the exports of Chile and Peru. The increase is exaggerated to some extent by price increases during the period. Schwedtman, "Lending Our Financial Machinery to Latin America," 250–51; report by William A. Deverall, Apr. 25, 1919, RG 182, Entry 151, Box 11, Bureau of Foreign Agents—Guatemala; Entry 192, Boxes 29 and 36, Bureau of Research and Statistics, for various country studies and studies on individual products, showing the impact of the war on Latin American markets; memorandum, "Economic Relations Between the United States and Latin America," Nov. 13, 1916, Fletcher papers; Ambassador Edwin V. Morgan (Rio de Janeiro) to SS, Dec. 12, 1917, RG 182, Entry 11, Box 6, Executive Country File—Brazil; Redfield to Whitbeck, assistant chief of the Division of Research, July 23, 1918, Entry 192, Box 8, Bureau of Research and Statistics—Brazil, commenting on an ONI report.

Hemisphere weakened United States security, and the War Trade Board shared this view. However, nothing could be done to relieve the situation. The Allied Maritime Transport Council drew up a comprehensive list of Latin America's needs and then turned it over to the War Industries Board and the War Trade Board. The fact that more than one agency was involved meant there was a certain amount of drift and indecision in carrying out the findings of the Allied Council.[26]

With responsibilities go privileges. People inside and outside the government thought that if the United States had to shoulder the heavy burden of Latin American economic dependence, it should also enjoy the fruits thereof. They took it for granted that United States merchants and bankers would replace Europeans in the Latin American economic process. Not surprisingly, Latin Americans and Europeans did not appreciate this logic. The first step in curbing European influence in the hemisphere was to make sure that Germany did not regain control over the property which her nationals had owned before the war. To that end, the United States convinced its allies in the hemisphere to establish offices for an alien property custodian to confiscate the property of enemy aliens and employ it in the national interest. In some cases, where they had many German ships in their harbors or particularly valuable German property within their borders, Latin American nations leaped at the suggestion.[27]

[26] Gay to McCormick, n.d., RG 182, Entry 192, Box 26, Bureau of Research and Statistics—Brazil; report of the Allied Maritime Transport Council, American Section, Statistical Division, "Relations Between the United States and other Countries Regarding Important Materials," n.d., the papers of Gordon Auchincloss, House Collection, Yale University, Drawer 54, File 4; Anderson diary, June 7, 1918; L. F. Schmeckeiber, "The Activities of the Government in Promoting Foreign Trade," *The Annals*, 83 (May 1919).

[27] Polk to Stabler, Mar. 28, 1918, Polk papers; Lansing to Leavell (Guatemala) for the Alien Property Custodian, Sept. 27, 1918, *Foreign Relations*, 1918, *Supplement*, II, 371; 1919, II, 287–302 and 400–409; Leavell to Lansing, from the Alien Property Custodian, Dec. 23, 1918, RG 182, Entry 151, Bureau of Foreign Agents, Box 11—Guatemala; Agent O'Brien to C. L. Jones, Nov. 22, Entry 151, Box 8, Bureau of

The issues were not so cut-and-dried in neutral nations, and the United States had to rely on the Enemy Trading List of firms and individuals suspected of harboring sympathies for the Central Powers—the famous "blacklist." American nations were forbidden to traffic with blacklisted firms except under a carefully supervised system of licensing. One government official considered the elimination of pro-German or pro-Austrian firms in South America by means of the blacklist "our most effective work." [28]

The first American blacklist was published on December 5, 1917 and contained 1,524 names, all firms and individuals in Latin America. Enforcing the Enemy Trading Act created dissension between American ambassadors and representatives of the War Trade Board. The former claimed that political expediency required "selective application" of the blacklist, whereas the latter argued for a "firm but just attitude" toward those who dealt with the enemy. Diplomatic personnel were, by and large, more lenient. The situation in Argentina was particularly sensitive because the representative of the War Trade Board, Consul General William H. Robertson, was opposed to the blacklist on principle. Relations with Argentina and Chile were complicated because both nations had large German colonies and both had products which the Allies needed for the war effort. Argentina had wheat and meat; Chile had the indispensable nitrates. Each wanted to use its raw materials as a lever to pry trading advantages out of the Allies.[29]

Foreign Agents—Bolivia; and Morgan to Lansing, Dec. 12, 1917, Entry 11, Box 6, Executive Country File—Brazil.

[28] Burwell Cutler, "The Problem of Government Control," *The Annals,* 83 (May 1919), 275; Bailey, *Policy Toward Neutrals,* 349 and 362; and Bailey, "The United States and the Blacklist During the Great War," *The Journal of Modern History,* VI (Mar. 1934); William O'Brien to G. T. Kirby, Dec. 13, 1918, RG 182, Entry 151, Box 8, Bureau of Foreign Agents—Bolivia; De Gorgorza to Kirby, Apr. 5, Entry 151, Box 17; and Barrett to McCormick, Aug. 22, Entry 151, Box 6.

[29] Stimson to SS, Sept. 29, 1919, RG 59, 810.00/a-35; Amory (Rio de Janeiro) to Stewart, director of the Bureau of Foreign Agents, Feb. 3, 1919, RG 182, Entry 151, Box 8; Anderson diary, May 29, 1918, on difficulties in Chile.

Argentina needed coal for heat and for operating its public utilities. The War Trade Board refused export licenses for coal intended for the Compañía Argentina Eléctrica (Argentine Electric Company), the major consumer of coal in Argentina, because it considered the company the most important German interest in the neutral world. The Argentine government made formal representations against the action of the War Trade Board. It insisted that the company had the right to receive coal from the Allies and refused to accept coal that was licensed for export to the government. The State Department suggested that coal for the company would be forthcoming if the Argentines could find some legal way to prevent the German stockholders from using the company's net earnings. When direct diplomatic representations proved futile, the Argentine government tried to negotiate a barter deal in which it agreed to provide wheat to the European market in exchange for coal. Herbert Hoover vetoed the plan. He did not want Argentina to supply more of the European cereals market than was absolutely necessary. Great Britain opposed the plan in order to block the United States from taking over the lucrative Argentine coal trade, even though Britain had neither the shipping to carry the coal to Buenos Aires nor the money to pay for the wheat. A compromise was worked out in 1918 whereby Argentina granted Great Britain, France, and Italy a credit with which these nations could contract for the purchase of Argentine wheat at a fixed price. In return for certain terms in the contract beneficial to American wheat exports, the United States agreed to grant the necessary export licenses for the coal and to assist in providing shipping. Argentina undertook, informally, to restrict the use to which the German stockholders could put the income of the electric company. The treasury was anxious to complete the negotiations and to grant Argentina most of what she wanted. Hoover simply wanted to hurt the Argentine wheat market; the War Trade Board led the forces of obstruction by refusing to commit itself to any deal with Argentina that provided coal for an enemy company. The State Department remained on the sidelines for the most part, content to watch the other agencies of the government thrash out the issues.[30]

Chile did not fare so well as Argentina. When the United States entered the war, the Allies coordinated their purchases of nitrate in the Nitrate of Soda Executive, which sat in London. The Nitrate Executive determined the amount of nitrate needed for Allied consumption, determined the price at which it should be purchased, and arranged for delivery to the consumers. Through their control over the sea lanes and their monopoly of commercial tonnage, the Allies were able to prevent Chilean nitrate from reaching the Central Powers. Nitrate was Chile's most valuable natural resource, and her entire economy depended upon the export earnings of the nitrate industry. To avoid being victimized by the Nitrate Executive, the producers of nitrate in Chile and the Chilean government formed a Chilean Nitrate Committee to sit across the bargaining table from the Nitrate Executive. Price was not a major problem for the negotiators. Chile had to sell her nitrate and the Allies had to buy; bargaining was perfunctory. A more delicate problem remained: what to do about those nitrate producers, representing 7 percent of the Chilean industry, controlled by German capital. Under the Trading with the Enemy Act, the War Trade Board demanded that United States companies refrain from trading with German-controlled nitrate companies in Chile. To make its demand effective, the board refused to grant export licenses for the petroleum that was necessary to operate the nitrate mines. The German-controlled companies countered by bringing suit in local courts for violation of valid contracts against the Union Oil Company of California and the International Petroleum Company of Canada, a Standard Oil of New Jersey subsidiary. They won the first round of their case: the oil companies were ordered to fulfill the terms of their contracts or have their stocks of fuel confiscated and

[30] Memorandum, Nov. 1, 1917, RG 59, 635.119/886; J. G. Lay to Polk, Feb. 21, 1918, Polk papers; Hoover to Polk, Oct. 5, 1917, RG 182, Entry 11, Box 1, Executive Country File—Argentina; Bailey, *Policy Toward Neutrals*, 332–33; Donald Scotts, member of the Shipping Control Committee to SecTreas, June 18, 1918, RG 39, Boxes 3 and 203, Country File—Argentina and South America; RG 59, 835.6131/–.

turned over to the slighted customers. The oil companies appealed the decision to higher courts in Chile and to the governments of Great Britain and the United States. This affair occupied the time of the United States government for three months in 1918.[31]

The War Industries Board felt that since it was charged with responsibility for the purchase and disposition of nitrates, it should control the negotiations with Chile. The War Trade Board refused to compromise the sanctity of the blacklist and would not grant the export licenses which the War Industries Board requested. The State Department tried to take over the negotiations with Chile in order to resolve the impasse and ended by bringing down on its head the anger of both Bernard Baruch, chief of the War Industries Board, and Vance McCormick, chief of the War Trade Board, two of the most influential men in Washington. The British, whose interests were also at stake, seemed content to sit by while their allies engaged in an acrimonious exchange. In July, Baruch finally took his case to the president and convinced him that any compromise of the enemy trading lists would be justified if it could guarantee an ample supply of nitrate. Despite this decision, War Trade Intelligence did not cooperate. On July 16, the Chilean government announced that the United States had stopped all shipments of petroleum to Chile. Failure to resume shipments immediately would mean stoppage of 75 percent of the nitrate industry and complete economic chaos in Chile. Baruch and Chandler Anderson, his legal adviser and top aide, acted quickly to take advantage of the president's decision in their

[31] RG 59, 825.6374; RG 182, Entry 11, Box 3, Executive Country File—Chile; Anderson diary, April to July, 1918; E. J. J. Bott, *El Comercio Entre los Estados Unidos y la America Latina Durante La Gran Guerra* (Buenos Aires, 1919); *La Prensa* (Buenos Aires), Oct. 28, 1918, 5:2–3; *La Epoca* (Buenos Aires), Jan. 14, 1:2–5, Jan. 15, 1:1–3, Jan. 16, 1:2–7, Jan. 17, 1:1–4, Jan. 18, 1:2–5, Jan. 19, 1918, 2:1, Republic of Argentina, Ministry of Foreign Relations, "Records Pertaining to World War I," Box 14, File I, t, 1 and Box 69, File XIX, 5; L. S. Rowe, *Early Effects of the European War Upon the Finances, Commerce and Industry of Chile* (New York, 1918); B. Schatsky, "La Neutralité du Chile Pendant la Guerre Mondiale," *Revue d'Histoire de la Guerre Mondiale,* 14 (1936), 123–44.

favor. They induced the Chilean government to take over the German-controlled nitrate mines for the duration of the war, operate them in accordance with agreements with the Nitrate Executive, and reserve all profits from the property until after the war. In return for the preservation of their assets, the German-controlled companies agreed to end all litigation against the oil companies. Once the Chilean government was in possession of the controversial properties, the blacklist no longer applied. At the eleventh hour, the Canadian government nearly upset the agreement by requisitioning the last International Petroleum tankers in service between Peru and Chile. Extreme pressure by the United States restored the service.[32]

Enforcing the blacklist had important repercussions for postwar policy. First, it led the Department of State to look beyond the Caribbean. Second, with several nations in the hemisphere, it left a legacy of strained relations which haunted the department for years. Third, and perhaps most important, it brought to the surface the fierce competition for Latin American markets between Britain and the United States. Because many of the Latin American markets into which Americans were now moving had been created and were controlled by British merchants, official efforts in behalf of American interests invariably were prejudicial to the British. The British quite expectably retaliated. Americans alleged that the British abused the censorship of American mail to the advantage of British business; that they refused to accept American goods in firms which they controlled, even if it meant postponing certain improvements or changes for the duration of the war; and that they used the blacklist to further the interests of British trade. The British complained loudly and bitterly of what they considered to be a very selfish disposition of American shipping. They accused the State Department of bad faith and accused

[32] Report from V. Loveday, London, to SecNav, July 16, "Records of the Navy Historical Section," National Archives Record Group 45, Box 220, Area Files—Southeastern Pacific. Hereafter these files will be referred to by record group and box numbers with an identifying area name. Bailey, *Policy Toward Neutrals*, 359, n. 40; Gibb and Knowlton, *Resurgent Years*, 102.

the Shipping Board of being as concerned with trade development as it was with winning the war. Counselor Polk stoutly defended the department against such charges:

> [We have] ruthlessly cut off our trade, particularly in South America. It is true that the State Department, and I may even go so far as to say I was responsible for it, tried to keep alive the fruit trade with Central America, not because we wanted to send anything there, but because the export of fruit was the sole means of support of several of these republics, and cutting off this trade would ruin them and would not reduce much in the way of valuable shipping. In spite of my contention, even this trade has suffered severely.

The United States maintained that it was in an essentially different position with regard to trade with Latin America and that it could not afford to alienate those countries. In an attempt to neutralize the United States' advantage, the British began to plan their postwar trade policy even before the United States entered the war. A policy of Imperial Preference was adopted in 1917, the British Trade Corporation was created the same year, and the Department of Overseas Trade a year later. The Maurice de Bunsen trade mission was sent to Latin America in 1918 to protect existing British markets and to insure that Britain would enjoy those markets after the war. American officials were uncertain how to counteract the scheme. One thought was to create a trade organization that would parallel the British councils, boards, and commissions. Another was to counter the De Bunsen trade mission immediately with a goodwill tour by a high-level cabinet minister. Nothing came of any of these plans, because fear of British trade was offset by the feeling that any such aggressive action would offend the British and damage the war effort.[33]

[33] Polk to Martin Egan, Oct. 15, 1918, Polk papers; Bailey, *Policy Toward Neutrals,* 421–22 and 426; F. J. Stimson, *My United States,* 376; statement of the representative of a large American company making a steel speciality, in Federal Trade Commission, *Report on Cooperation in American Export Trade,* I, 74, quoted in C. W. Phelps, *The*

The Anglo-American trade rivalry was often in danger of getting out of hand. Men in the field and junior officials of the Trade Adviser's Office in the Department of State had a tendency to give higher priority to extension of American economic influence than to cooperation with an ally, and they frequently recommended economic reprisals against the British. The War Trade Board generally insisted that winning the war was more important than some present or future trade advantage. As the war drew to a close, Americans

Foreign Expansion of American Banks (New York, 1927), 72–73; Egan to Polk, Sept. 21, 1918, Polk papers; Barrett to WTB, in Stimson's Dec. 9, 1918, RG 59, 763.72112A/5043; Robertson to SS, Aug. 21, 1918, 635.4115/8; Stimson to SS, and SS to Stimson, Jan. 1919 and Sept. 1919, 631.4117/3 and 810.00/a-35; Amory to SS, May 15, and to WTB, Dec. 16, 1918, RG 182, Entry 11, Box 2, Executive Country File—Brazil and Entry 151, Box 8, Bureau of Foreign Agents—Brazil; memorandum from Finch to Whitbeck, July 16, Entry 192, Box 29, Bureau of Research and Statistics—South America; Stabler to Polk, Feb. 8, 1919, Polk papers, discusses competition in Peru; James Ferrer, Jr., "United States—Argentine Economic Relations, 1900–1930" (Ph.D. dissertation, University of California, Berkeley, 1964), 118–22; discussion of British trade measures in Julius Klein, chief of the Latin American Division of the Bureau of Foreign and Domestic Commerce to commercial attaché in Brazil, Thomas McGovern, Oct. 10, and 18, 1919 RG 151, Box 2232, 432—Brazil; Joseph C. Baldwin, Jr. to Polk, Feb. 5, 1919, Polk papers; Stimson to SS, May 1, 1917, "Records of the Department of the Navy," National Archives Record Group 80, File 4793-121. Hereafter, these records will be referred to by record group and file numbers. For further information on the trade rivalry, see memorandum by Solicitor Lester H. Woolsey, May 17, 1917, *Foreign Relations, 1917, Supplement 2,* II, 865–70; W. B. Colver, "Recent Phases of Competition in International Trade Promotion," *The Annals,* 83 (May 1919); P. H. Middleton, "British Foreign Trade Promotion," *The Annals,* 94 (Mar. 1921); Benjamin Gerig, *The Open Door and the Mandate System* (London, 1930), 77–79; the Naval Intelligence Register, "British Trade After the War," "Records of the Department of the Navy," ONI, National Archives Record Group 38, 6272-E, B-6-a. Hereafter these records are referred to by record group and file numbers, and the name of the report where it is relevant. On the De Bunsen mission see RG 38, C11540, c-10-v; and *La Prensa* (Buenos Aires), May 25 to July 17, 1918. Discussion of retaliation is in Anderson diary, May 1, May 26, and July 18, 1918; Special Agent Howland to G. T. Kirby, July 26, 1918, RG 182, Entry 151, Box 6, Bureau of Foreign Agents—Argentina; memorandum by A. N. Clevon, n.d., RG 182, Entry 192, Box 13, Bureau of Research and Statistics—Brazil; Latin American Division memorandum by Stabler, May 14, 1918, RG 59, 033.1132/5.

in Latin America became frantic in their efforts to make their government see that it must act in order not to lose an opportunity "we have waited fifty years for. . . ." And, with the war nearly won, some government officials seemed more sympathetic to such pleas than they had been earlier, as in these instructions to the consul in Birmingham, England:

> Let me assure you that we are particularly interested in the reports of the activities of the English in preparing for postwar trade, a matter which is, of course, now of much more importance to us than was the case when our chief and practically sole duty seemed to be to win the war.[34]

Americans thought the British merchants had an advantage because they had the strong support of their government. British government officials were reportedly joining the boards of major companies in Latin America; British nationals held vital positions in American firms. One American businessman in Bolivia complained of these practices, linking the strategic importance of trade and communications:

> One of the worst phases of their contemptible and underhand maneuvering is through the cable offices. I am satisfied that the British representatives in foreign countries have a corruption fund which they use in part to buy information about commercial matters which pass over the foreign cables. They even manage to get British managers in charge of the American cable offices in foreign countries . . . and unless our important cables

[34] Robertson to SS, Aug. 21, 1918, and attached minutes by trade adviser, WTB, and counselor, RG 59, 635.4115/8; Stimson to SS, Jan. 16, 1919, WTB to SS, and SS to Stimson, 635.4117/3; SecCom William G. Redfield to the Dexcar Trading Company, Oct. 23, 1918, RG 151, Box 2231, File 431—Argentina; C. L. Jones to Howland, Nov. 5, 1918, RG 182, Entry 151, Box 6, Bureau of Foreign Agents—Argentina; Morgan to SS, Jan. 23, 1919, Entry 11, Box 2, Executive Country Files—Brazil; reply to consul in Birmingham, England, Mar. 9, 1920, RG 59, 164.2/71.

about our negotiations for important new business is disguised in the form of privately arranged code, it is immediately communicated to the British Minister who makes use of the information for British interests.[35]

The president was so upset over the ill feeling developing between the allies that he asked George Creel to publicize a series of statements by high officials of the American government to the effect that relations between Great Britain and the United States after the war would continue to be marked by cooperation and goodwill. He feared an open commercial war "of the severest sort" in which he expected Great Britain to "prove capable of as great commercial savagery as Germany has displayed for so many years in her competitive methods." Secondary officials in the Foreign Office were as competitive as their American counterparts. For the most part, cabinet-level politicians tried to dampen the ardor of their subordinates. Wilson even thought of rejecting the new British ambassador, Sir Auckland Geddes, because Geddes was thought to represent the commercial policies and not the political policies of the British Empire. Undersecretary Polk was able to convince the president that it would be an unfriendly act to prevent Geddes' appointment and that it would be better to have Geddes in the United States, where he could be watched, than in Great Britain or Canada, where he could speak out whenever he pleased. When Polk raised with the British chargé the question of a ruthless trade war which would "seriously interfere" with the relations between the two countries, that official "merely looked a little depressed and said nothing." A month later, Polk raised the same issue with an old friend, Sir William Wiseman, who told him anti-American feeling in England was tremendous. Polk said such feeling "was based for the most part on the fear of trade conquest by the United States" and pointed out that "we were not

35 Lawrence E. Bennett to John Barrett, Mar. 26, 1921, Barrett papers; Stimson to SS, Jan. 24, 1919, RG 59, 635.4117/7; Robertson to SS, Aug. 22, 1918, 635.4117/1; memorandum, Sept. 27, 1924, 824.6354/62; Amory to WTB, Nov. 4, and Burnett to WTB, Dec. 30, 1918, RG 182, Entry 15, Box 6, Bureau of Foreign Agents—Argentina.

really very much to be feared." The United States military
viewed British activities in the hemisphere with marked un-
easiness. They objected to the sale by the British government
of military equipment to the governments of South America;
they objected to a new British coaling station in Peru; and
they urged the United States government to offset British
influence in the hemisphere by sending United States naval
missions to countries in the hemisphere.[36]

The naval mission seemed an ideal vehicle for the State
Department's aggressive economic policy. If the United States
could secure contracts with individual Latin American countries to send missions of high-level naval personnel to supervise the reorganization of their navies, it would cripple the
British and French influence over those navies and go a long
way toward guaranteeing that those nations would soon turn
to the United States to purchase ships, ordnance, and supplies for their navies. The missions also could help the
United States use its influence "toward the betterment of
the international situation in South America." The navy went
along with this policy reluctantly, explicitly denying that
there was any great military advantage to be derived from
the missions, though acknowledging that they might further
"the policy of the Government to cultivate close diplomatic
and commercial relations with South American countries."
In the case of Peru, the navy argued that the time was not
propitious for the establishment of a naval mission. It was
overruled by the State Department, and, at the latter's request, Congress passed on June 5, 1920, a bill authorizing
military personnel to accept office in a foreign government
for the purpose of taking on duties of naval and military missions. When Daniels left office, the navy became more enthusiastic about missions. In 1924, Secretary of State Charles
Evans Hughes summarized the government's policy:

[36] Creel to Baruch, Aug. 26, 1918, RG 63, CPI 1-A1; Wilson to Polk,
Mar. 4, and Polk to Wilson, Mar. 5, 1920, Polk papers; Polk diary, Mar.
4 and Apr. 12, 1920; SecNav to SS, June 14, RG 80, 6077-153; and report
of military attachés in Latin America, Dec. 31, 1920, 28642-35; file
5654. I am indebted to Professor Wilton B. Fowler for information on
the British Foreign Office.

On several occasions this Government has had an opportunity to be helpful to certain Latin American Governments by detailing officers from the United States Army or Navy to assist in organizing or training their military forces. While not desiring in any way to encourage the increase of armaments, this Department has felt that a more efficient and economical organization of their existing forces would be a real service to the Government concerned, especially in those countries where a more efficient military force might be helpful in promoting political stability. It has felt also that this was a service which should, if possible, be performed by the United States rather than by European governments.[37]

After the war, British and American interests came into conflict in every area of the world. Where the vital strategic interests of the United States were at stake, the goodwill between the two countries was put aside and the former allies fought with every peaceful means available. The Great War left a legacy of expanded economic activity and concern for such things as trade, shipping, petroleum resources, communications facilities (chiefly cables), and investment capital such that those who formulated foreign policy after the war had to consider them as part of the national interest. Protection of the Panama Canal no longer was sufficient. Americans were so impressed with the importance of petroleum, cables, and capital that they built postwar policy in Latin America around a determination to dominate the possession and use of all three in the entire hemisphere. The war also stirred up the debate over the proper relationship between private interests and the government, and this debate affected the definition of the new strategic objectives and the manner in which they were achieved. Deficiencies in shipping during the war caused the same kind of worry as inadequate supplies of

[37] Daniels to Lansing, Dec. 24, 1919, and Lansing to Daniels, Jan. 17, 1920; memorandum by L. A. Bostwick, naval operations, Dec. 12, 1919, RG 80, 4492-76 and 77; Colby to Representative Thomas S. Butler, June 2, 1920, RG 59, 810.30/3; Hughes to Weeks, Jan. 9, 1924, 810.20/3; file 813.105; Phillips diary, Sept. 17, Nov. 19 and 20, 1923.

petroleum or poor communications. The navy and the War Trade Board particularly were concerned with the lack of reliable shipping in the hemisphere. Shipping was not kept on the list of strategic objectives because the merchant fleet accumulated by the United States during the war proved adequate to postwar needs.

CHAPTER 2

The Transition to Peace:
The Democratic Phase

The Great War had a tremendous impact upon the American economy. The war effort cost the United States $24 billion and at its peak absorbed one quarter of the national income. Demand in the American economy increased $31.5 billion. Industrial output doubled from 1914 to 1921; American tonnage in foreign trade increased more than 10 times; and exports to the rest of the Western Hemisphere increased from $652.5 million to $1.6 billion, while imports rose from $650 million to $1.6 billion.

The most dramatic economic change was in international status from debtor nation to the world's greatest creditor. On July 1, 1914, American indebtedness to foreigners exceeded the debt of foreigners to Americans by approximately $3.7 billion. By December 31, 1919, the situation had more than reversed itself. The United States had total net assets on private and government accounts of $12.6 billion. Before the war the United States was involved in no intergovernmental debts. After the war foreign governments owed the United States government $9.6 billion. Investment and foreign commerce in the United States were dominated by foreign banks as late as 1913. By the end of the war, New York City had replaced London as the financial center of the world. With very few exceptions, New York's banking houses controlled foreign and domestic bond issues. When the United

States entered the war the best investment opinion held that $500 million was the limit to the nation's borrowing capacity; yet the public debt rose from less than $1 billion in 1914 to over $25 billion at the end of the fiscal year 1918–19. The federal government adopted the latest publicity and sales techniques to encourage the public to buy Liberty Bonds and Victory Bonds. The Victory Bond loan of over $5 billion was sold in 1919 to nearly twelve million individual subscribers. The popular ownership of securities was revolutionized by the wartime finance. One prominent financial expert estimated that there were two hundred thousand holders of securities in the United States before the war and over twenty million afterward. The little investor did not step in immediately. The banks bought the first Liberty Bonds under pressure from the government, and they, in turn, had to find permanent holders.[1]

United States economic expansion in the Western Hemisphere after 1914 was due primarily to the collapse of European financial and commercial power which the war precipitated, not to specific acts of the United States government. United States direct investments in Central America alone increased from $40 million in 1912 to $93 million in 1920, and United States trade with the Caribbean area increased 400 percent in the same period. As a direct result of the war, the United States was able to increase its share of the Mexican market from 57 percent to 68.3 percent. Great Britain, the chief competitor of the United States, suffered a severe loss in its own share of the Latin American market. Britain's share of Mexican imports fell from 12 percent to 7.8 percent. Its percentage of Latin American imports generally fell from 29 to 20. At the same time, the United States' share of this total Latin American market increased from 18 percent to

[1] G. M. Jones, "The Declining Independence of the United States," *The Annals*, 83 (May 1919), 30; C. W. Phelps, *The Foreign Expansion of American Banks* (New York, 1927), 87; Joseph Dorfman, *The Economic Mind in American Civilization*, 4 vols. (New York, 1959), IV, 4; H. Parker Willis and Jules I. Bogan, *Investment Banking* (New York, 1936), 235–37; Charles Cortez Abbott, *The New York Bond Market, 1920–1930* (Cambridge, 1937), 55–61; M. F. Jolliffe, *The United States as a Financial Centre, 1919–1933* (Cardiff, 1935), 3.

42 percent. In the ten years after 1914, the United States' "stake" in Latin America increased nearly 350 percent, while Britain's increased only 18 percent. The pattern of United States trade with Latin America was remarkably consistent. Exports to the major countries in the hemisphere increased approximately four times from 1912 to 1920, Argentina and Mexico taking the most from the United States in both years. The pattern of imports from Latin America was not so consistent. Argentina enjoyed the greatest percentage increase, beginning in 1912 with only $29 million worth of sales and ending, in 1920, with $207 million. In 1912, Brazil sold the most to the United States, by far, $123 million. In 1920, it still was on first place, but with sales of $227 million, its lead had been cut. The chart on page 41 indicates the trend of Imports into and Exports from the United States from/to Latin America, 1910–1927. It is not possible to determine if all of these figures are based upon constant prices. We know government trade statistics from the period are inflated because they do not account for rising prices. The discrepancies can be enormous, as in the following: Using actual prices, imports in 1914 were $1.2 billion and $4 billion in 1920, an increase of 244 percent; exports in 1914 were $1.7 billion and $5.5 billion in 1920, an increase of 224 percent. Restating the 1920 trade figures in 1914 prices cuts the increase in half —imports = $2 billion and exports = $2.3 billion. Added to this is the fact that the United States enjoyed considerable trade expansion in the six-year period prior to 1914. Nevertheless, expansion from 1914 to 1920 was greater than expansion prior to 1914. More important for this study, the expansion was different qualitatively as well as quantitatively.[2]

[2] J. W. Angell, *Financial Foreign Policy of the United States,* 79–80; Callcott, *Caribbean Policy,* 461 and 312; articles by W. C. Wells and Simon Litman, in *The Annals,* 94 (Mar. 1921); Herbert Feis, *The Changing Pattern of International Economic Affairs* (New York, 1940), 110, n. 1; data from Department of Commerce, Bureau of Foreign and Domestic Commerce, *Statistical Abstract of the United States* (Washington, D. C.: United States Government Printing Office, 1918 and 1923); J. R. Smith, "The American Trade Balance and Probable Trade Tendencies," *The Annals,* 83 (May 1919), 114; Max Winkler, *Investments of United States Capital in Latin America* (Boston, 1929), 9. On

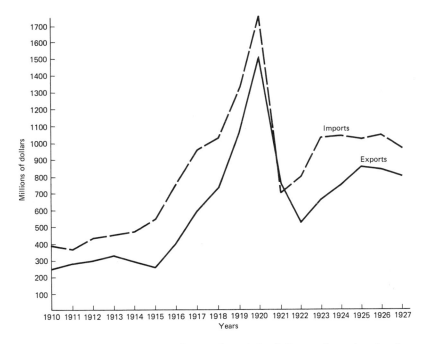

Imports into and exports from the United States from/to Latin America, 1910–27. Adapted from Department of Commerce, Bureau of Foreign and Domestic Commerce, *The Statistical Abstract of the United States,* for the years 1910–18, 1919–23, and 1924–27. (Washington: United States Government Printing Office, 1918, 1923, and 1928.)

The role of the United States government in this increase of American economic power was as significant as it was inevitable. By means of a multiplicity of wartime agencies, the government controlled the movement of capital, the disposition of shipping tonnage, the distribution and pricing of many basic commodities, the fluctuation of exchange rates, the use of communications networks, and the exploitation of natural resources. Every detail of international economic relations was considered a vital part of the national interest. By 1919 the government was accustomed to committing its power and prestige to economic affairs, and businessmen took

the problem of rising prices, see National City Bank study in *The World's Week,* XLI, 2 (Dec. 1920), 118.

the active participation of their government for granted. Business men and government officials, particularly those in the State and Commerce Departments, were anxious to take advantage of Europe's weakness by continuing the expansion of the United States' economic influence, which had been facilitated by the war, through retention of at least some of the wartime administrative machinery for their benefit. The American Club of Buenos Aires petitioned the United States government to continue the Committee on Public Information, "thereby increasing American prestige in the Argentine." John Barrett, as secretary general of the Pan American Union, devoted considerable energy to the campaign to maintain United States commercial interest in Latin America. While his office worked to supply information to the United States delegation to the Paris Peace Conference, Barrett toured the country speaking to business groups about the fabulous opportunities available in Latin America. These men were supported by economists who warned that a great volume of foreign trade and investment was necessary to stimulate the economy and maintain the wartime level of production and employment. According to one expert, America "cannot be isolated and commercially independent." [3]

The transition to a peacetime economy was softened by a continuation of the government's extraordinary wartime expenditures. Whereas prewar spending reached a high of $760 million in 1915, monthly disbursements of the government exceeded this figure every month of 1919 through August.

[3] RG 59, 103.93/1472; Barrett's speech, *The New Pan American Opportunity,* Jan. 1, 1919; and letters to Barrett from Lawrence E. Bennett of the Ulen Contracting Company, May 14, 1917; Walter Sanford, Jan. 9 and 20, 1919; John Gasque, Apr. 12, 1919, all in the Barrett papers. Similar attitudes by government officials in report by Henry Amory, Nov. 4, 1918, RG 182, Entry 151, Box 6, Bureau of Foreign Agents—Argentina; William Beer to Franklin K. Lane, Dec. 2, Entry 192, Box 29, Bureau of Research and Statistics—South America; Roy G. Blakey, "Government Restriction and Promotion of Foreign Trade," *The Annals,* 94 (Mar. 1921), 205. W. A. Williams, "The Legend of Isolationism in the 1920's," *Science + Society,* XVIII (1954), is a different interpretation of these events.

The deficits of December 1918 and January 1919 were higher than those of any war month and higher than government expenditures for any year before the war. For this reason, one economist said the period of the war extended into the middle of 1920, when a depression cut short the trade boom.[4]

The immediate task for the United States economy after the Armistice was to reconvert industry to peacetime production and provide employment for the millions of workers released from service in the armed forces. The federal government provided no leadership in this area, and there was a six-month period of hesitation and uncertainty during which businessmen tried to adjust themselves to peacetime conditions. Production dropped off in all basic industries, and unemployment mounted. Thereafter, demand rebounded quickly, ending the recession and driving the economy to new heights in 1919. The Gross National Product in 1919 was $66.4 billion higher than in 1918. United States trade in 1919 amounted to $11.8 billion, as compared with only $8.8 billion in 1918 and $4.2 billion in 1914. The boom continued at an accelerated pace into 1920. Prices rose owing to overordering and general speculation. There was more plant expansion in 1919 than in any year of the war, and money was easy. The prop for the boom was continued government spending—the deficit financing by the Treasury Department and the reconstruction loans to Europe. The boom collapsed when these forces ceased to operate in 1920.[5]

The impetus of the war effort strengthened the argument in favor of continuing government support of private inter-

[4] Grosvenor Jones of the Department of Commerce, in *The Annals*, 83 (May 1919), 22–34; H. R. Mussey, "The New Normal in Foreign Trade," *Political Science Quarterly*, XXXVII, 3 (1922), 369–88.

[5] See Everett E. Hagen and Paul A. Samuelson, *After the War: 1918–1920* (Washington, D. C., 1943); John D. Hicks, *Rehearsal for Disaster* (Gainesville, Fla., 1961), 1–32; George Soule, *Prosperity Decade: From War to Depression: 1917–1929*, vol. 8 of the *Economic History of the United States* (New York, 1947); Dorfman, *Economic Mind*, IV, 3–6; Jolliffe, *United States as a Financial Centre*, 43–44; Feis, *The Changing Pattern*, 27 and 85; trade statistics from *Statistical Abstract of the United States, 1923*; and statistics on GNP from Simon Kuznets, *National Product since 1868* (New York, 1946).

ests overseas. It was hard for government officials to stop thinking of commerce in broadly strategic terms just because the Armistice had been signed. The drive to achieve the specific strategic objectives of self-sufficiency in fuel, communications, and investment capital carried over into government trade policy. Moreover, continuation of the blockade of Germany lent credence to the argument that wartime conditions were still in force. On occasion, the United States did use the wartime inter-Allied bureaucratic machinery to further the interests of United States commerce. As late as January 1919, the Allied Meat and Fats Executive was exerting pressure on the neutral nations of Europe to discourage them from purchasing meat in South America while inducing them to satisfy their needs in the United States in order to help create a market for North American pork. Part of the sympathy for continued restrictions on enemy trade to support United States trade stemmed from the belief that trade went hand in hand with investment and that support for one benefited the other. Congress had demonstrated its acceptance of this argument by creating the War Finance Corporation in April 5, 1918 and by passing the Export Trade Act just five days later. The former was intended to facilitate export of American agricultural and industrial products necessary for the prosecution of the war and to ease the work of postwar reconstruction by granting long-term credits to Americans. The latter authorized the formation of combinations engaged solely in export trade. These two, together with amendments to the Federal Reserve Act authorizing investment trusts with the broad purpose of supporting United States export trade and the laws on shipping and marine insurance passed shortly after the end of the war, were tangible evidence of interest in the promotion of foreign trade.[6]

    [6] Norman Davis to WTB, Jan. 25, 1919, RG 182, Entry 11, Box 1, Executive Country File—Argentina; link between trade and investment in testimony before the Federal Trade Commission, *Cooperation in American Export Trade*, vol. I, 75, quoted in D. M. Phelps, *Migration of Industry to South America* (New York, 1936), 73; C. D. Snow, "Governmental Foreign Trade Promotion in the United States," *The Annals*, 94 (Mar. 1921); G. F. Meyer of the Standard Oil Company of New York to P. E. Whitham, Department of Commerce, Sept. 28, 1920, RG 151, 312—General, Box 1652.

The expansion of United States economic influence outside the Caribbean was a fact, and one not displeasing to government officials. It behooved the Department of State to fix priorities to guide relations with the rest of the hemisphere. The assumption was that the pattern of those relations would be different from the pattern of relations with the Caribbean protectorates. South of the Caribbean, trade and investment would facilitate more intimate relations, eliminating the need for exercising more direct forms of influence. Trade and investment could also be the means of eliminating unwanted competition from European powers, as when department officials took advantage of a state visit by Brazilian President-Elect Epitacio da Silva Pessôa, in June 1919, to help Charles Schwab of the Bethlehem Steel Company discuss the terms of a large arsenal contract. The department was anxious to prevent the British Vickers, Ltd., from getting the business. Assistant Secretary Breckinridge Long was much impressed by Schwab's statement that Brazilian iron and manganese ores were of very high grade and that "the ones who control [them] will control the world in 75 to 100 years." [7]

Such energetic cooperation with business was not considered official government policy in the year following the war. A few months before the Pessôa visit, the State Department tried to get the Navy Department to ferry a group of men "interested in sugar development in the Caribbean" from Guantánamo to Port-au-Prince. The navy declined on the grounds that this would be an improper use of United States sea power, even though the chief of Naval Operations was a "strong supporter of the doctrine that the trade follows the flag." A policy memorandum by the State Department solicitor opposing representations before the Venezuelan government to protest laws designed to inhibit foreign investment

[7] Hoffman Philip (United States minister in Colombia) to John Barrett, enclosed in RG 59, 710.11/409; the diary of Breckinridge Long, June 25, 1919, LC; *Foreign Relations,* 1919, I, 204–18. For other examples of United States government support for private interests see J. F. Dulles to SS, May 17, 1924, RG 59, 814.6463Em7/106; Latin American Division memorandum, Sept. 5, 1918, 813.51/–; and Z. L. Cobb to Polk, Dec. 6, Polk papers; speech by Foreign Trade Adviser J. G. Lay before the Second Pan American Commercial Conference, June 5, 1919, Fletcher papers.

in Venezuela, written just before the Armistice and still in
effect a year later, made it clear that promotion of American
foreign trade and investment was an objective of very low
priority for the Wilson administration. There was considerable tension between the official policy and the sympathies
many officials had with promoting American foreign trade
and investment, and the latter succeeded in making the State
Department the most effective spokesman in the government
for American trade interests. An internal debate was held on
the merit of continuing wartime controls and maintaining
wartime identification of private and public interests. For at
least a year after the war, the government's attitude was ambiguous, clouded by conflicting tendencies to lend support to
private interests and to end the wartime cooperation with
the private sector.[8]

There were two developments arising out of the war which,
after a period of hesitancy and drift, helped to fix the course
of United States policy along lines more congenial to those
who favored supporting business interests in Latin America
than to those who preferred to see the government retire to
the sidelines. The first was the wartime organization of the
United States government, already mentioned, which led to a
broader spectrum of relations with the governments of the
hemisphere than had existed previously. The second was the
increasing sophistication of United States government information about Latin America and the gradual rationalization
of gathering information to suit the needs of businessmen.
These two developments contributed to the definition of an
aggressive policy for support of private interests overseas.

One of the most obvious ways in which United States government agencies affected relations with Latin America was

[8] Polk to Daniels, Jan. 14, 1919, and Daniels to Polk, Jan. 16, RG 80,
5526–172; Freidel, *Ordeal,* 21; solicitor's memorandum, July 19, 1918,
RG 59, 831.602/22; report from Consul General Robertson in Buenos
Aires, June 30, 1920, RG 59, 635.119/916; Morgan to SS, Jan. 7, 1919,
RG 182, Entry 38, Box 3, "Cables Received from U. S. Foreign Service
Representatives—Brazil." For conflicting views on continuing the black-
list see RG 182, Entry 151, Bureau of Foreign Agents, passim, and
Clarence Woolley to Polk, June 26, 1919, RG 182, Entry 11, Box 16,
Executive Country File—Mexico.

through the Shipping Board. So long as the board was responsible for the disposition of United States merchant shipping, incidents involving those ships were automatically incidents between governments and not matters of purely private interest. The State Department was asked to intercede when, two years after the war, labor disputes in the port of Veracruz prevented ships under the control of the Shipping Board from sailing. The United States response, designed to stir the Mexican port authorities "to take action to have goods promptly removed from steamers and warehouses," was a total embargo on cargo bookings to Veracruz. The officials of the Shipping Board had a greater claim upon State Department support than did any private citizen. In cases involving routine legal difficulties, the Department of State had to decide if the political aspects of the situation permitted strong representations in favor of the Shipping Board and often found itself in a position where it was caught between an angry foreign government and an angry Shipping Board. On one such occasion, the State Department managed with difficulty to convince the Shipping Board to abide by the findings of the Argentine courts.[9]

The State Department was never loath to act energetically in cases where United States private interests were seeking to dislodge German investments or interests which had been sympathetic to the Germans during the war. The department committed its influence and prestige wholeheartedly to the efforts of the Electric Bond and Share Company in Guatemala to take over properties formerly controlled by the German-owned Empressa Electrica del Sur, and it did the same for United States interests in Peru which were trying to gain control over the Gildermeister sugar properties. The State Department also appeared sure of its ground in cases that were direct continuations of wartime activity, such as the negotiations with Chile over the disposition of nitrate. These negotiations have already been considered for their importance to the blacklist during the war. When the war ended and the Allied Nitrate Executive disbanded, the British

---

[9] Shipping Board to SS, Nov. 18, 1920, RG 59, 812.504/274; RG 59, 335.115C66.

dumped their surplus nitrate on the European market. The British tried to come to terms with Bernard Baruch, but the War Industries Board had been disbanded, and they could not reach an agreement with the State Department. To counteract the effects of the British dumping, the Chilean government asked the Nitrate Producers Association to limit production and regulate export prices. American companies complained to the Department of State that they were being forced to join the association in violation of United States antitrust laws. The department instructed Ambassador Joseph Hooker Shea to protest the formation of the association. The Chilean government's proposals foundered in the legislature in 1919, and the Chilean producers moved to protect themselves through a private association.[10]

The Nitrate Producers Association also tried to force American firms to join by threatening them with a price war. This threat proved ineffective, and it then tried to support its price control by having the Chilean Congress pass discriminatory taxes against the recalcitrant Americans. This failed also. The major American interests considered their position insecure because they believed they could not hold out much longer and because they were fearful that they would violate American anti-trust laws if they joined the association. At their request, the State Department once again informed the Chilean government of its interest in the matter.

The legal issues were unclear. Although the Commerce Department had promised to work in Congress for protection for the American firms in the event they were forced to join the association, the Federal Trade Commission refused to comment before the companies had actually committed the acts which might or might not be in violation of the law. The State Department continued to make mild representations in favor of the American companies. These prevented the Chilean Association from taking any further atcion. In 1922, the American companies succeeded in enlisting the aid

[10] The Guatemalan incident is RG 59, 814.6463Em7/14–36; Stabler to Polk, Feb. 8, 1919, Polk papers, summarizes the Peruvian case; the Chilean case is RG 59, 825.6374/161–673.

of Consul Homer Brett in Santiago. Brett asked the department to support a special tariff on all nitrate from monopoly-controlled suppliers such as the Chilean Nitrate Producers Association. This plan was a favorite with Secretary of Commerce Herbert Hoover, who was opposed to all natural-resource monopolies. Because of Hoover's influence and congressional pressure, Brett's suggestion received careful attention from the Department of State. The Economic Adviser's Office passed on it, though with little enthusiasm. Once it was in the Latin American Division, however, it was subjected to strong criticism. An attack on Chile's nitrate industry would have grave political consequences; the Chilean Association never had a complete monopoly because there were so many kinds of artificial nitrates; and without the association, the industry would be subject to disastrous depressions. The assistant secretary accepted these arguments and instructed the economic adviser to inform Brett that his idea was deemed inexpedient.

While the department had decided against taking official action in opposition to the Chilean Nitrate Association, the American ambassador continued to support the American firms informally, and Hoover supported Henry Ford's idea of manufacturing nitrate at Muscle Shoals to protect the United States from what he called the "British-controlled Nitrate Association." The Chilean ambassador lodged vigorous protests against these activities, and the State Department eventually decided that the Chilean nitrate industry was too sensitive for diplomatic interference. In 1924, when the United States Supreme Court found that participation in the association would not violate the Sherman Antitrust Act, the department ordered the American ambassador to end his informal defense of the independent American firms and as much as suggested that the Americans join the association. The department simply washed its hands of the matter. The need for nitrates was no longer vital, and the political disadvantages of vigorous governmental interposition far outweighed any gains that might be made by a few American firms. Other examples of activities begun during the war and continued in the Harding administration were purchases from Cuba and Argentina by the Sugar Equalization Board.

The second development arising out of the war was the revolution in the information-collection procedures of the United States government. Before the war, Latin America was very nearly a terra incognita for the United States. In order to do its job, the War Trade Board had to learn the details of economic activity in every country in the hemisphere. How else could the board make intelligent decisions on export licenses and give useful advice to the War Industries Board and the Shipping Board to help those agencies control trade and plan for the ships to carry the goods needed for that trade? The Bureau of Research and Statistics did pioneering work in the collection of data on Latin America and tapped the rich resources of the newly established Bureau of Foreign and Domestic Commerce in the Department of Commerce. As part of its effort to reestablish its primacy in the field of international relations, the State Department took the lead in the systematic collection of all possible kinds of data about Latin America. When the military asked for confirmation of the fact that the United States did dominate hemispheric trade, it provided information to the Military Intelligence Division of the Department of the Army on foreign investments in Latin America. Later, it did a survey for the Department of Labor on opportunities for investment and employment in Argentina.

To meet its own growing needs for information, the Department of State circulated a series of instructions to all its representatives abroad calling for systematic reports on political, commercial, financial, and economic conditions in the countries to which they were accredited. These reports were to be far more elaborate than any required before the war. As early as February 1917, the department requested reports on postwar trade possibilities in various areas, and, in a consular circular of July 1918, it requested reports on the plans of neutral governments and commercial organizations for carrying on trade after the cessation of hostilities. These efforts, together with the inheritance of the War Trade Board files after the war, prepared the State Department for a more aggressive role in helping United States interests find and exploit new opportunities in Latin America.[11]

The termination of hostilities generated other forces which inhibited the department from immediately assuming its new role. Some people believed that the government should stop meddling in the economy. Even the president was of two minds on the question, and he quickly became so involved with affairs in Paris that he did not provide his subordinates with clear guidelines for policy. The cry "Bring the boys home!" conveyed the impression that the American people were tired of foreign adventures. Congress made it perfectly plain that the responsibilities of protectorates were undesirable, so that even advocates of an aggressive campaign to spread American influence in the Western Hemisphere understood that there would be limits to the government's participation, although there was disagreement over what these limits should be. While the debate over policy undoubtedly contributed to the hesitancy which characterized general economic foreign policy through 1919 and part of 1920, a more important cause was the speed with which the United States dismantled its war machine and the administrative incapacity that gripped the State Department in the wake of demobilization. Scarcely two weeks after the Armistice, the British representative in the United States expressed his alarm that, with the president out of the country, there would be no one in the United States with any authority to act and that "the whole war organization would collapse, and there would be no machinery left by which to work back from the war basis to the peace basis." The War Industries Board closed shop officially on January 1, 1919, when Bernard Baruch resigned; the War Trade Board was shifted over to the State Department on June 30; Herbert Hoover left the Food Administration on July 1; Harry A. Garfield was forced out of the Fuel Administration by the

[11] Report by H. T. Collings, n.d., RG 182, Entry 192, Box 8, Bureau of Research and Statistics—Argentina; RG 59, 812.503/16 and 20; report of Lt. Warren C. Graham, June 28, 1920, RG 38, ONI Register 13577, B-7-d; William Barnes and J. H. Morgan, *The Foreign Service of the United States* (Washington, D. C., 1961), 192–93.

end of 1919; and the Railroad Administration folded on March 1, 1920. But these dates indicate the formal ending of business. Efficient conduct of operations ceased much earlier. Most of Baruch's staff left for a Christmas holiday and never returned, and the War Trade Board made itself ineffective long before June 30, 1919. Even the State Department, which was charged with absorbing the international obligations of all these boards and agencies, began to lose its wartime staff immediately after the Armistice and to fall into something bordering on chaos. This was perfectly plain to department officials, whose job it was to carry on after the war, and to men in the field attempting to do business with Washington. The department's mail had increased to 900,000 pieces per year as compared to a prewar rate of 200,000. The staff had increased so rapidly during the emergency that business was never conducted with model efficiency; after the war, the work did not decrease, while the executive staff—those working for the secretary, the undersecretary, the three assistant secretaries, and the solicitor—went from ninety-three to twenty-three in less than a year. The results of such overwork were predictable. Chandler Anderson, not a sympathetic observer, reported that "At the Department, I found nothing of interest except the usual lack of intelligence, which is always amusing." To compound the personnel problems, many of the department's best men were sent to Paris to help prepare for and conduct the peace conference. This added demoralization to disorder in the Department of State in Washington. Everything in the home office seemed pedestrian.[12]

For almost a year after the Armistice, the Department of State went into a decline. At Paris, the department and the secretary of state were totally eclipsed by the president and Colonel House. In Washington, the department became a messenger service for the Peace Commission and for the var-

[12] Anderson diary, May 7 and Nov. 23, 1918; Hicks, *Rehearsal for Disaster*, 6–7, Clarence Woolley to Polk, June 26, 1919, RG 182, Entry 11, Box 16, Executive Country File—Mexico; Carr diary, Feb. 6, Aug. 13, and Aug. 30, 1918; Auchincloss to Carlyle Barton, Nov. 28, and Barton to Auchincloss, Dec. 6, 1918, Auchincloss papers; John W. Davis to Polk, Jan. 4, 1919, Polk papers.

ious war boards with agents in Paris. The Latin American Division was reduced to gathering information. The very few memoranda of the division on policy questions during this period were filed without discussion; there was virtually no dialogue within the department on Latin American policy. Things got so bad that, by April 1919, Polk, acting secretary in Lansing's absence, spent nearly half of his time on routine passport matters. This was indicative of the department's plight. It galled Polk and everyone in his office who was forced to share in his frustration. They blamed it on the "almost total lack of system and absence of centralization of control." [13]

In the middle of 1919, Polk was sent to Paris to replace Lansing. The secretary's presence in Washington did not improve matters, as he and the president were not on speaking terms after their falling out at Paris. Besides, Lansing was so tired from his work at Paris that he was often away from his office. One of Polk's former aides visited the department in September and found it "dead." He reported to Polk, "The Secretary was away, you were away, [Solicitor] Woolsey was away, [Assistant Secretary] Long was away, and [Assistant Secretary] Adee was in seclusion." The only man of authority on the scene was Assistant Secretary William Phillips. Lansing was sensitive to what he considered the shabby treatment he had received at Paris and began to consider resigning as early as August 1. His friends could not understand why he remained in office. Wilbur Carr noted in his diary on two occasions during the summer that Lansing thought the president was beginning to consult with him more than he had in the past. This may have been a brave attempt by the secretary to bolster the morale of his staff. He felt compelled by a strong sense of duty to stay at his post until the department was capable of carrying on without him and until the president's programs were brought to fruition. He set October 1 as his target date for resignation and undoubtedly would have resigned some time in October if it

[13] Carr diary, July 10, 1918; and Phillips diary, July 10, 1918; L. E. Gelfand, *The Inquiry* (New Haven, 1963), passim; G. Howland Shaw to Auchincloss, Apr. 16, 1919, Auchincloss papers.

had not been for Wilson's collapse on October 2. As he put it, in a desk memorandum on October 6,

> I am most anxious to leave an office which no longer has any attractions for me. . . . I am sick of being treated as a school boy or a rubber stamp. I have lost my great regard for the President—I say it with real regret because he is eaten up with egotism, a prey to vanity, and has become almost impossible.

Because of the president's illness, however, he would suppress his personal feelings and "stick to my job doing the best I can in the circumstances." [14]

Woodrow Wilson suffered a cerebral thrombosis on October 2, 1919, while touring the country to gain support for the League of Nations. His illness left him broken in body, although within a very short time he was capable of performing the obligations of his office a part of every day. As early as mid-November, it was clear that, for brief periods at least, he was able to control large bodies of material and reach firm decisions which he could then leave to loyal subordinates to execute. His stroke exacerbated certain personality traits which made his relations with Lansing impossible. After his collapse, the president was often irascible, suspicious, morose, and overemotional. He could not forgive Lansing for calling cabinet meetings during his illness and did his best to force the secretary of state to resign. He refused to answer communications sent to the White House by Lansing and would not even see him. He did not ask for a resignation; he merely waited for it to be submitted. Conduct of United States foreign relations was embarrassed further by the fact that the president's wife and his private secretary, Joe Tumulty, disliked Lansing and did their ut-

[14] Anderson diary, Aug. 27; Auchincloss to Polk, Sept. 25; Polk to Davis, Jan. 17, 1920, Polk papers. Colonel House referred to the department as "a thoroughly bankrupt concern." House diary, Nov. 30, 1919, quoted in Harold B. Whiteman, Jr., "Norman H. Davis and the Search for International Peace and Security, 1917–1944," Ph.D., dissertation, Yale University, 1958.

most to keep him from the president. The painful irony was that Lansing, who was looking for an excuse to resign, could not see that the president was as anxious to have him go as he was to be gone. The White House bypassed the department so completely that even loyal Wilsonians complained that they "did not have the vaguest idea what the President was going to do" on many vital issues of foreign policy. Wilson realized that this situation could not continue and let it be known that Lansing's resignation would be welcome. The latter complied on February 13, 1920, and Polk once again became acting secretary. Lansing was heartily glad to be free and was amazed at the "clumsy way" in which the president had handled the incident.[15]

Wilson wanted a secretary of state who thought as he did, or who would agree to do so. He selected Bainbridge Colby, a former "Bull Moose" Republican, a member of the United States Shipping Board, and a corporation lawyer. The press was generally critical of the appointment. Only the *New York World,* a faithful Wilson organ, greeted the announcement with anything like warm praise. Many papers reacted calmly, taking the appointment as confirmation of the president's desire to be his own secretary of state; others could not understand how the president could appoint a man so lacking in qualifications for the job. The most hostile papers used Colby as a means to throw poisoned barbs at the president. The *Boston Evening Transcript* went so far as to imply that the appointment pleased Joe Tumulty. That would be the final curse for the paper's Boston Brahmin readership. Wilbur Carr thought it was due "to the same motive that

[15] Cary Grayson, *Woodrow Wilson: An Intimate Memoir* (New York, 1959); W. M. Bagby, *The Road to Normalcy; the Presidential Campaign and Election of 1920* (Baltimore, 1962), 58–59, explains much of Wilson's behavior after his collapse by the illness and the physical-psychological syndrome it brings with it. He refers specifically to Walter C. Alvarez, "Cerebral Arteriosclerosis," *Geriatrics,* 1 (1946), and to David Lawrence, *The True Story of Woodrow Wilson.* Lansing's resignation is in Polk to Davis, Jan. 17, 1920, Polk papers; Private Memorandum, Dec. 4, Dec. 10, 1919, and Feb. 13, 1920, Lansing papers; Daniels, *Years of War,* 519–26; Long diary, Feb. 3; "Record of United Press International Interview," Sept. 27, Colby papers; Carr diary, Feb. 18, Polk diary, Apr. 2.

guides a man to select a wife—congeniality and lack of irritating qualities." [16]

Colby and Wilson got along well together. Their letters were warm and personal and give no evidence of the slightest disagreement or difference of opinion. Wilson told a reporter that, in Colby, "for the first time I have a man who can write a note for me . . . heretofore, I have always had to write them myself." When he had been in office for a month, Colby told the president, "My enjoyment of this post will be in direct proportion to the extent to which I feel I am carrying out your wishes and meeting your expectations." His fellow workers in the State Department ridiculed this behavior. One career diplomat said that he was overly fastidious and that he would make a "regular tempest in a teapot" out of minor issues. Breckinridge Long, a Wilsonian political appointment, felt such subservience would lead to no good:

> Colby is scared to death of the President. . . . He alludes to the words of the President in the Lansing correspondence, about a mind that "goes along," "forestalling judgement," etc.—and will never send back a note from the President suggesting he change his decision. He says the President "jealously guards his prerogative of appointment" etc.—and fears to make recommendations to fill the existing vacancies. He is *quite* frightened. The Department—and the Administration—are certainly bound for trouble if this continues.[17]

[16] *New York World,* Feb. 26, 1:1 and 12:1; *New York Times,* Feb. 26, 1:8 and 10:1; *The Outlook,* Mar. 10, 408; *Literary Digest* (Mar. 13), 22–23; *Current Opinion* (Apr. 1920), 479–82; and *Boston Evening Transcript,* Feb. 25, pt. 1, 1:5, 12:3,4, and pt. 2, 2:2; Carr diary, Feb. 27; John Spargo, "Bainbridge Colby," in S. F. Bemis, ed., *The American Secretaries of State and Their Diplomacy,* 10 vols. (New York, 1927–29), X; and Graham H. Stuart, *The Department of State* (New York, 1949), 257.

[17] "Record of United Press International Interview," Sept. 27, and Colby to Wilson, Apr. 1, 1920, Colby papers; Wilson to Polk, Feb. 24; G. Howland Shaw to Polk, Sept. 12, Polk papers; Long diary, May 12, 1920. In view of the materials in the Colby papers and the evidence cited here, it is difficult to believe that Colby played as active a role in formulating Wilsonian policy as is suggested by Daniel M. Smith, "Bainbridge Colby and the Good Neighbor Policy, 1920–1921," *Missis-*

This malaise was widespread among Wilson's foreign-policy advisers, nearly all of whom opposed the president's decision to fight for the peace treaty without revisions. Wilson
and Colby did not find the State Department, in 1920, a
powerful instrument or one that was easy to use. In addition to expressing its disagreement with the president on how
the League of Nations should be handled, and aside from
being overworked and understaffed and having been demor-
alized by the peace conference, the department was in the
throes of an internal battle for reform of the diplomatic
and consular services and of an external battle with the
Commerce Department for control over foreign relations.
Even those who opposed Wilson's concept of collective security recognized that the United States had emerged from the
war with new economic and political status. If advantage was
to be reaped from that heightened status, the United States
required a more efficient means of collecting information
from abroad and of protecting the nation's interest—public
and private—in foreign countries. Secretary Lansing told a
congressman, at the end of 1919, "such great changes have
been wrought that occurrences now in the remotest regions
of the earth have an immediate effect upon the material interests of the United States which can be safeguarded only
by the most competent and efficient watchfulness." [18] Because
the Department of State was charged by the Constitution
with responsibility for conducting the foreign relations of
the nation, and because the overseas operations of the War
Trade Board, the Committee on Public Information, and
other agencies were being transferred to the State Department its officers argued that any measure to improve the
efficiency and competence of the conduct of foreign relations

---

sippi Valley Historical Review, 50, 1 (June 1963); and "Aftermath of
War: Bainbridge Colby and Wilsonian Diplomacy 1920–1921," *Memoirs*
of the American Philosophical Society, 80 (May 1970), which appeared
too late to be used in this study. Colby was a faithful follower rather
than an intimate adviser and originator of policy.
[18] Lansing to Congressman Stephen G. Porter, Dec. 6, Lansing papers;
Polk diary, Mar. 3 and 16; Anderson diary, Mar. 10; Dwight W. Morrow
to Charles F. Choate, Jr., Nov. 11, Dwight W. Morrow papers, Amherst
College; Polk to Davis, Dec. 8, 1919, Polk papers.

should enhance the influence and primacy of the department. They wanted to create one foreign service to tie the consul, with his new orientation toward economics, to the old diplomat, and to keep both activities in the Department of State. On the assumption that a good foreign service would help in the fight for overseas markets, powerful business groups actively supported the reform movement. Conscious of this support, Lansing told Congressman Porter that he wanted to build up a real "business organization."

Far more important to smooth execution of policy than proposed structural changes within the department was the power struggle going on between the State and Commerce Departments over which should enjoy greatest influence in international economic relations. The State Department had responded to the new importance of economic affairs by increasing the staff of the Office of the Foreign Trade Adviser and by building a library of valuable information on the economic affairs of every country under the sun. Responding to the same stimulus, the Commerce Department increased the number of commercial attachés abroad and demanded more detailed reports from them. The State Department complained that the attachés did not give proper attention to the political aspects of their positions and often hampered delicate negotiations. The Commerce Department accused the State Department of holding up communications from the attachés under the guise of artificial political issues.[19]

While the argument raged over which department should control the commercial attachés and the dissemination of economic information, the real bone of contention was political influence, and here the State Department got much the better of the deal. The Office of the Foreign Trade Adviser was able to extend its control over the wartime intergovernmental committees to the postwar Foreign Trade

---

[19] For example, the debate over a Commercial Traveler's Treaty with Argentina, RG 59, 810.51A/79; and memorandum, Apr. 16, 1920, RG 151, Box 917, 151.2—Economic Liaison Committee. More generally, Klein's memorandum, Oct. 8, 1918, RG 151, Box 911, 151—General; and C. D. Snow, "Governmental Foreign Trade Promotion," 112.

Committee and the Economic Liaison Committee. The former was designed to assist in the formulation of economic foreign policy, and the latter was established on the expert level in order to provide information necessary to the Foreign Trade Committee. Both were controlled in 1918 and 1919 by Wesley Frost of the State Department, who attempted to use his position to dominate all aspects of economic foreign relations. The Commerce Department was angry at this grab for power, but it was effectively stymied by the State Department's control over the cable facilities of the entire government and by the greater influence which the State Department could command with President Wilson. Even the Treasury Department protested Frost's activities. Official correspondence belies the tensions which are given vent to freely in intradepartmental communications.[20]

Secretary of State Lansing pressed his department's advantage before congressional committees investigating the reorganization of the government. He urged that all aspects of foreign relations—commercial and political—be concentrated in the State Department, and he held that the postwar situation demanded that extension of foreign trade be made contributary to the furtherance of general policy and shaped in deference thereto. Lansing lobbied in the Senate and House and succeeded in winning from Secretary of Commerce Redfield the admission that the State Department was the proper organization for the coordination of the foreign relations of the United States. Beyond that, his efforts were fruitless. The Republican Senate was determined to cut all appropriations, and—in the face of such hard facts as the rise in cable costs from $184,000 in 1914 to $975,000 in 1919—to be especially

[20] Memorandum, July 9, 1920, "General Records of the Department of the Treasury, Correspondence of the Secretary," National Archives Record Group 56, Box 212. Hereafter these records will be cited by group and box numbers. Acting Secretary of Commerce E. F. Sweet to SS, Sept. 13, 1918, RG 151, Box 917, 151.2—State Department; Jones to Rowe Jan. 25, and Rowe to Jones, Jan. 28, 1919, Box 925, 152—Treasury; Klein to Jones, Oct. 8, 1918, and memorandum by F. R. Eldridge, Jr., Dec. 11, 1920, Box 911, 151—General. Cutler to Lay, June 6, 1919, Box 911, 151—General; Frost to Eldridge, June 21, 1920, Box 915, 151.12—General Information, are examples of gentle official correspondence.

severe on all requests for funds directly related to foreign affairs.[21]

The depression of 1920 crippled inter-American trade. In an effort to still the complaints against United States businessmen for their failure to meet their commitments in Latin America, the State Department asked the Federal Reserve Board to inform the countries of Latin America about the difficulties in the United States investment market. The department also had to meet complaints by Americans prompted by cancellation of orders by Latin Americans. At the end of the year, the department circularized all consular officials for data from their district on specific commodities which were needed in the United States. It was the intention of government to stimulate the production of those commodities in order to promote exports from Latin America to the United States; United States exports to Latin America would, in turn, benefit and lift the American economy out of its depression.[22]

This consular instruction indicates how firm the policy to protect and favor United States business interests in Latin America had become by 1920. That it was accepted as policy and no longer the whim of a few individuals within the government can be seen by the favorable response of the Navy Department to a request by the State Department for the use of naval vessels by an American company. The help was for a company doing a survey of the Magdalena River which would "greatly facilitate the commerce of the United States with Colombia." The navy responded with alacrity, instructing the commander of the Special Service Squadron in the

[21] Lansing to the Senate Committee on Foreign Relations, Jan. 22, 1920, Senate Document 190, 66th Cong., 2nd Sess., 8; Lansing to Congressman Rogers, Jan. 21, in *Hearings before the Committee on Foreign Affairs on H. R. 17 and H. R. 6357*, 68th Cong., 1st Sess., 32, both quoted in Tracy H. Lay, *The Foreign Service of the United States* (New York, 1925), 197; Lansing's letters to Congressman Porter, Dec. 6, 1919, Senator Lodge, Feb. 18, and Congressman Dickinson, Mar. 23; and Lodge to Lansing, Feb. 16, 1920, Lansing papers.

[22] Circular instruction, July 1; general instruction, consular, No. 765, Dec. 16, 1920, RG 59, 811.503/54a and 164.2/126a; business complaints in P. S. Smith to T. R. Taylor, Feb. 9, and Taylor to Smith, Mar. 23, 1921, RG 151, Box 2232, 432—Brazil; Box 2231, 431—Argentina.

Canal Zone to render all possible assistance to the firm in question and assuring the secretary of state that the navy would "accord all reasonable attention to such requests. . . ." [23]

How are we to explain the transition from hesitancy to firm support for American business interests overseas? This policy evolved slowly, without guidance from the president, largely in response to administrative needs of the department itself and to the expanding needs of the American economy. It was encouraged by the fact that during the period of its greatest debility, the department's daily work was in the hands of career men who viewed Latin America as a sphere of United States special interest which merited a more forward stance by the United States government than might be called for in other areas of the world. These career men remained at their posts while the upper ranks of the department were decimated by resignations or upset by the constant traveling between Washington and Paris. To protect what they felt was their just control over foreign affairs and to withstand the attacks of the Department of Commerce and business-minded congressmen, the diplomats had to show themselves willing to defend the rights of Americans abroad. The more sensitive the department's position in Congress, the more aggressive the diplomats would be. The competition with Great Britain produced the same effect: it led the department to commit more of its prestige and influence to private interests, so long as it was clear that those interests coincided with the national interest.

The department's willingness to go to the aid of private American interests throughout the hemisphere contrasted sharply with a growing disposition on the part of the American people to avoid foreign entanglements. The struggle for the League of Nations broke Woodrow Wilson's health. It also seemed to drain him and the United States of idealism and energy for international good works. By the time the country had gone through the war, the league fight, and the Red scare, "it lost most of its desire to face squarely the challenge to the old order." The American people were

23 SS to SecNav, Oct. 5, and SecNav to SS, Oct. 9, RG 80, 5341–74.

unwilling to commit the power and prestige of the United States in the unsettled squabbles of Europe and Asia. Even when they consented to lend Europe their dollars to repair the physical damage of the war, they would not become involved in the larger, more disturbing issues of economics and politics. In the Western Hemisphere, this attitude was reflected in a desire to withdraw from involvement, to shun crises which might force the commitment of the nation's power and prestige. It was one thing to help American bankers and businessmen find new markets in Latin America; it was quite another to protect American interests to the point of intervention, which was understood to mean the formal assumption of dominance, as in Haiti, the Dominican Republic, or Cuba; or of military incursion, as in Mexico.

It was an axiom of United States foreign policy that the nation had special interests in the Caribbean which it would protect by any means necessary, including force. On several occasions, the United States had occupied militarily another sovereign state, usurping the political, economic, and civil functions of the intervened nation. After the war, Wilson decided that the United States must avoid such intervention in the Caribbean and must, wherever possible, terminate existing occupation of dependent states in the hemisphere. The decision to eschew intervention stemmed from his desire to make Caribbean policy consistent with the idealism of United States involvement in the European war and from his dissatisfaction with United States failures in the region and with the procedural solution to the problems of political underdevelopment. His preoccupation with the League of Nations, his illness, his final disillusionment with the American people, and the fact that he was under bitter attack during the campaign of 1920 for his interventions helped shape the president's new attitude toward the use of American power in the hemisphere. The new attitude was essentially isolationist, a disposition to withdraw from involvement. It is in this sense that Wilson's handling of relations with Latin America after the war serves as the origin for Franklin Roosevelt's policy of the "Good Neighbor." The posture of one and the policy of the other were designed to prevent the recurrence of imperial relationships that were admitted to be inadequate to the needs of United States foreign policy. Pressure on the United States by Latin American nations was another factor leading the State Department wherever possible to avoid the responsibility of formal dominance. The war set loose Latin American hostility to American "imperialism" and posed for the State Department the problem of establishing a level of diplomatic meddling that would protect America's expanding interests in the hemisphere without giving offense to sensitive nations and without leading to unwanted responsibilities.[24]

As soon as it was obvious that the war in Europe was drawing to a close and that the United States would have to participate in a peace conference, the Latin American Division of the Department of State applied itself to the problem of how to reconcile United States attitudes with respect to the Western Hemisphere with the policies of the United States in the Great War. There was a strong sense of guilt in the department and a fear that the Latin American nations would make things difficult for the United States at Paris. Far from embarrassing the United States, the Latin American nations proved staunch supporters of the Wilsonian plan for a League of Nations, and in return, the United States went out of its way to insure the representation of Latin America at the first meetings of the league.[25]

[24] Leuchtenburg, *Perils of Prosperity*, 6; private memorandum, May 6, 1919, Lansing papers; Joseph Robert Juárez, "United States Withdrawal From Santo Domingo," *HAHR*, 42 (1962). Freidel, *Ordeal*, 83, argues that these issues had only a negligible effect on the vote. Wilson's change of heart concerning intervention is in George F. Kennan, *The Decision to Intervene* (Princeton, 1958), passim; and Newton Baker to Wilson, June 19, 1918, Wilson papers, LC, Series IV, Case File 64. For hostility to American imperialism see articles by Antonio Escobar and Enrique José Varona, *Revista de Filosofía* (La Plata), 14, 15, 16 (1921–22); Antonio Orzábal Quintana, "El Imperialisimo Yanqui en Santo Domingo," *Nosotros* (Mar. 1921); Max Henríquez Ureña, "Optimismo, Idealismo, Patriotisimo," *Cuba Contemporánea*, XXIV (1920); Tulio M. Cestero, *Estados Unidos y Las Antillas* (Madrid, 1931); Cosme de la Torriente, *Cuba y los Estados Unidos* (Havana, 1929); press release, Oct. 17, 1920, Barrett papers.

[25] Latin American Division memoranda prepared for the projected peace conference are by Ferdinand Mayer, Sept. 9, RG 59, 710.11/377;

Many people in the United States feared that the League of Nations would usurp control of the Monroe Doctrine and that the league would be used by European countries to extend their influence in the Western Hemisphere. In fact, the league generally left hemispheric matters to the United States, although not all of the Latin American nations were pleased that this was so. Members of the Pan American Union were concerned lest the proposed League of Nations detract from their status in the hemispheric organization and reduce the effectiveness of their hemispheric body. John Barrett brought this to the attention of the president and the Department of State, while, at the same time, he prepared a series of high-flown memoranda for the peace conference extolling the virtues of Pan Americanism as the prototype for the new world League of Nations.[26]

Wilson's submission to the Senate demand to include in the Covenant of the league a statement explicitly recognizing the Monroe Doctrine prompted a marked change in the relations between the United States and Latin America. Nations which had been very enthusiastic over Wilson's project for a society of nations changed their mood completely when the Monroe Doctrine was added to the Covenant, despite the fact that Wilson had always favored what amounted to multilateralization of the doctrine. Latin Americans realized, perhaps, that Wilson would leave office one day and that his successor could return to the traditional unilateral interpretation of the doctrine; so that having it written into the Covenant would place Latin America in a position of inferiority in the community of nations. They were upset, also, by statements Franklin Roosevelt made

---

and J. H. Stabler, Nov. 29, 1918, 710.11/380½; United States–Latin American cooperation at Paris is discussed in Rowe to Lansing, July 3, and Lansing to Rowe, July 19, 1920, and the private memorandum of May 8, 1919, Lansing papers.

[26] Polk to Wilson, Apr. 3, 1920, Polk papers; Anderson diary, Mar. 1919; Barrett to Tumulty, Feb. 28; Harry E. Bard, secretary of the Argentine-American Chamber of Commerce, to Barrett, Dec. 12, 1919; "The Attitude of the Latin American Countries During the War," "The Pan American Union—A Working League of American Nations," and "Practical Pan Americanism—Past, Present, and Future," Barrett papers.

during the campaign of 1920 justifying the league on grounds that the United States controlled more votes in the Western Hemisphere than Britain in her empire.[27]

In February 1920, the minister from Salvador, Juan Francisco Paredes, tried to embarrass the United States by requesting an official interpretation of the Monroe Doctrine. As it was about to be transformed by the sanction of the nations "into a principle of universal public law *juris et de jure,*" the minister asked the secretary of state to "set forth the authentic idea of the Monroe Doctrine, as the illustrious Government of the White House understands it in the present historic moment and in its intentions for the future." After some discussion, Chief of the Latin American Division Rowe and Acting Secretary Polk decided to frame an answer from pertinent parts of the president's address to the Second Pan American Scientific Congress, January 6, 1916, and thereby indicate publicly that the president's views had not changed. Their response to Minister Francisco Paredes was approved by the president on February 19, and it was sent on March 26 as a circular telegram to all United States missions in Latin America.[28]

When the League of Nations was rejected by the United States Senate, Pan Americanism was revived as a means of channeling the interests of the nation in international matters. The machinery of the Pan American movement was also convenient to the purposes of the State Department in

[27] For Latin American praise of the League of Nations see: Stimson to Lansing, June 17, 1918; Debillier (Santiago) to Lansing, June 14; Leavell (Guatemala) to Lansing, June 15; Handley (Lima) to Lansing, Sept. 1; Goding (Guayaquil) to Lansing, June 15, RG 59, 710.11/364, 362, 367, 339, 371. For additional comments on Latin American attitude toward League of Nations, see Warren Kelchner, *Latin American Relations with the League of Nations* (Boston, 1930); and the author's unpublished paper, "Egoísmo: Argentine Foreign Policy Under Hipólito Yrigoyen." Complaints about including the Monroe Doctrine in the League Covenant came in 1919 and 1920 from Mexico, Argentina, Colombia, Costa Rica, and Brazil, 710.11/388–394, 399, 414½, 421, 423, and 435. See, also, Don Ignacio Calderón, "The Pan American Union and the Monroe Doctrine," *Journal of International Relations,* X, 2 (Oct. 1919), 133–37; Freidel, *Ordeal,* 81.

[28] *Foreign Relations,* 1920, I, 223–25, 227; Rowe to Polk, Feb. 20, RG 59, 710.11/433.

advancing the economic interests of the United States. In this way, the Second Pan American Financial Conference, which met in Washington during January 1920, was used as a means of bringing American bankers together with their potential customers among the Latin American delegates.

This was an empty gesture. The real interest of the Wilson administration was not in the machinery of a moribund Pan American movement but in the realities of United States relations with the individual countries of the hemisphere. It was in these relations that Wilson's disposition to avoid intervention acquired substance, not so much by the withdrawal of American troops from the Caribbean protectorates, as by repeated decisions to avoid acting in a manner that would increase United States involvement in Caribbean affairs. Wilson had come to understand that, unless the government took positive measures to restrict the nation's involvement in the internal affairs of unstable nations, that involvement might escalate until it became formal dominance or control. Thus the State Department, despite provocation, refused to intervene in Mexican or Costa Rican affairs and avoided invoking the Platt Amendment with its commitment to intervene in Cuban affairs. The desire to restrict American involvement lay behind the decisions to withdraw, whenever possible, from Haiti and the Dominican Republic. While in Haiti only the smallest beginning was made, a plan to reorganize the administration of United States occupation, a more significant step was taken in the Dominican Republic, where the military government was subordinated to the civilian representative of the State Department and a plan of evacuation was formulated.

In Costa Rica, the new objective almost immediately came into conflict with the older policy of nonrecognition, and it was given higher priority. On the advice of his Latin American Division, Wilson had refused to recognize the regime of Federico Tinoco, who had taken over the Costa Rican government in January 1917. Wilson remained firmly opposed to this usurper throughout the war, despite the fact that Tinoco was pro-Ally and that what Wilson considered the "legitimate" government was notoriously pro-German. He took every opportunity to weaken the Tinoco regime, but he would not allow what he considered intervention of any kind in the internal affairs of Costa Rica. He repeatedly refused to aid a "legitimist" revolution. This restraint, coming as it did on top of Wilson's public opposition to Tinoco, was incomprehensible to the diplomatic representatives of the United States government in Costa Rica. They labored to the utmost to bring about the active intervention of the United States in the face of the State Department's steadfast refusal. From January to July 1919, dispatch after dispatch from San José contained references to violence in the capital or to some other danger to American life and property, the traditional reasons for American intervention. The failure to comprehend Wilson's subtle distinction between acceptable and unacceptable meddling led to confusion. Commanders of naval vessels in the area embarrassed the Department of State by exchanging salutes with Costa Rican port authorities. The secretary of the navy tried to excuse the officers by saying they were not kept informed of conditions in Central American countries.[29]

The agent of the Costa Rican government in Washington, Carlos Lara, complained that Consul Benjamin Chase was attempting an "unjustifiable interference" in Costa Rican affairs and that he was spreading false representations and rumors against the Tinoco administration. He also accused the Nicaraguan government of giving protection to Costa Rican revolutionaries on Nicaraguan soil. Acting Secretary Polk responded to the second complaint. On May 3, he instructed the minister at Managua, Benjamin L. Jefferson, to keep the department informed and to do everything in his power to prevent the outbreak of hostilities between the two nations. The instructions continued:

> The Department does not wish to be placed in the position where it can be criticized for failure to urge upon President Chamorro the careful fulfillment of

[29] The incident is in *Foreign Relations,* 1919, I, 800–850; SS to SecNav, Dec. 24, 1918, RG 80, 14417–19; Polk diary, June 1919; memoranda, May 14 and June 25, Fletcher papers.

his duty to prevent expeditions being organized on the
territory of Nicaragua and his duty to remain strictly
neutral in any struggle between Tinoco and his opponents.

The complaint against Chase, a representative of the
United States government, was more touchy and more difficult to handle. Chase was becoming insistent. On May 7,
he termed the situation in San José "more serious" and urged
that "prompt and adequate measures be immediately taken
for the protection of American lives and property in Costa
Rica." On May 10, Minister Jefferson relayed a message
from the consul at Corinto which Chase had sent through a
passing ship's captain: "I am cut off from all communication.
Advise the Government of the United States that I am men-
aced by Tinoco with assassination should United States tug
appear."

The State Department was not impressed. Polk asked Chase
to verify the report, but the consul would not attempt to
prove his allegations until his informants were secure from
reprisals. Polk's patience seemed at this point to have come
to an end. He cabled Chase that the presence of warships
would be interpreted as an attempt by the United States to
undermine the influence of Tinoco and that the landing of
marines was out of the question unless some actual danger
threatened Americans. Furthermore, he told Chase, the department could do nothing in the situation because he had
given it no definite information as to why he considered the
situation dangerous. To eliminate the uncertainty in its communications with the field, the department sent Ezra M.
Lawton, consul at Guatemala City, to assist Chase. While he
did his best to calm Chase, Polk dealt firmly with Tinoco's
representative in Washington. He warned Agent Lara that
"if any Americans were in jeopardy we would at once send
ships to Costa Rican ports and if necessary send an expedition to the capital." This was a bluff. Polk was working to
avert just such a contingency.

Chase did not give up. Early in June 1919, he reported
violence in San José, and, without clearance from the depart-

ment, he called for help from the gunboat *Castine,* then lying off the coast. The commander of the gunboat, obviously not attuned to the State Department's policy, informed Washington and steamed for Puerto Limón. Unconvinced of any real danger, Polk had the navy stop the ship and again telegraphed Chase for more information. Later the same day (June 14, 1919) he sent positive orders that "under no circumstances should the Marines land," and he told Chase bluntly that he was rattled and must "keep cool." Chase asked if the department would consider a tender from Costa Rican citizens of a request for intervention. In reply, the department told him curtly to "keep out of such projects." Chase had so alienated the Costa Rican government that, when Tinoco made inquiries through the Chilean ambassador at Washington and proposed to end the crisis by resigning, he insisted upon a condition precedent that Consul Chase should be put in jail! This was rejected, but the department thought wistfully of the quiet it would bring.

The policy of watchful waiting bore fruit. Lawton arrived in San José in the middle of June. His reports to the department belittled Chase's earlier accounts of violence and chaos. The situation remained quiet through July, but the call to the *Castine* had given heart to the Costa Rican opposition. Joaquín Tinoco, head of the army, was assassinated on the streets of San José on August 11, and Federico fled the next day. The department continued to negotiate for a compromise solution, but Wilson would not compromise. After October, he was unable to give the matter his attention. A "legitimate" government was elected in December, and the department decided to recognize it. Because of Wilson's illness, however, and the many changes in the upper echelons of the department, recognition was delayed until August 1920.[30]

The Costa Rican case is instructive because it demonstrates a determination to avoid intervention, even at the

[30] Fletcher to Polk, July 15, Fletcher papers; and Anderson diary, Oct. 22 and 23, Nov. 26 and 30, Dec. 1, 10, and 30, 1919; file of newspaper clippings on the revolt in Anderson papers, Box 61; Munro, *Intervention and Dollar Diplomacy,* 418.

cost of undermining previously established policy of non-recognition. In addition to Costa Rica, in 1919 the Wilson administration gave nonintervention higher priority than opposition to unconstitutional governments in Peru when the United States recognized Augusto B. Leguía; and in 1920, when the United States accepted revolutionary governments in Honduras and Guatemala.[31]

The decision to avoid intervention in Costa Rica was made easier by an absence of political pressure on the administration and by the smooth passage of events in Costa Rica. The first significant step toward curtailing American involvement was taken in Mexico, in December 1919, when the president specifically countermanded an ultimatum by Secretary of State Lansing which implied that the United States would follow any rejection of its terms with strong action. In the face of violent opposition at home, strong disagreement by his own advisers, and an unsympathetic government in Mexico, Wilson refused to allow forceful intervention in the internal affairs of Mexico. His decision in 1919 followed a similar one in 1916, when he refused to go to war with Mexico over a raid by Pancho Villa on Columbus, New Mexico.

Relations with Mexico had been an open wound from the beginning of Wilson's administration, and by 1916, the American people had grown restless with a situation that did not lend itself to rapid or facile solution. Not even recognition of the Carranza government in October 1915 seemed to help. The United States policy of "watchful waiting" was under constant pressure from a vociferous group that demanded war with Mexico to "teach them a lesson," "salvage American dignity," and "save American honor." The majority of the Congress and the public opposed war but insisted on some positive step to resolve the differences between Mexico and the United States. Watchful waiting in this case

[31] The decision to recognize Leguía is explained in Breckinridge Long to Wilson, September 1919, Long papers. J. C. Carey, *Peru and the United States, 1900–1962* (Notre Dame, Ind., 1964), 34–38, implies that economic "interests" were behind Leguía and won recognition for him. The evidence in the State Department records does not lead to this conclusion, and even Carey's own argument is inconclusive.

was a policy of inaction. As Pershing led his troops deeper into Mexican territory, against the wishes of the Mexican government, the tension in the United States rose to an unbearable level.

Finally, on June 21, 1916, at Carrizal in the state of Chihuahua, one of Pershing's patrols had a bloody engagement with Carranza's troops. Wilson's first response on June 2, made almost against his will and mainly to forestall an outcry in the United States, was to demand immediate release of American prisoners. His real objective was to find a way to withdraw the Pershing expedition without alienating the public. While he awaited a reply to the ultimatum, he tried to reassert his control over Mexican-American relations. He did so by making a moral virtue of inaction. He was able to cut the ground from under the faction which called for war and to ease tension generally by convincing the American people that their power and their dignity demanded patience, not war; that their honor would be served better by tolerant friendship toward Mexico than by armed intervention. A conciliatory Mexican response on June 28 to his ultimatum of June 25 made his task easier and enabled him to overcome a deep-seated feeling of hopelessness and frustration in the Department of State.

Wilson explained his policy to the American people in two widely publicized speeches, to the Associated Advertising Clubs on June 29 and to the New York Press Club on June 30. In the second speech, he said:

> The easiest thing is to strike. The brutal thing is the impulsive thing. No man has to think before he takes aggressive action; but before a man really conserves the honor by realizing the ideals of the Nation he has to think exactly what he will do and how he will do it.
>
> Do you think the glory of America would be enhanced by a war of conquest in Mexico? Do you think that any act of violence by a powerful nation like this against a weak and distracted neighbor would reflect distinction upon the annals of the United States?
>
> I got off the train yesterday, and as I was bidding

good-by to the engineer he said, in an undertone, "Mr.
President, keep out of Mexico." And if one man has
said that to me, a thousand have said it to me as I have
moved about the country. . . .[32]

These speeches had the desired effect. They regained for
the president the control over Mexican policy that he had
momentarily lost, captured public opinion in the United
States, and enabled Mexico to reopen negotiations without
loss of face.

In Mexico, as in Costa Rica, avoiding intervention was a
matter of patience. In the aftermath of the unhappy punitive
expedition, Wilson had stated that he would not allow military intervention in the affairs of Mexico. While the war
diverted attention from Mexico, Germany managed to keep
Mexican-American relations uneasy by effective propaganda
and subversive diplomatic maneuvers. Such undercover
activities were hardly necessary. By the end of the war, the
behavior of the Carranza government had convinced United
States officials it was "so hopelessly stubborn and stupid that
we shall never get anywhere until they are kicked out."
Senator Fall's subcommittee kept the attention of the public
focused on Mexico after the Armistice and served as a forum
for the most bitter critics of the Wilson administration. Fall
himself favored armed intervention to protect American
interests, and he had the warm support of the petroleum
industry and of many people with financial interests in
Mexico. Wilson refused to budge. He drew a sharp contrast
between "the policy of armed intervention" and that of
diplomatic interposition. He "would not countenance armed
intervention in the affairs of another state." Nor, on the
other hand, would he forfeit the right of diplomatic interposition in behalf of American citizens, "a distinctly friendly
method of supporting legitimate national interests in order

[32] Link, *Wilson,* IV, 317–18; V, 54–55; Grayson, *An Intimate Memoir,*
29–30; the author's "Inhibitions Affecting the Formulation and Execution of the Latin American Policy of the United States," *Ventures,* VII,
2 (fall 1967), 74–79; Freidel, *Apprenticeship,* 262; Launa M. Smith,
American Relations with Mexico (Oklahoma City, 1924), 188, 208, and
243.

to avoid injustice." This was a distinction accepted under international law at the time; it was reiterated by Secretary Hughes.[33]

Whether or not interposition was a "distinctly friendly" method of protecting the rights of Americans in Mexico depended upon one's point of view. Certainly, the Carranza government did not look upon it as such. To Wilson's way of thinking, however, it definitely was more friendly than military intervention. Wilson did not realize, when he determined upon a firm separation of intervention and interposition, that the latter was subject to abuse and that, in order to make effective his decision to avoid intervention, it would be necessary to circumscribe quite narrowly the kinds of action that properly might be taken by the Department of State under the rubric "interposition." Wilson personally fixed a hierarchy of priorities among objectives and modes of action to guide Mexican policy after the war. There was nothing in the president's policy, except the disposition to avoid increasing American commitments, to indicate what response the United States would make elsewhere in the hemisphere, where the alternatives would not be so unambiguous and the consequences of action would not be so clear.

Scarcely a month after the Armistice, people in the United States with a stake in Mexico organized the National Association for the Protection of American Rights in Mexico, which served as a lobby in the United States Congress and in the Department of State. At the same time, they launched a vigorous publicity campaign in the public press in favor of intervention. Many officials within the State Department sympathized with the basic objectives of the association—the protection of United States rights and interests. As relations between the two countries grew more tense through the spring and summer of 1919, because of numerous depredations and a breakdown in the talks between the Mexican

[33] Anderson diary, Dec. 5, 1918; Fletcher to Lansing, Jan. 7, 1919, RG 59, 103.93/1443; Auchincloss to Shaw, Nov. 28, Auchincloss papers; Polk diary, June 21, and July 9; memorandum by Boaz Long, Jan. 23, Harrison papers; Fletcher to Polk, July 24, Fletcher papers; "Investigation of Mexican Affairs," United States Congress, Senate Document No. 285, 66th Cong., 2nd Sess., "Preliminary Report and Hearings," II, 3166.

government and the oil companies, there was an all-pervading sense that intervention was inevitable. Bernard Baruch advised Henry Fletcher at the end of August to stay at his post in Mexico City because "it looked to him as if intervention was coming, and after intervention a governor general would be needed there." Intelligence sources reported from Mexico that Carranza was giving serious thought to the situation "arising from the threat of intervention." The Senate called for a report from the president on United States–Mexican relations. Caught up in the crisis, policymakers in the State Department assumed ever more firm tones in their correspondence with Mexican officials. They felt it was their duty to keep the Mexican government "alive to its responsibilities" so that it would "feel acutely the seriousness of the present situation." They must make it clear that "the Department is gravely concerned over the Mexicans' apparent inability to discharge effectively their obligation to preserve law and order." [34]

Such a policy required the utmost delicacy in execution and, if intervention was to be avoided, a firm commitment to the president's objectives. Adjusting the pressure applied to the Mexicans went well enough so long as it was in the hands of Frank Polk, who was sincerely opposed to intervention. When Polk went to Paris in the middle of July, control over Mexican policy passed to Henry P. Fletcher and to the secretary of state. Fletcher believed that intervention was desirable. Lansing was out of patience with the Mexicans and was determined to allow no further stains on the national escutcheon. Wilson, unaware that his senior policy advisers were out of sympathy with his objectives, gave his approval to a public announcement which stated that if the Mexican government did not mend its ways, the United States "may be forced to adopt a radical change in policy with regard to Mexico." This aggressive stance boomeranged and contributed to a crisis in Mexican–United States relations.[35]

[34] Fletcher to Adee, Sept. 30, 1919, Fletcher papers. Anderson diary, Aug. 27; report of Aug. 27, RG 38, ONI Register 12087, C-10-j; memorandum, July 30, Fletcher papers.

[35] Polk diary, June 14 and July 9, 1919; private memorandum, Nov. 28, 1919, Lansing papers. Fletcher's views are in his letter to Lansing,

On October 19, Consular Agent William Jenkins was kidnapped from his post in Puebla. He was released a week later. The kidnapping was part of a plot by rebels in the Puebla region to demonstrate to the American government that the Carranza government was not able to protect foreign nationals. It seemed to have the desired effect, for on October 25, Senator Myers of Montana introduced a resolution calling for armed intervention. Debate on this resolution was forestalled by the release of Jenkins just one day later and by the State Department's efforts to bury the issue. The incident entered a new phase when the Carranza government arrested Jenkins briefly for questioning on November 15 and then arrested him again on November 19 on charges that he had conspired with the rebels and had faked the kidnapping to embarrass the central government. Lansing was "surprised and incensed" by these actions and on November 20 instructed American Chargé George T. Summerlin to demand the immediate release of Jenkins. Lansing prepared further instructions which said, in part, that if his demands were not met, "the United States will be compelled to sever its diplomatic relations with Mexico and that, if necessary, will take steps to protect the rights of its citizens in Mexico." [36]

While his demands were still outstanding, Lansing had an interview with the Mexican ambassador in which he paraphrased his ultimatum and added:

> the patience of this country was nearly exhausted and had almost reached the breaking point, the tide of indignation among the American people might overwhelm and prevent further diplomatic discussion and force a break in our relations and . . . a break would almost

---

Nov. 21, Fletcher papers. Fletcher had been a constant advocate of a hard line in Mexican relations. He had Leon J. Canova, then chief of the Mexican Division, collect memoranda covering the period 1915–17, which supported the case for intervention. These are filed under Feb. 10, 1918, Fletcher papers.

[36] Charles C. Cumberland, "The Jenkins Case and Mexican–American Relations," *HAHR*, 31, No. 4 (Nov. 1951); *Foreign Relations*, 1919, II, 578–90; draft instructions, Nov. 21, Fletcher papers.

inevitably mean war . . . [which] would be carried to an
end with all the power of this nation.[37]

The tide of indignation was rising high indeed! Newspapers
called for intervention to restore the nation's honor; even
those which did not urge intervention saw that war was
imminent. Only the staunchly Wilsonian *New York World*
blamed Fall and Hearst for scaring up a conflict with Mexico;
and the *New York Times* seemed alone in its call for modera-
tion in the face of extreme provocation.

Congress returned on December 1 from its recess, and
immediately the jingoists sounded alarms for the national
honor and called upon the president to take decisive action.
On December 1, the text of Lansing's ultimatum was made
public. On December 3, Senator Fall submitted a resolution
calling for severance of diplomatic relations and followed
it with a demand for military intervention. Lansing and
Fletcher supported the Fall Resolution. They avoided bringing the issue to the attention of the president because they
feared that in the president's illness, Mrs. Wilson and Tumulty, who opposed a bellicose attitude, would dictate the
nation's policy. The president, hurt that Lansing had called
meetings of the cabinet during his illness, was now made
furious by the uncompromising handling of the Jenkins case.
He ordered the ultimatum of November 20 retracted and had
the State Department advise the Senate to delay action on
the Fall Resolution until the Mexican government had a
chance to act. Through the intercession of private Mexican
citizens, Jenkins was released from jail on December 5, and
the Fall Resolution was tabled.[38]

[37] Private memorandum, Nov. 28, Lansing papers; *Boston Evening
Transcript,* Nov. 17, pt. 2, 2:1; Nov. 28, 12:1; Nov. 29, pt. 3, 2:2;
Chicago Tribune, Nov. 18, pt. 2, 8:2; Nov. 22, pt. 1, 8:2, Nov. 24, pt. 1,
8:1, Nov. 28, pt. 1, 2:6; *Atlanta Constitution,* Nov. 28, 10:1, *New York
Times,* Nov. 22, 12:2. Expectations of war are in *Boston Evening Tran-
script,* Nov. 29, pt. 1, 1:6; *Chicago Tribune,* Dec. 1, pt. 1, 5:1; *New
York World,* Dec. 5, 14:1; *Atlanta Constitution,* Nov. 25, 3:3.
[38] *Washington Post,* Dec. 11, and private memorandum, Dec. 4, Lan-
sing papers; Daniels, *Years of War,* 521–22; Julius W. Pratt, "Robert
Lansing," in S. F. Bemis, ed., *The American Secretaries of State,* X, 169;
Foreign Relations, 1919, II, 589.

The crisis had passed. As he had in 1916, at the height of tension over the Pershing expedition, Wilson managed to regain control over the conduct of United States foreign policy and prevent a total breakdown in relations with Mexico. Negotiations over the Jenkins kidnapping dragged on for another year; Ambassador Fletcher continued to urge severance of relations as the only way to get what was wanted out of Carranza; Fall, Lodge, and others continued to rant and rave on the floor of the Senate against the administration's policy—all to no avail. On December 9, the Senate voted to leave disposition of the matter in the hands of the executive, and there it remained. Having made the crucial decision, Wilson was content once more to leave execution of his policy in the hands of the State Department. Fletcher and Lansing were muzzled, and both were out of the government by the middle of February. Wilson called Fletcher a "quitter" because he had given up the effort to gain American objectives by peaceful means. For the same reason, he blocked the appointment of Fletcher's first secretary, George T. Summerlin, as assistant secretary of state. Colby was faithful to Wilson in his efforts to cope with the trying situation. Where Lansing had been quick to send naval vessels at the first sign of trouble, Colby delayed responding to requests for naval vessels and sent ships only when violence in several of the western provinces threatened American lives. This can be considered a desperate preventive measure rather than the first step toward intervention. As soon as it was possible, he asked Secretary of the Navy Daniels to remove the vessels.[39]

On May 21, 1920, relations with Mexico passed into a new phase with the assassination of President Carranza. Now the United States was faced with the decision of whether to recognize Carranza's successors, substitute President Adolfo de la Huerta and newly elected President Álvaro Obregón. Supporters of the hard line urged the government to demand satisfaction from Mexico before recognition would be granted. That Wilson did withhold recognition from the Obregón regime caused most observers to overlook the im-

[39] Memorandum, Dec. 22, 1919, Fletcher papers; Wilson to Colby, Apr. 13, 1920, Colby papers; *Foreign Relations,* 1920, III, 133–61.

portance of his earlier decision against intervention. He had
always wanted to teach the Mexican leaders to behave like
"gentlemen," and nonrecognition gave him a chance to try
what he considered some friendly interposition. Nonrecognition was, for him, a peaceful means of achieving his long-
term objective in Mexico—peace and democracy. Wilson
would bargain, and bargain hard, but he would not allow the
bargaining to force the United States to the point of intervention. This had the effect of inhibiting the Department
of State in pressing United States demands on the Mexican government. The United States would not commit its
power and prestige to influence the internal affairs of another sovereign nation. In this case, nonrecognition was a
"friendly" form of interposition.

Wilson's decision to reverse Lansing's ultimatum is all the
more significant in view of the forces working against him
at the time. The majority of the press favored a strong policy,
even intervention; his chief advisers in the State Department
offered him only the alternative of force leading directly to
intervention; and, at the height of the crisis, Congress was
outspoken in its demands for intervention. Wilson acted in
the face of all this opposition. In avoiding intervention, he
overcame enormous pressure. Once he had acted, the public
and Congress were satisfied to have him proceed in his own
way to a solution of the difficulties with Mexico.[40]

[40] Open letter from Fletcher to Colby, July 11, 1920; Woolsey to
Fletcher, July 12, Fletcher papers; Henry Morgenthau to Lansing, Mar.
27, Lansing papers; John Barrett to Morgenthau, Mar. 26, Barrett
papers; *Journal of Commerce and Commercial Bulletin*, July 9, 6:3.
Another inhibiting factor working against Wilson was the obsession of
many United States representatives in Mexico with "reds." They saw
them everywhere and painted dark pictures of conditions in Mexico.
See, for example, the military intelligence report of May 19, 1919, RG
59, 812.504/185; Consul Dawson's (Tampico) report of July 23, 812.504/
224; Chargé Hanna's Nov. 10, 812.504/276; and Vice Consul Harper
(Ciudad Juárez), Apr. 8, 1921, 812.50/80.

CHAPTER 3

The Transition to Peace:
The Republican Phase

All of the problems growing out of the war—the economic and political legacies of the war—were passed on by the Democrats to the Republicans. The United States' stake in Latin America continued to increase after 1921, rising to a peak in 1924. By that year credit was easy, long and short-term rates were down, and banks had an extraordinary supply of funds. The outflow of American capital for investment abroad jumped from $390 million in 1923 to $1.2 billion in 1924. Of the $10 billion invested abroad by Americans in 1926, over $4 billion was in Latin America. Also in that banner year of 1924, Latin America accounted for more of the foreign corporate flotations on the American market than did any other area of the world. Two years later, Latin American capital flotations publicly offered in the United States amounted to $459 million; $318 million were government issues, and $141 million were corporate issues. Countries that had borrowed little or nothing before floated enormous loans through American banking houses. The famous Bolivian 8's were taken by Stifel-Nicolaus and Equitable Trust in 1922. Colombia, which had done its borrowing in Britain before the war, now got nearly all of its new capital from the United States. Of the $236 million in Colombian securities floated during the 1920s, more that $215 million was taken by Americans, $171 million of which was secured by public funds and guaranteed by the Colombian government.[1]

An interesting aspect of this craze for borrowing was the prevalence of refunding. Nearly 50 percent of government loans and 20 percent of corporate loans to Latin America in the decade after the war were for this purpose. Frequently such schemes entailed the establishment of some sort of financial control by the lending agency—either a financial commission, a financial adviser, or a customs receivership. By 1925, United States citizens had served or were serving in some supervisory capacity in Colombia, Peru, Panama, El Salvador, Nicaragua, Guatemala, Bolivia, Haiti, the Dominican Republic, and Cuba. Often the financial adviser or commissioner was appointed with the approval of the Department of State or was nominated by the department.

The United States' economic stake was more than stocks and bonds; it was also trade and direct investment, and these, too, continued to grow after 1921. New patterns traced during the war continued through the 1920s. To take one example, in 1927 trade with Argentina was nearly double what it was in 1913; the value of American exports had increased four times, and, most importantly, the United States share of the Argentine market increased from 14.7 percent in 1913 to 24.7 percent in 1925, while Great Britain's fell from 31 percent to 19 percent. United States capital invested in Argentina rose from $40 million in 1912 to $600 million in 1928. United States investment in Colombia was little more than $3 million before the war. By 1920 it had swollen to $20 million, and by 1926 it was $80 million. United States trade with Colombia

[1] Abbott, *Bond Market,* 84. These Department of Commerce figures are lower than *Moody's* or the *Foreign Securities Investor* because they do not include short-term loans to foreign companies; the difference amounted to $400 million in 1924. See: Dunn, *American Foreign Investments,* 14; C. W. Phelps, *Foreign Expansion of American Banks,* 123; and Latin American Division memorandum, unsigned, "Investment in Certain Latin American Countries," n.d., RG 59, 811. 503110/11; U. S. Department of Commerce, Bureau of Foreign and Domestic Commerce, Trade Information Bulletin No. 503, *The Balance of International Payments of the United States in 1926* (Washington, D. C., 1926), 30–32; Rippy, *Capitalists and Colombia,* 152–59 and 162–63; RG 39, Box 29—Colombia.

was worth $61 million in 1913, $155 million in 1920, and
$219 million in 1926.

Direct investment abroad took four principal forms: activities primarily related to the extraction and processing of
mineral products and other raw materials, either for export
or domestic use (Anaconda Copper and Standard Oil); activities primarily related to processing products of agricultural
or pastoral origin (Armour and Company and United Fruit);
the furnishing of public services (International Telephone
and Telegraph); and general manufacturing. The last heading might include complete manufacture of a product in
branch plant (Firestone Tire and Rubber Company); production of some assembly units and importation of others (Otis
Elevator Company); minor production, assembly, and service
operations in subsidiaries of public utilities (Brazilian Traction and Light and Power Company, Ltd.); or production of
a trademarked item by native concerns through contractual
arrangements (Colgate Palmolive-Peet Company). By 1929,
Americans had invested in 1,164 companies worth $3.5
billion.[2]

Americans were convinced that the incoming Harding
administration would be sympathetic to the interests of busi-

[2] This investment was divided in the following manner:

TABLE 1

	Manufacturing	Distribution	Agriculture
Value	$231 million	$119 million	$817 million
Number	153	230	177

	Mining	Petroleum	Public Utilities and Transportation
Value	$732 million	$617 million	$887 million
Number	152	154	126

	Miscellaneous	Total
Value	$116 million	$3,519 million
Number	172	1,164

Organization of American States, Inter-American Economic and Social
Council, Economic Research Series, *Foreign Investments in Latin
America* (Washington, D. C., 1955), 12; Department of Commerce, Bureau of Foreign and Domestic Commerce, Trade Information Bulletin
No. 731, *American Direct Investment in Foreign Countries* (Washington, D. C., 1930), 18–19.

ness and would devote more of its time to economic affairs than had the previous administration. Business interests looked forward to the change in Washington with undisguised enthusiasm. The Harding government was credited in advance with all manner of triumphs in the foreign field. One commentator predicted that United States troubles with Mexico would end on March 4, 1921, because the Mexicans would not dare trifle with a Republican administration. Another referred to the Harding cabinet as "all that could be desired or asked for." There was a strong feeling that the Harding administration would eschew concern for political forms and put economic relations ahead of the diplomatic niceties. Men in both political parties with an international bent accepted this as a fact. For them, the election of 1920 was the final sad proof that the greatest loss caused by the war was "idealism destroyed." Forced out of the Democratic camp by Wilson's uncompromising attitude on the League of Nations or alienated by what they took to be his dictatorial and extravagant behavior in conducting the war, many conservative internationalists looked to Harding as the lesser of two evils. Privately, they told one another that Harding was an oaf or that he had no foreign policy. They winced when he made egregiously stupid public statements about the financial problems growing out of the war or about collective security, but they hoped for the best and continued to support him. On several occasions, men who were in the Wilson administration and would serve in the Harding administration felt compelled to issue angry statements correcting and denouncing the Republican candidate. At one point in the campaign, the *New York Times* asked editorially how "the solid businessmen of New York" could listen without complaint to the Republican candidate "who thus showed that he did not know—or did not care—what he was saying when he dropped into national finance." The *Times* implied that these same businessmen would not accept such nonsense from a Democrat. Perhaps, the *Times* suggested, "the large business and banking interests are consoling themselves with the thought that, between November and March, there will be an interval during which the great minds of the Republican Party may undertake Harding's education in finance." [3]

During the campaign, Harding confused his followers on his foreign policies. On the Mexican issue, he declared that he would rather "make Mexico safe and set it aglow with the light of new world righteousness, than menace the health of the republic in old world contagion." At the same time, he denounced Wilson's moral diplomacy, "the rape of Hayti and Santo Domingo." He criticized the League of Nations in harsh terms, yet spoke of a need for an "Association of Nations." He invited to the porch of his house in Marion, Ohio, men of widely disparate views and, after each meeting, issued a statement that gave the impression he was on the same side of an issue as the man to whom he had just spoken. The result of such behavior was complete befuddlement, and men in both parties were convinced that foreign affairs were not given much weight in the balloting. [4]

President Harding left foreign policy to his secretary of state, Charles Evans Hughes. Hughes described the relationship years afterward:

> I realized that I must take a full measure of responsibility when I felt definite action should be taken, I did not go to him with a statement of difficulties and ask him what

[3] *Wall Street Journal,* Jan. 7, 1:4; Feb. 18, 2:4; Mar. 1, 1921, 1:4; Henry Bruère, "Constructive versus Dollar Diplomacy," *The American Economic Review,* XIII, 1 (March 1923); private memorandum, May 6, 1919 and Feb. 16, 1922, Lansing papers; Morrow to Lamont, Aug. 30, and Lamont to Morrow, Sept. 1, 1920, Morrow papers; S. Parker Gilbert to Houston with press release of statement by Gilbert, Sept. 30, RG 56, Box 212; *Journal of Commerce and Commercial Bulletin* (New York), Oct. 20, 7:5; *New York Times,* Sept. 30. On the 1920s, see: John D. Hicks, *The Republican Ascendancy, 1921–1933* (New York, 1960); Frederick Paxson, *American Democracy and the World War, Postwar Years: Normalcy, 1918–1923* (Berkeley, Calif., 1948); Leuchtenburg, *Perils of Prosperity;* Bagby, *Road to Normalcy.*

[4] Leuchtenburg, *Perils of Prosperity,* 107; Freidel, *Ordeal,* 83; John W. Davis to Lansing, Dec. 31, 1920, and Lansing to Davis, Nov. 5, 1920 and Apr. 14, 1921, Lansing papers; J. C. O. Laughlin to Leland Harrison, Jan. 13, 1921, Harrison papers; Morrow to Lamont, Aug. 16, 1920, Morrow papers.

should be done, but supplemented my statements of the facts in particular cases by concrete proposals upon which he could act at once, and to which he almost invariably gave his approval.[5]

Whenever Harding did communicate with his secretary of state in any but the most formal manner, his letters were almost timid and apologetic. Hughes reciprocated by keeping out of domestic politics—he said he was not aware of the misdoings of the "Ohio Gang" surrounding Harding. Harding was in awe of Hughes. The man exuded moral authority. His career, his reputation, even his physical presence with his full beard and his head always held high, bespoke probity and competence. When he became secretary of state, Hughes was in the middle of a public career that spanned nearly forty years, capped by a decade as chief justice of the Supreme Court. He already had been counsel in the special investigations of the gas and insurance companies in New York, twice governor of New York, associate justice of the Supreme Court, unsuccessful presidential candidate, chairman of the Draft Appeals Board in New York, and one of the leaders of the American Bar. He brought to his new job an extraordinary intelligence, a highly developed sense of duty, a self-containment that made him seem aloof and detached, a distaste for common politics, and a genius for effective administration. His powerful intellect and memory

[5] Biographical notes, 253a, Hughes papers; Harding to Hughes, May 5 and Nov. 28, 1922, Hughes papers. See David J. Danelski, *A Supreme Court Justice Is Appointed* (New York, 1965), 20–24, for an analysis of Harding's character; for Hughes's appointment, see: *New York American,* Feb. 21, *Brooklyn Eagle,* Feb. 20, *Buffalo Express,* Feb. 21, clippings in the Hughes papers; Barrett to Hughes, Jan. 16, Barrett papers; on Hughes as SS, see: Merlo J. Pusey, *Charles Evans Hughes,* 2 vols. (New York, 1951), II; Dexter Perkins, *Charles Evans Hughes and American Democratic Statesmanship* (Boston, 1956); Betty Glad, *Charles Evans Hughes and the Illusions of Innocence. A Study in American Diplomacy* (Urbana, Ill., 1966); Charles Cheney Hyde, "Charles Evans Hughes," in Bemis, ed., *American Secretaries of State,* X; J. C. Vinson, "Charles Evans Hughes, 1921–25," in Norman A. Graebner, ed., *An Uncertain Tradition: American Secretaries of State in the 20th Century* (New York, 1961). David J. Danelski and Joseph S. Tulchin are preparing a critical edition of the Biographical notes for publication.

never ceased to amaze his colleagues; it also allowed him to make his judgments based on his own examination of the record. Above all, he was a lawyer, an advocate. He dealt with the problems of international relations as if they were cases at the bar. One of his aides captured the essence of the man: "Mr. Hughes took a lawyer's delight in plumbing the depths of any problem. No detail escaped him. After having mastered every aspect with startling rapidity, he then formed an opinion to which he held tenaciously." [6] This quality made Hughes less than diplomatic in his dealings with Latin American representatives. He had no patience with circumlocutions and could make dilatory negotiators writhe with embarrassment.

It has been suggested that, had Hughes been more of a politician, more of a realist, he might have accomplished more as governor and as secretary of state and he might have defeated Woodrow Wilson for the presidency in 1916. This is by no means clear. He was elected and reelected governor on a progressive platform with the backing of a conservative Republican state machine. He got Theodore Roosevelt to endorse his candidacy both times even though Roosevelt disdained Hughes as a mugwump and gladly would have thrown his support to another candidate. He could not because Hughes was a winner. While governor, Hughes won a number of battles with the conservative legislature and neutralized the power of the Republican machine, largely through skillful use of press conferences and public disclosure of political maneuvering which traditionally had been considered behind the scenes. Hughes ran a shrewd campaign in 1916, changing his tactics to suit the situation and inducing Wilson to adopt the slogan, "He kept us out of war," which the president loathed. Except for an egregious error in California, he probably would have been elected president. His misunderstanding with Hiram Johnson was not so much Hughes's fault as it was the failure of his campaign manager. Even Hughes admitted later that had he not been swayed by feelings of

[6] William Phillips, *Ventures in Diplomacy* (Boston, 1952), 113; transcript of meeting with Panamanian minister, Dec. 15, 1921, Hughes papers.

personal loyalty to a friend and had he selected another campaign manager, he might have been president. After the election he continued to be prominent in Republican affairs. He joined with other party leaders to sign the famous round robin on the League of Nations, hoping to force the president to accept certain reservations to the peace treaty. His speeches during the campaign of 1920 were sharp and telling. Hughes knew how to appeal to popular sentiments and was not afraid to do so if he felt it was necessary.[7]

As secretary of state he was extremely cautious in his political activities. He felt the public was not competent to judge the highly technical issues of foreign policy; yet he was determined to act as an advocate for the United States within the limits set by public opinion. The public was not concerned with boundary disputes in Latin America or with the fine points of petroleum concessions overseas, and in these areas Hughes was an aggressive advocate. When dealing with sensitive public issues, such as reparations, the League of Nations, and the World Court, Hughes moved carefully and slowly. Even during the fight over the World Court, when Hughes was convinced his position was morally and legally correct, he did not take his case to the people and fight to the end, as was typical of him while governor of New York. He believed that his role must be to educate the public to a more intelligent understanding of the issues, not by means of impassioned speeches, but by calm and reasoned argument. The sweetest fruit of this strategy was the Dawes Plan. Whenever he could not conduct the foreign relations of the United States free from domestic political influences, Hughes demonstrated acute sensitivity to the climate of public opinion. He bowed meekly to the dictates of Congress in the Japanese Immigration Act of 1924, although he considered the measure a hindrance to amicable relations with Japan. He skillfully used American public opinion to second his challenge to the delegates at the opening session of the Washington

[7] Robert F. Wesser, *Charles Evans Hughes. Politics and Reform in New York 1905–1910* (Ithaca, N. Y., 1967); T. L. Woodruff to Hughes, Apr. 2, and Hughes to Woodruff, Apr. 4, 1908; file "The Campaign of 1916," Hughes papers.

Arms Conference, calling upon them to follow the American lead in ending the naval arms race. The public response to his moralistic appeal influenced the negotiations that followed. Hughes was using in international politics the same technique he had found so successful as governor of New York. One can criticize Hughes for a lack of crusading zeal and for failure to make the American people aware of their new responsibilities in the postwar world, but given the spiritual exhaustion of the American people and their disillusionment with international crusades, it is difficult to fault Hughes for not being realistic enough. He had a sophisticated understanding of American power and of the limits imposed upon the secretary of state in its use.

Hughes believed in government by experts—within the limits set by public opinion—and, despite Harding's political habits, he had the highest percentage of professional diplomats since the Taft administration and an unusual number of professionals in the department at all levels. Four under-secretaries—Davis, Fletcher, Phillips, and Grew—and seven assistant secretaries—Dearing, Harrison, Wright, MacMurray, Carr, Adee, and Bliss—supervised the execution of policy, at one time or another, during Hughes's term of office. This rapid turnover in the upper echelons of the department, combined with a great degree of stability among the drafting officers of the geographical divisions, the foreign trade adviser's staff, and the solicitor's office, was an important factor in the continuity of policy from one political administration to another. Subordinate officials were allowed to direct most of the foreign relations of the United States, and, as a result, few changes were made unless the secretary interested himself personally in the case. A contemporary student of the department observed this:

There is no more superficial assumption than that basic foreign policy changes from administration to administration. Temper and tone change, emphasis is often shifted here and there, but in its fundamental character American foreign policy changes surprisingly little. There are important differences in administrations as they conduct foreign affairs, but on close examination, they usually will be found to concern principally details.[8]

The personnel in the Diplomatic Bureau, the Consular Bureau, and the Solicitor's Office were virtually unchanged from 1918 to 1922, although the solicitor himself was a political appointee. Changes in the rosters of the vital Latin American Division and the Office of the Foreign Trade Adviser were made well before March 1921. Of the five men on the trade adviser's staff during the transition between administrations, four—Arthur C. Millspaugh, Arthur N. Young, W. W. Cumberland, and Wallace McClure—joined before the end of 1920, whereas Stanley K. Hornbeck, the only officer to enter in 1921, had been serving as a government economist since 1918. In the Latin American Division, Sumner Welles, the division chief, and John H. Murray served under Wilson, and Stewart Johnson and Charles B. Curtis were career officers on duty in the department. The division's economists, Dana G. Munro and William R. Manning, had been transferred from the Trade Adviser's Office, where they had been in charge of Latin American affairs. Only Morton D. Carrel seems to have been a political appointee. He had served in the department before 1913 and left during the Wilson administration to represent a New York bank in Latin America.

Many of the diplomatic officers had similar backgrounds or shared experiences. One group called itself "The Family" and lived at 1718 H Street, Northwest, just around the corner from the old State Department. This particular group was composed of Harvard graduates, wealthy, socially prominent, and very strongly Republican. In addition to the diplomatic officers, it included an assistant secretary of the treasury, an official in the War Department, a former governor general of the Philippines, and an officer of the Federal Reserve Bank. The State Department members included Henry Fletcher, Fred Dearing, William Phillips, and Leland Harrison. The

[8] Hulen, *Department of State,* 58; John Spargo to Colby, June 2, 1921, Colby papers; Department of State *Register,* 1918–1930, 13 vols. (Washington, D. C., 1918–1930).

social background of these men and their personal financial responsibilities placed them in frequent and easy contact with many important bankers and financiers. Although business, as such, never interested them, their familiarity with some business leaders eased communication between the public and private sectors.[9]

The continuity of personnel helped maintain policy by reducing the effectiveness of political lobbying. A Republican congressman from Pennsylvania, George S. Graham, counsel for John H. Amory and Company of New York, whose valuable petroleum concession in Costa Rica was threatened with annulment, petitioned the department for support in 1920 and was refused on grounds that the concession was controlled by British oil interests. He waited until after the election and wrote the department criticizing Wilson and the "prejudiced" officials. The letter was referred to the department's petroleum expert, Arthur C. Millspaugh, the same officer who had rejected the earlier request. Millspaugh took the case directly to the secretary, and Graham was turned down again.[10]

When left to their own devices, the experts did, on occasion, commit the department to action that was inconsistent with the administration's intentions. For example, during the negotiations for a loan to Guatemala in 1923 and 1924, several American banks competed for the business. Hughes was determined to remain aloof and favor no one American interest over any other, even though he disapproved of the bankers who seemed about to get the loan. He did not even want to advise the Guatemalan government of his attitude. Dana Munro, the Central American desk officer, and Minister Arthur Geissler considered it more important to block the unfair loan than to maintain the department's neutrality. Geissler informed the Guatemalan government of the secretary's attitude, and negotiations for the loan were broken off. Assistant Secretary Harrison, who was charged with respon-

[9] Harrison papers; Fletcher papers; Waldo H. Heinrichs, Jr., *American Ambassador, Joseph C. Grew and The Development of United States Diplomatic Tradition* (Boston, 1966), passim.
[10] File RG 59, 818.6363Am6/41 and 82.

sibility for matters pertaining to loans, might easily have prevented Munro and Geissler from flouting the secretary's wishes if he had supervised the correspondence between the department and the field more closely.[11]

Continuity of personnel affected policy in one other way; it gave experienced officers sufficient influence within the department to restrain the more enthusiastic men in the field. The department took a broader view of foreign relations than the field and often gave greater consideration to the interests of Latin American nations. This restraint complemented Secretary Hughes's cautious use of United States power. He encouraged it in the face of critics who held that it was a sign of weakness and who resented the fact that the professionals were not more responsive to pressure.[12]

Criticisms of the State Department notwithstanding, businessmen took their problems to the government without hesitation. To be sure, they had done so before March 1921 and had received help, but now there was a sense that the government as a whole was closer to them and more responsive to their needs. In Herbert Hoover, particularly, they felt they had a friend, and, far more than they had before, they used the Department of Commerce to bring their complaints to the attention of the Department of State. Insofar as the State Department was concerned, businessmen got a more sympathetic hearing only for a short while after March 1921 before relations began to deteriorate. Part of the blame for this lay with the business community. Relations between government and business on matters of common interest in foreign affairs were complicated by competition among American interests in Latin America, as in the Guatemalan loan negotiations of 1923 and 1924, or by the disputes between banks over a Uruguayan loan or among American oil men in Venezuela over dredging the Maracaibo Channel. Differences between American bankers and manufacturers were bothersome. The latter, working through the National Foreign Trade Council, urged the government to make it a "condition-precedent" for loans to foreign governments that

[11] RG 59, 814.51Am4/32 and 35.
[12] RG 59, 835.516/61; 814.51/356; Anderson diary, Apr. 24, 1924.

the proceeds from those loans would be spent in the United States. Hoover endorsed this plan, but bankers opposed it; so the State Department did no more than publicly state that it "would be highly pleased" if the proceeds were spent in the United States.[13]

Quite often, the cooperation between business and government necessary for dollar diplomacy broke down because business did not find it convenient to be restricted by the government's foreign policies. The Department of State was trying to eliminate British (and other non-American) influence from Latin America as well as to encourage American enterprise and was irked when Americans cooperated with British firms and hired British nationals to manage their affairs. In the years immediately following the war, business and government had been equally anxious over British trade competition in Latin America. As American economic influence became more pervasive, businessmen grew less fearful and more willing to work with the British if it was to their advantage. For strategic reasons, the government remained firm in its antipathy to non-American influence in the hemisphere, preferring to remain aloof from a situation rather than aid Europeans. The only clear case of the State Department actively helping British interests occurred in 1923, when a British oil concession was threatened by the Venezuelan government; the aid was given reluctantly, under pressure, to aid Americans in their negotiations for entrée to the Turkish Petroleum Company in the Near East. Relations between the government and American business interests in Latin America became increasingly strained through the 1920s.[14]

[13] Phillips diary, Feb. 9, 1923; L. H. Taylor, counsel for the Guerrero Mining Company, to Hoover, n.d. (1921), RG 151, Box 1510, 271—Mexico; Lamont to Morrow, March 11, 1921, Morrow papers; Woolsey to Francis White, Oct. 11, 1922, RG 59, 813.41 United Fruit/orig.; Dearing to E. T. Gregory of the First National Corporation, Jan. 7, 1922, 833.51/173; 800.51/381 and 482.

[14] For criticisms of Anglo-American cooperation see: Consul General Robertson (Buenos Aires) to SS., Aug. 22, 1918. RG 59, 635.4117/1; letter from Julius Klein [on Bolivia], Aug. 4, and economic advisers' memorandum by Young, Sept. 27, 1924, RG 59, 824.6354/57 and 62; and [on Brazil] Phillips diary, Apr. 16, 1923.

Although they were not always willing to be governed by the State Department, many American businessmen hired former officials of the Department to maintain good relations with it. Julius G. Lay left the Foreign Trade Adviser's Office to join the New York banking house of Speyer and Company and was extremely useful in bringing his firm's business to the attention of the department. Fred M. Dearing worked for the International Petroleum Company between stints in the department. During the Wilson administration Morton D. Carrel worked in Latin America for a large New York bank and in 1923 left the department again to work for the Ulen Corporation, which was expanding its Latin American business. J. Herbert Stabler left the department in 1919 to help All America Cables extend its system to the east coast of South America and then joined White, Weld, and Company. Frank L. Polk and Lester H. Woolsey, for their respective firms, represented many businesses before the department. The law partnership of Lansing and Woolsey represented United Fruit, International Railways of Central America, Radio Corporation of America, Tropical Radio, New England Oil Company, and many others. Polk was a member of the same New York law firm as John W. Davis, and they represented the International Paper Company, Vanadium Company of America, American Metals Company, All America Cables, Commercial Cables, and other companies. Both Polk and Woolsey had the advantage of taking their business directly to the undersecretary or to an assistant secretary and of being fairly certain they would get immediate action. Those who were not members of the in-group received curt treatment and were upset by this discrimination. On occasion, the department made use of these former government officials in the business world by asking them to take advantage of a loan or a concession of some kind that it thought should be in American hands.[15]

[15] Harrison to White, Sept. 29, 1922, Harrison papers; Phillips diary, Jan. 6, July 11, Oct. 10, and Dec. 4, 1923; Harrison to Samuel Edelman, Apr. 1922, Harrison papers; Carr diary, Sept. 27, 1924. Department initiatives are in folder marked "Chile" in the Morrow papers; Dearing to Harrison, Aug. 29, 1922, Harrison papers; Latin American Division memorandum by White, Nov. 16, 1922, RG 59, 823.51/294.

The obvious ties between government and business in international affairs have led to countless allegations that United States involvement in foreign countries was motivated by economic considerations and that business controlled the State Department. This is an unrealistic analysis. First, the documents provide little evidence to support it and much to contradict it. Second, with the exception of Cuba, there is very little correlation between the degree of pressure exerted by the United States government and the extent of economic penetration by American interests. Trade and investment did not follow the troops into Haiti, Santo Domingo, Nicaragua, or any of the other Central American protectorates. It is precisely in those areas of Latin America where there was little likelihood of military or political intervention that economic factors seem to have been much more important in determining the conduct of United States foreign relations. Just as before the war it had been considered in the national interest to keep peace in the Caribbean Danger Zone, it was considered in the national interest after the war to extend—to all parts of the hemisphere—American cable facilities, the influence of American bankers, and American control over petroleum reserves.[16]

In this sense, the economic foreign policy of the United States after World War I can be considered a form of dollar diplomacy, the alliterative term used to describe the tie between economics and foreign policy whereby the influence of the government was employed "to protect and promote the investments of citizens of the United States abroad," and which was characterized "by at least a threefold purpose: financial advantage, strategy, and benevolence." Dollar diplomacy in this sense was extended after the war from particular reference to the Caribbean to include all of South America. This willingness to commit the prestige of the United States government to promote and protect American

[16] Angell, *Financial Foreign Policy*, 28 and 81; Montague, *The United States and Haiti*, 253, n. 47; Munro, *Intervention and Dollar Diplomacy*. For accounts of United States imperialism during this period that follow an economic deterministic line see Nearing and Freeman, *Dollar Diplomacy*; Rippy, *Capitalists and Colombia*; and Marsh, *Bankers and Bolivia*.

economic influence in the Western Hemisphere conflicted with the strong postwar isolationist tendency to restrict formal commitments of American power. The nation's experience had been that minor or partial assertions of responsibility in the Caribbean led to increasing commitments of American power until, in several cases, the United States was forced to assume complete control over the internal affairs of the protectorate state. For a variety of reasons—military, political, and economic—the United States was unwilling to repeat this pattern of increasing involvement outside the Caribbean. The hostility in the United States toward formal or institutional commitments further inhibited the indiscriminate use of American power in Latin America. The pattern of constant, seemingly inexorable increases in American involvement in the internal affairs of Latin American nations was broken after the war because the European threat was gone. The crushing logic of the United States' responsibility for stability in the Caribbean was vitiated by Europe's weakness and by America's new strength and far-flung affairs. American diplomats came to understand that it was not necessary to exercise formal imperial control over the Latin American nations in order to protect American security in the hemisphere. Thus, during the period 1918–25, while the scope and requirements of national security expanded, formal commitments of American power tended to contract.[17]

Latin American issues were not considered among the most pressing questions left by the Wilson administration. In fact, the Department of State's memorandum for the new secretary on matters which would require early action contained no mention of Latin America. The five pressing issues were: the controversy over the general question of mandates, the status of the island of Yap, the Chinese Eastern Railroad, the Langdon incident, and the contract of the Federal Wire-

[17] Rippy, *The Caribbean Danger Zone* (New York, 1940), 134; Arthur P. Whitaker, "From Dollar Diplomacy to the Good Neighbor Policy," *Inter-American Economic Affairs,* IV, 1 (summer 1950); speech by F. M. Huntington Wilson, May 4, 1911, quoted in Callcott, 309; President Taft's message to Congress, 1909, quoted in Huntington Wilson, *Memoirs of an Ex-Diplomat* (Boston, 1945), 210–11; Munro, 530–46.

less Company for the erection and operation of radio stations in China. To the extent that the secretary's attention was given to these issues, control over Latin American questions was left in the hands of the department's experts. For a year after he took office, Hughes made no move to coordinate Latin American policy, preferring to deal with Latin American issues on an *ad hoc* basis. For the most part, he accepted his predecessor's decisions and followed the lines of policy laid down before he entered office. Often, however, though he made no changes in policy—that is, in the standards or order of priorities by which choices among alternatives were made—he lost patience with the leisurely pace of diplomacy and acted vigorously to impose what he considered to be legal and just solutions. In this way his personality affected the execution of policy, so that he would produce different results from his predecessor, though he used his predecessor's policy.

The first problem Hughes dealt with, the Costa Rican–Panama boundary dispute, was a case in point. The career officers in the department were conscious of the fact that they could do little to bring the dispute to a conclusion during the interregnum between administrations. The night after Harding's inauguration, Hughes took home the relevant files, spread them all around him, and spent the entire night studying them. In the morning he had reached his decision and went right to work as soon as the Senate had confirmed his nomination. He pushed toward a solution with a directness that bordered on the undiplomatic. His conclusion—that the old award of United States Chief Justice Edward D. White was legally correct and should be enforced—was the same as Secretary Colby's. Where Colby had been content to tell the Panamanian government that the United States "could not but view with the gravest apprehension any developments which will disturb the peace and tranquility of Central America," Hughes flatly told both parties to the dispute that the White award must be accepted. The tone of Hughes's note was far more brusque than Colby's. They differed also in transmitting the texts of messages which American ministers were to deliver to the disputing governments. Chandler Anderson was the representative of the Costa Rican government in this affair, and he seems to have enjoyed the ear of officials in the department on every possible level. Anderson had as ready access to Secretary Hughes as he had had to his good friend, Secretary Lansing. Anderson's advice was for a strong stand by the United States in order to settle the issue in a hurry.[18]

Hostilities in the border area did cease, but Panama still refused to accept the terms of the White award. Hughes summoned the Panamanian minister and told him that if the territory were not given to Costa Rica, "The Government of the United States will find itself compelled to proceed in the manner which may be requisite in order that it may assure itself that the exercise of jurisdiction is appropriately transferred." Panama continued to stall, and Hughes threatened to allow Costa Rica to take control of the territory by force. When the Panamanian minister inquired if this meant the United States would allow the renewal of hostilities, the secretary stated unequivocally that "the United States cannot permit a renewal of hostilities by Panama against Costa Rica by reason of Costa Rica's now taking peaceful possession of that territory." Panama capitulated.

Hughes used the same blunt methods to reestablish diplomatic relations with Mexico. In 1920, the State Department drew up a Treaty of Amity and Commerce, acceptance of which was to serve as the basis for recognizing the Obregón government. The Mexicans wanted recognition first and a treaty afterward. Hughes followed Colby's lead and began by leaving negotiations in the hands of the Division of Mexican Affairs. After a few months without progress, Hughes became peeved with Mexican intransigence. In June, he asked the Mexican government how it had justified recognition by definite action taken to adequately protect the rights and interests of American citizens. Not bothering to wait for an answer, on June 7 he issued a statement to the press which

[18] *Foreign Relations,* 1921, I, 177, 181–83, 212, and 225–27; Anderson diary, Nov. 9 and Dec. 10, 1920, Jan. 5 and 21, Feb. 5, 26, and 27, Mar. 1, 2, 7, and 11, 1921. See also Anderson to Octavio Beeche, Mar. 4 and 12, and to P. Perez-Zaledón, Mar. 16, 1921, Anderson papers, Box 56.

outlined the United States policy: "Whenever Mexico is ready to give assurances that she will perform her fundamental obligation in the protection both of persons and of rights of property validly acquired, there will be no obstacles to the most advantageous relations between the two peoples." He adhered firmly to this policy and convinced the Mexican government that his purpose was unalterable. Two years later, after a series of minor concessions on both sides, Mexico retreated from its position, gave the necessary guarantees, and diplomatic relations were renewed.[19]

Hughes was as convinced as Colby had been that recognition of the Mexican government was necessary for the preservation of normal relations between the two nations. The difference between the two men was that Hughes placed greater emphasis on the protection of the rights of American citizens. His "hard line" was supported by Henry P. Fletcher and George T. Summerlin, the former ambassador to Mexico and the chargé d'affaires in Mexico City who had been violently opposed to Wilson's policy of patience. Hughes was willing to follow Fletcher's advice and speak harshly to the Mexicans in order to get what the United States wanted. The strong words and the two-year delay brought the Mexican government to a willingness to compromise.[20]

Hughes was proud of his Latin American policy. When he gave Frank B. Kellogg material for a speech during the latter's unsuccessful senatorial campaign of 1922, he listed ten

[19] *Foreign Relations,* 1921, II, 406–7; record of interviews between undersecretary and representative of Mexican government, Aug. 9 and 30, and Sept. 23, 1920, Davis papers. Other examples of Hughes's brusque, legal style of negotiating: record of interviews with the minister from Panama, Apr. 7, 1921, and Dec. 15, 1923, Hughes papers; *Foreign Relations,* 1921, II, 610–11; discussion of Guatemalan railroad concessions, May–June, 1921, RG 59, 814.77/62 to 69, in which notes to the minister to Guatemala included the formal text of the protest to be delivered to the Guatemalan government. This was very unusual, as Minister McMillan had previously enoyed the latitude of formulating his own notes.

[20] Fletcher to Summerlin, Mar. 27, 1922, M. E. Hanna to Fletcher, Feb. 28, Fletcher to Hughes, Feb. 28, and Summerlin to Fletcher, Sept. 10, 1923, Fletcher papers. On the widespread public opinion in favor of recognition and the resumption of normal relations, see Barrett to Harding, Mar. 20, 1922, Barrett papers.

major accomplishments of the Harding administration. Six
of them had to do with Latin America. They were: settling
the Costa Rica–Panama boundary controversy; general improvement of United States relations with Latin America;
adjustment of the Tacna-Arica controversy through a conference in Washington; the protection of American property
rights in Mexico; perfecting arrangements for the termination of the military government in Santo Domingo; and
Haiti, "where, despite the great difficulties of the situation,
we have perfected administration and are devoting ourselves
in every practicable way to the assistance of the Haitian people." In later years, he accepted Samuel Flagg Bemis' esti-
mate that it had been his policy "to liquidate United States
imperialism as promptly as political stability should seem
to be established and the safety of foreign nationals reason-
ably assured." Hughes considered himself a peacemaker, a
"big brother" who could settle disputes among the little
brothers. Hughes told an audience in Philadelphia at the
end of 1923:

> It is the policy of this Government to make available its
> friendly assistance to promote stability in those of our
> sister republics which are especially afflicted with dis-
> turbed conditions involving their own peace and that
> of their neighbors. . . . In promoting stability we do
> not threaten independence but seek to conserve it. We
> are not aiming at control but endeavoring to establish
> self-control. We are not seeking to add to our territory
> or to impose our rule upon other peoples. . . . The
> United States aims to facilitate the peaceful settlement
> of difficulties between the governments in this hemi-
> sphere. . . . We are seeking to establish a *Pax Ameri-
> cana* maintained not by arms but by mutual respect and
> good will and the tranquilizing processes of reason. . . .[21]

[21] Charles Evans Hughes, "The Centenary of the Monroe Doctrine,"
The Annals, supplement to vol. CXI (Jan. 1924), 16–19; Harding to
Hughes, May 5, 1922; Hughes to Kellogg, July 17, 1922, Hughes papers;
biographical notes, 320 and 324–28; Hicks, *Republican Ascendancy,*
153; and Hyde, "Charles Evans Hughes," 349. Democrats had accepted
the "big brother" label during the 1920 campaign, Freidel, *Ordeal,* 81.

Most of his peacemaking efforts were devoted to the Central American republics, which were the weakest and least stable in the hemisphere. Central America and the Caribbean in general had long been acknowledged by others as a United States sphere of influence which required special policies. Danger to the Panama Canal diminished markedly after the war; yet the Isthmus was still of vital interest for the security of the United States, and the Department of State was under pressure to keep peace in the region. Following in the footsteps of his predecessors, Hughes declared at Philadelphia that disturbances in the Caribbean were of "special interest" to the United States "for the purpose of being assured that our own safety is free from menace."

The small nations of Central America seemed forever at odds with one another. In the two years after the war, the State Department handled five different boundary disputes between various Central American nations and stepped into a dozen angry exchanges in order to prevent them from getting out of hand. Secretary Lansing and Undersecretary Polk adopted a firm legalistic stance in coping with these problems and tended to push persuasion to the edge of coercion in order to settle differences between disputants. In the period following the Armistice, the Department of State had so many other obligations, and these two men were kept so busy, that they could not give their undivided attention to any disturbance or dispute.

Chandler Anderson, who represented Costa Rica, Nicaragua, and Guatemala in different boundary disputes, was convinced that the Wilson administration, after Lansing resigned, deliberately avoided pushing Central America to settle disputes. There is some evidence that the State Department was reluctant to make any commitments that would bind the incoming administration.[22]

Conditions in Central America in 1920 and 1921 were unusually chaotic, and the United States government felt that it was responsible for the restoration of stability in the area. Relations between Nicaragua and Honduras were particu-

[22] Anderson diary, Mar. 12, 1921.

larly bad. Emigrants on both sides of the border were making life miserable for both governments. In September 1921, the navy sent ships of the Special Squadron to Bluefields, Nicaragua and to Ampala, Honduras, and the presence of the ships was credited with quieting the two local situations. War threatened again in December when the Guatemalan government was overthrown by the Liberals, and the Conservative governments of Nicaragua and Honduras offered to intervene in the name of the recently revitalized Central American Union. Secretary Hughes rejected this offer, and the Central American Union collapsed as much through United States neglect as through Guatemala's withdrawal.[23]

With the collapse of the Central American Court along with the Union, the Department of State in Washington was the only body with machinery for the investigation and peaceful settlement of Central American disputes. The burden was too much for the department. It had had a modicum of success as a supplement or adviser to the Central American Court and to direct bilateral negotiations. Now the staff of the department had full responsibility for negotiations between Costa Rica and Panama, Costa Rica and Nicaragua, Nicaragua and Honduras, and Honduras and Guatemala. The secretary had given his personal attention to the Costa Rica–Panama dispute and was about to produce a settlement between the disputants, but it was impossible to expect him to intervene directly in every single dispute. Too many other things demanded his time and energy. As early as February 1922, Sumner Welles of the Latin American Division proposed a general Central American conference to facilitate settlement of all outstanding disputes. The arguments in favor of a conference were twofold. First, it was hoped that minor commitments of United States prestige would obviate the need for major commitments of United States forces to maintain the peace. Second, although the Central Amer-

[23] Vice Consul T. W. Waters (Bluefields) to Hughes, Sept. 7, 1921, RG 59, 817.00/2813, quoted in Virginia L. Greer, "Charles Evans Hughes and Nicaragua, 1921–1925," (Ph.D. dissertation, University of New Mexico, 1954), 42.

ican agreements of 1907 still formed the basis of United States policy in Central America, these treaties had lost much of their usefulness. Furthermore, as the United States was not a party to them, it could not enforce their provisions. It was hoped that a general conference would revise the old agreements.[24]

Hughes had little patience with the disputatious politicians of Central America, and, after struggling for a year to end innumerable boundary disputes, he accepted the proposal for a conference. The presidents of Nicaragua, Honduras, and Salvador met on board the U.S.S. *Tacoma* in Fonseca Bay to discuss their difficulties in the presence of United States diplomats. Once the three presidents were together, the Americans insisted that they reach an agreement before disembarking and that a provision be inserted into the *Tacoma* agreement of August 20, 1922, which called for a general regional conference to be held in Washington at the end of the year. As Hughes explained to Harding, "The conditions existing in the countries of Central America for some time have made it appear advisable for the United States Government to take some steps looking to the establishment of more peaceful and stable relations among them." The Conference on Central American Affairs convened on December 4 and lasted a little over two months. The United States was represented officially by the secretary of state and Sumner Welles.[25]

Hughes found that he had to allay the Central Americans' fears of the United States and convince them of the essential community of interest that had brought them all together before the participants would begin to discuss their differences. He assured them:

[24] Anderson diary, Feb. 2; Latin American Division memorandum, Feb. 6, RG 59, 813.00/1196; Welles to Harding, Mar. 1, 1922, 813.00 Tacoma/7; Greer, "Charles Evans Hughes and Nicaragua," 51.

[25] The correspondence on the *Tacoma* agreement is printed in *Foreign Relations, 1922,* I, 418–29; proceedings of the conference are printed in Department of State, *Conference on Central American Affairs, Washington, December 4, 1922–February 7, 1923* (Washington, D. C., 1923).

The Government of the United States has no ambition to gratify at your expense, no policy which runs counter to your national aspirations, and no purpose save to promote the interests of peace and to assist you, in such manner as you may welcome, to solve your problems to your own proper advantage. The interest of the United States is found in the peace of this hemisphere and in the conservation of your interests.

The conference produced several treaties designed to end the border troubles in the region. They provided for nonrecognition of unconstitutional regimes and for the creation of an international Central American tribunal and an international commission of inquiry. These treaties, together with the United States policy of withholding recognition from unconstitutional governments, became part of the machinery for keeping the peace in Central America.

Though Hughes thus seemed to be adopting Wilson's prewar policy of denying recognition to politically unacceptable governments, he was unhappy with it. He feared it would force the United States into unwanted interventions and would complicate commercial relations with unrecognized governments. Gradually, he returned to pre-Wilsonian standards for according recognition, using nonrecognition mainly as a weapon for economic purposes. When, for example, the unrecognized Orellana government was having financial difficulties because it could not get its gold deposits out of United States banks and could not float a loan, Chargé Charles B. Curtis was instructed to inform the Guatemalan minister of finance that it would be impossible to secure a loan from foreign bankers until the country's financial system was reformed. Curtis suggested that an American financial expert supervise the reorganization. Recognition followed a promise to make the necessary reforms. By the end of Hughes's tenure in office, the desire to limit American involvement, even at the expense of representative democratic constitutional government, was stated in a policy memorandum written at the secretary's request by the chief of the Latin American Division, Francis White:

The United States will get better results if we do not make long pronouncements but let the natives work out their solution with help and assistance from our diplomatic representatives, but without tying our hands to any given course of action should the people of the country be able to come to some solution which gives promise of affording a period of stability even though it should not fall in with our ideas of a representative democratic constitutional government and even should it not be in accordance with their own written constitution.[26]

The only element of Wilsonian policy which Hughes rejected outright was the interpretation of the Monroe Doctrine. Far from being a regional understanding, Hughes said, the doctrine was a national policy, "an assertion of the principle of national security," and one which did not exhaust American rights or policies. What action the United States should take in any exigency did not depend upon the Monroe Doctrine. It "may always be determined on grounds of international right and national security as if the Monroe Doctrine did not exist." Therefore, the traditional Latin American policy of the United States was justified by the demands of national security and by the practice of international law. Hughes denied that the League of Nations could have required the United States to submit its policies regarding American questions to the league or to any of its agencies, and he insisted "that the United States of America may oppose and prevent any acquisition by any non-American power by conquest, purchase, or in any other manner of any territory, possession or control in the Western Hemisphere."

In view of Hughes's strong feelings on the subject and the very obvious differences between the Republican and Democratic interpretations of the Monroe Doctrine, it is a tribute to bureaucratic perseverance that the Department of State continued after 1921 to use as its official interpretation of the Monroe Doctrine Woodrow Wilson's address to the Sec-

[26] White to Grew, Nov. 7, 1924, RG 59, 711.13/65; *Foreign Relations,* 1922, II, 712–17; 1923, II, 575–77; RG 59, 814.51/333–38.

ond Pan American Scientific Congress of 1916. Drafting
officers in the department followed established policy until
explicitly ordered to change. Hughes's interpretation of the
Monroe Doctrine did not permeate the divisions of the department until 1923, when the secretary made a series of
speeches on the centenary of Monroe's famous message to
Congress. The changeover began in February 1923 when
Solicitor Hyde prepared a memorandum for United States
delegates to the Fifth Pan American Conference, to be held
in Santiago, Chile.[27]

There was no general reappraisal of Latin American policy under Secretary of State Hughes until February 1922.
The memoranda prepared for him at that time stressed the
importance both of United States business activities in Latin
America and the part the department should play in helping
those activities. Dana G. Munro dealt with the Caribbean
and Morton D. Carrel with South America. Munro, whose
memo had been drafted a few months earlier, urged the department to interest American bankers in meeting the capital
needs of the region and to see to it that loans were used to
effect the economic and financial reforms so much desired by
the department. Helping Americans broaden investments in
the Caribbean was subordinated to preventing any unstable
financial conditions which might lay the republics open to
political unrest and complaints from European powers.
Munro was anxious to have American bankers provide the
capital needed by Caribbean countries in order to refund
their external debts and to see American interests control
their national banks and manage the stabilization of their
currencies.

Munro felt that the Department of State should take the
lead in working toward a proper solution to Central American financial problems. He believed United States bankers

[27] Material on Hughes's view of the Monroe Doctrine is taken from
Hughes, "Centenary of the Monroe Doctrine," and the *Pathway of Peace*
(New York, 1925), 113–63; Hyde, 334–49; Beerits memorandum, "Latin
American Intervention and the Monroe Doctrine"; press release of
speech delivered in New York City, Jan. 1920; Hughes to Hale, July
24, 1919, Hughes papers; discussion of how to answer inquiry from
Miss Virginia Lindsay, Apr. 1921, RG 59, 710.11/515; 710.11/586.

were holding back out of "a feeling of uncertainty in regard to the support which they might hope to obtain from the Department in the event of difficulties with the debtor governments." He urged the department to end this uncertainty by giving sufficient assurances to prompt bankers to accept minimal guarantees from Central American nations. This would eliminate the need to have United States bankers dominate debtor nations, a relationship which had never produced anything but ill will toward the United States. Munro was careful to emphasize that such guarantees by the United States government would not be a radical departure in policy; that they were merely an acknowledgment of a situation that had become familiar during the period of Bryan's secretaryship of state. The memorandum also followed closely along lines laid down by the Latin American Division in 1918 as part of the planning of postwar policy. The emphasis on extending the United States' financial influence was so great among some diplomatic representatives in the Caribbean that they considered their greatest service to American commercial interests to be not in actual commercial matters but in the final arrangement and execution of loan negotiations.[28]

Morton D. Carrel entitled his memorandum, "A Summary of the Questions Pending Between the United States and the Republics of Latin America," and dealt almost exclusively with opportunities for loans and investments. Every one of the countries required money for refunding accumulated debts or for financing major public works. The credit standings of some of them were such that they would have no trouble obtaining funds, but others would require assistance of some kind from the United States government before the loans could be made. Carrel was not sure "just how far the United States Government should go" to bring about the loans, but he was certain that it should do something to

[28] Latin American Division memorandum by Munro, Nov. 9, 1921, RG 59, 813.51/5; memorandum by Carrel, Feb. 27, 1922, 710.11/568; memoranda by J. W. Jenks, Mar. 4, and Hallett Johnson, Sept. 5, 1918, 811.51/2058 and 813.51/–; Minister Montgomery Schuyler's dispatch, Oct. 15, 1923, 711.162/2.

take advantage of the South American needs for money in order to help Americans looking "for profitable commercial and investment opportunities." Carrel and Munro made it clear that they were doing nothing more than urge action they considered consistent with existing policy.

"Just how far the United States Government should go" to further private American interests was a question that could only be answered with reference to the strategic considerations of each case. When the issue was considered of sufficient importance—as in the three vital areas of cables, loans, and petroleum—the department could interject itself in private discussions with unseemly energy. Less than a month after the change in administrations, Peru was reported to be about to sign an exclusive contract with the British Marconi Company for operating the domestic telegraph and postal services. Secretary Hughes immediately instructed the American ambassador in Lima to delay the contract by any means until All America Cables, which controlled cables into and out of the country, had a chance to bid on it, and to prevent infringement of American rights in the premises. Ambassador William E. Gonzales managed to delay the contract, only to learn that the American cable company had told President Leguía that it was not interested in the business. The department was extremely embarrassed because the information came to the legation from the Peruvian foreign minister. The cable company had not bothered to inform the ambassador or the department.[29]

There were other occasions in which the department considered a contract, concession, or development project so important an objective that it made representations even before the supposedly offended American national or company had a chance to complain. Soon after Hughes entered office, Guatemala threatened to allow the International Railways of Central America concession to lapse. The Latin American Division thought the department should express

---

[29] *Foreign Relations*, 1921, II, 666–70. The same overanxiety is reflected in the State Department's efforts to maintain United States control over Bolivian petroleum reserves, Nov. 1924–Jan. 1925, RG 59, 824.6363/48-51.

its disapproval of this course of action. Without waiting for the railroad to make an appeal for help, the department contacted former Solicitor Lester H. Woolsey, who was counsel for the United Fruit Company, which had at one time controlled the railroad. Somewhat startled by the department's forwardness, Woolsey said that he knew nothing of the matter but promised to consult with the railroad company. He reported that it had indeed been thinking of protesting the action of the Guatemalan government and, encouraged by the department's initiative, was now giving the matter serious consideration. Before the railroad had a chance to act, the department instructed Minister Benton McMillan to convey the "great interest" of the United States in the completion of the railroad by the American interests engaged in its construction. The decision was made by the secretary himself, with the solicitor's aid. He left aside the Latin American Division. He was unconcerned to wait for the railroad to complain formally, so that the United States government protest might be justified by a claim of denial of justice. The railroad finally requested help a week later. As the Guatemalan Congress continued to block the renewal of the concession, the State Department notes became more and more insistent. Left to the solicitor, who handled all formal representations, the dispute might have led to a serious breakdown in the relations between the two countries. However, the Latin American Division, with a broader view of policy, was brought back into the discussion. It persuaded the secretary that the department's objectives could be secured by means less likely to embarrass relations between the two countries. With the department's help, the railroad and the Guatemalan government were able to come to a settlement of their dispute.[30]

Outside the strategically sensitive areas of communications, petroleum, and bank loans, such forward, aggressive action by the department was the exception rather than the rule. By and large, the department preferred to keep out of disputes between United States nationals and foreign governments. When called upon for legitimate reasons, the depart-

[30] RG 59, 814.77/62–92.

ment responded. It sought to limit the number of times it was called by not proffering information to private interests, except in unusual cases, and by quickly publicizing adverse economic conditions in a Latin American nation so that private interests would avoid the situation and not become involved in unnecessary disputes. In time, Hughes became less and less willing to see the department participate in disputes between Latin American governments and American business interests. He relied more heavily on the Latin American Division, which gave greater weight to political considerations and the niceties of diplomatic relations. The economic adviser and most American ministers were more concerned with the United States' economic influence in the hemisphere. In 1923, the department was waiting for the Costa Rican government to ratify a protocol to begin negotiations on the canal route along the Costa Rica–Nicaragua boundary, and the American minister in San José was urging extreme pressure on the Costa Rican government to complete ratification. But Dana Munro, the Central American desk officer in the Latin American Division, argued that the protocol had been originally signed to meet Costa Rica's wishes and did not confer any benefit upon the United States, so that it was foolish to impose it on Costa Rica. His view prevailed.[31]

The following year the economic adviser, in cooperation with the Bureau of Foreign and Domestic Commerce, was trying to sign most-favored-nation treaties with all the nations in the hemisphere. Salvador was reluctant to sign because it gave preference, by special treaty, to luxury articles from France and because its Congress demanded a *quid pro quo* from the United States in the form of having its sugar placed on an equal tariff footing with Cuban sugar. The economic adviser did not care to prolong the negotiations. He instructed Chargé Benjamin Muse to point out to the Salvadoran government that its coffee entered the United States free of duty and that the United States Executive, under Section 317 of the Tariff Act of 1922, was empowered to increase the duty on the products of countries which dis-

[31] RG 59, 711.1828/5–7.

criminated against American commerce. Political pressure in Salvador continued to prevent the exchange of notes, and after several fruitless exchanges the economic adviser wanted to serve Salvador with an ultimatum. Munro counseled restraint. He argued that the loss to American businessmen would be greater as a result of an increase in the tariff on coffee than it would be without a treaty and that the damage to United States prestige would outweigh any benefits that might accrue from the treaty. He could see no reason to single out a small country, with which United States relations were so close, for the first application of the penalty provisions of the tariff law. Once again, his views prevailed. Similar incidents arose over a tangled exchange situation with Argentina in which the department felt Argentina was justified in protecting itself; and over a report from Consul General Dawson in Mexico requesting that confidential information go to an American company, in which Assistant Secretary Harrison and Secretary Hughes decided that the department could not assume the responsibility of sending such a message.[32]

One excellent example both of the continuity of policy from one administration to another and of the shifting importance of economic and political factors in foreign relations was the attitude of the State Department toward the dispute between American nitrate companies and the Chilean Nitrate Producers Association. By 1924, the department had ordered the American ambassador to end his defense of the American companies and had washed its hands of the matter. The need for nitrates was no longer vital, as it had been during the war, and the political disadvantages of vigorous governmental interposition far outweighed any gains that might be made by a few American firms.

Morton Carrel's important memorandum of February 1922 on Latin American policy placed great stress on using South America's shortage of capital to create opportunities for United States direct investment and trade. There is ample evidence that American industry did benefit from

[32] RG 59, 711.162; economic adviser's memorandum (on Argentina), June 22, 1921, 611.359/73; Nov. 23, 1922, 812.50/122 (on Mexico).

loans to foreign governments, but it is difficult to find clear
examples in which the department used the link between
finance and investment. It used the loan to Cuba as an instrument of policy, but this was to secure desired political
and financial reforms, not to guarantee investment opportunities for Americans. And though the department was
urged on numerous occasions to make "the encouragement
of capital investment . . . a national policy," in Cuba and
in Central America, at least, its first concern was with financial stability and not with investment.[33]

By establishing its order of priorities in this fashion, the
State Department ran counter to the announced objectives
of the Department of Commerce and its secretary, Herbert
Hoover. Hoover is said to have taken his position in the
Harding cabinet on the condition that he would have a voice
in all economic policies. For him, the top priority was the
health of the domestic economy. Wherever and whenever the
domestic economy required it, Hoover was an uncompromising advocate of expanding United States economic influence
abroad. He conceived of his department as an agency for
furthering the commercial activities of the United States.
During his tenure in office, the Bureau of Foreign and Domestic Commerce, directed by Julius Klein, enlarged its field
force, established branches in fifty foreign cities, was re-
organized to serve the needs of American business, and made
a great clearing house of information and advice for American industry and finance and a buffer between private American interests and their foreign counterparts. In contrast to
the State Department's policy of informing businessmen of
unstable political and economic conditions in Latin America,
the Commerce Department was extremely reluctant to discourage selling or shipping into the markets of unstable
countries. The Bureau of Foreign and Domestic Commerce
considered it its duty to "assist businessmen to take these
so-called revolutions less seriously than they are now being
taken," because exaggerated reports of revolutionary activity

[33] R. F. Smith, *The United States and Cuba,* 83; *Foreign Relations,*
1921, I, 697 ff.; 1922, I, 1004 ff.

alienated business interests already established in the affected markets.[34]

Latin America, said Hoover, was especially important as a preserve of American capital. Loans to the republics of this hemisphere were doubly valuable because they contributed "to the elevation of standards of living, [and] to peace and economic stability." Just after he took office he told reporters, referring to Latin America, "the more our intercourse expands, the more certain is the development of our long established friendships." The fundamental principle of Hoover's policy was untrammeled trade—the "open door." He advocated the right of American industry to obtain raw materials without restraint, and he opposed loans by Americans to foreign raw-materials monopolies. For him, the Department of Commerce was the executive arm of the American people in the fight against monopolistic prices and practices. He urged retaliation by the United States in the form of conservation, high tariffs, import restrictions, and the development of substitutes. He urged American businessmen to form buying pools and asked Congress to make them legal. He fought foreign cartels by inducing other nations to produce the monopolized commodities. In one highly publicized incident, the Department of Commerce was successful in preventing American banks from lending money to Brazil to help finance the coffee valorization scheme.[35]

Hoover envied the British government's control over the export of capital and urged, unsuccessfully, that American loans include the condition that United States products be

[34] Joseph Brandes, *Herbert Hoover and Economic Diplomacy* (Pittsburgh, 1962), 30; C. H. Cunningham, commercial attaché in Havana to R. F. O'Toole, chief, Latin American Division, Bureau of Foreign and Domestic Commerce, Oct. 30, 1924, RG 151, Box 2230, 430.30—Cuba. State Department's attitude is in RG 59, 812.50/81–122, and 835.516/83 and 102. On relationship between the Bureau of Foreign and Domestic Commerce and businessmen, see T. R. Taylor, of the bureau's Latin American Division, to Wilbur Carr, Oct. 17, 1921, RG 151, Box 1654, 312—Argentina.

[35] Klein, 164–65; Alexander DeConde, *Herbert Hoover's Latin American Policy* (Stanford, Calif., 1951), 6; Williams, *Economic Foreign Policy*, 402; Brandes, 63–83.

purchased wherever possible. Banks in the United States opposed such controls and had the support of Secretary of the Treasury Andrew Mellon. The State Department was never anxious to meddle in disputes between private interests and, in this case, did not welcome making additional commitments to American business abroad or relish the thought of enforcing the condition. Under Hoover's guidance, the Department of Commerce became an effective instrument of United States foreign investment and trade and played an increasingly important role in the nation's foreign affairs. In 1921, the average number of inquiries to the Commerce Department on international problems was 700 per day; by 1928 it had increased to 10,300 per day. This increase in the Commerce Department's influence was won at the expense of the State Department, which did not give way with good grace. At the beginning of the Harding administration, there had been every indication that cooperation between the two departments would be unusually good. Several career diplomats had worked with Hoover in Europe and had formed a very high opinion of him. Hugh Gibson, for one, idolized him. When Leland Harrison returned to Washington in 1921 to become assistant secretary of state, he anticipated a smooth relationship with the Commerce Department because his close friend, Christian A. Herter, was to be Hoover's chief assistant, and he promised Gibson he would work closely with Hoover. But Harrison's enthusiasm diminished rapidly. Herter had little scope for independent action, and his friendship with Harrison could not insure cooperation between the State and the Commerce Departments. Hoover insisted on being informed of all developments in international affairs and would not leave his office without making arrangements for a constant flow of information to him, wherever he was. In little more than a year Harrison was disillusioned with Hoover's empire-building.[36]

[36] See John Barrett to Klein, Mar. 27, 1925, Barrett papers; Klein, 198; Harrison to Gibson, Mar. 21, 1921, Herter to Harrison, Mar. 24, 1923, and Harrison's memorandum of Nov. 7, 1922, Harrison papers; Carr diary, May 4, 1921; Phillips diary, Feb. 11, 1924; Brandes, 151–91.

It was difficult to stop Hoover. He had the powerful backing of Congress and the business community. He was able to expand his department's sphere of influence because of the uncharted divide between purely commercial affairs, the constitutional mandate of the Department of Commerce, and foreign affairs, the province of the Department of State. Since there were no ground rules for the separation of responsibility with regard to international economic affairs, Hoover expanded his influence whenever he could and into whatever areas were vulnerable. A few months after taking office, he moved to take control of the Inter-American High Commission when Secretary of the Treasury Mellon, the titular head of the commission, indicated a lack of interest in its work. Hoover claimed the commission fitted perfectly into his program for bringing about greater stability in the financial relations between the United States and the other republics of the Western Hemisphere. The commission was one of the few active institutional manifestations of inter-American cooperation. Latin Americans respected it because they felt they had some influence over its deliberations. The State Department, which had considerable interest in its work, opposed Hoover vigorously. Its protests were in vain. A few months later it received a mimeographed postcard announcing that the High Commission would henceforward operate in the Department of Commerce Building.[37]

Part of the explanation of Hoover's success in taking over the High Commission was Hughes's reluctance to engage in petty fighting for political influence. Another reason was the strict neutrality maintained by the working staff of the commission, led by the Executive Secretary Leo S. Rowe and his assistant, C. E. McGuire. These two men had run the commission since its inception and had worked in the Treasury Department for many years. It made no difference to them who sat in the chairman's seat, so long as they were allowed to run the commission as an international agency, completely independent of domestic politics. Rowe and McGuire were sadly mistaken in Hoover. The secretary of commerce domi-

[37] Carr to Fletcher, Oct. 20, 1921, and SecCom to SS, Jan. 1, 1922, RG 59, 810.51/1048 and 1049; DeConde, 6.

nated the first meetings he chaired and took steps to make
the commission an appendage of his department. Rowe and
McGuire continued to perform their duties, trying desperately to maintain the independence of their organization.
They passed resolutions to this effect in their executive meetings and attempted to secure legislation from Congress which
would guarantee independent existence for the commission.
All measures failed, and both men resigned in October 1922,
leaving the field to Hoover. Once the commission was made
a fief of the Department of Commerce, Latin Americans lost
interest in it. Efforts to revive it were to no avail, as they
originated in the Department of Commerce and only emphasized to the Latin Americans that the commission was
no longer their organization.[38]

The State Department was vulnerable to encroachments
by the Department of Commerce in the early years of the
Republican ascendancy because it was still in the throes of
the reorganization begun during the previous administration. Until the Rogers Act of 1924 consolidated the Diplomatic and Consular Services into one Foreign Service, the
State Department was uncertain in its handling of economic
information. Though diplomats, who dominated the State
Department, resented Hoover's attempts to take over the
Consular Service, they were not willing to instill that service
with sufficient importance and prestige to quiet Hoover once
and for all. In a very perceptive memorandum, Robert Lansing attributed the State Department's loss of prestige to its
inflexibility in a period of great change. The department
was "in a rut, and a very deep rut at that," bogged down in
"dust-covered precedents." It is no wonder that American
businessmen turned to the Department of Commerce for support in their foreign activities. They were made to feel that
the State Department gave precedence to political relations
between countries, and they resented the fact that their chief
difficulty was "in persuading their own Government that

[38] Minutes of the meetings of the American Section of the International High Commission RG 43, Entry 308, Box 45; McGuire to Rowe,
July 20, 1922, Entry 305, Box 10; Guillermo Sherwell (Rowe's successor) to Grosvenor Jones, Nov. 20, 1922, Entry 305, Box 15.

they are honest and acting in good faith." Lansing's recom-
mendations were designed to save the Department of State
before it was too late. He urged the appointment of officials
"who know something about business and business methods
. . . who formulate policies on principles of commerce and
trade and not alone on principles of international law and
diplomacy." [39]

During the first few years after the war, the Department
of State had gotten all the best in its competition with the
Commerce Department. It had established its suzerainty over
international economic issues through the Economic Liaison
Committee. One of Hoover's first moves was to undermine
the Economic Liaison Committee and to insist upon receiving all economic reports passing through the Department of
State. This diluted the power of the foreign trade adviser,
whose best economists were transferred into the geographical
divisions of the department. Once this was accomplished, the
initiative passed to Hoover and Julius Klein in the Commerce Department, and they used it to good advantage. In
the correspondence between the two departments, which had
been diffident on the part of the Commerce Department and
aggressive on the part of the State Department, the Commerce Department now was confident of its position and
made demands upon the State Department. The latter resented the fact that most of the former's information was
collected by State Department officials, who never received
credit for their work, and that the Commerce Department
was woefully indiscreet in its use of confidential information. The State Department claimed that it provided the
Commerce Department with 93,364 separate services in 1923.
The State Department's Consular Service had made a profit
of over $1.5 million in that year, while the Department of
Commerce's Foreign Service cost the government over $1
million. After one particularly embarrassing incident, Francis White burst out, "confidential information should never
be sent to Commerce!" The two departments never agreed
on the relative importance of economic and political factors

[39] Memorandum by Dr. A. C. Millspaugh, Apr. 19, 1922, Harrison
papers; private memorandum, Feb. 16, 1922, Lansing papers.

in foreign relations, and, as a result, there was considerable
confusion in the distribution of responsibility between them.
On occasion there was outright hostility. Ambassadors were
sensitive of their positions as leading representatives of the
United States in foreign lands and were quick to report any
arrogance or seeming slight by representatives of the Department of Commerce. Once the Commerce Department established its primacy in the field of international economics, it
began to cut its ties to organizations that might compete
with it. One of the first to suffer was the Pan American
Union.[40]

By the end of the Harding-Coolidge administration, the
Department of Commerce had established its hegemony in
the field of economic affairs, even those affairs with obvious
international ramifications. The Department of State gradually withdrew from the forefront in the fight to expand
American economic influence abroad and relinquished its
leadership to the Department of Commerce. Only with reference to petroleum, cables, and bank loans—considered strategically vital—did the State Department hold tenaciously to
its control. So long as international commerce touched the
vital interests of the United States, it was still the province
of the State Department, and it would brook no encroachments. The Commerce Department seemed to accept this,
as there is little evidence of competition in formulating policy for these issues where the department had clearly formulated objectives. Once these objectives were achieved or
secured, the State Department was content to withdraw in
favor of the Commerce Department. As it withdrew, it mod-
erated its support for American private interests in foreign

[40] Carr diary, Mar. 30, Apr. 11, May 4, and Sept. 26, 1921; Klein to
Carr, Sept. 6, 1922; F. R. Eldridge to A. N. Young, Jan. 31, 1923; Department of Commerce memorandum, Apr. 10, 1924, RG 151, Box 911,
151—General; Phillips diary, Feb. 11, 1924; Tracy Lay, *Foreign Service
of the United States*, 200–201; C. D. Snow, "Governmental Foreign
Trade Promotion Service in the United States," *The Annals*, 94 (Mar.
1921); Francis White's memorandum, Apr. 14, 1925, RG 59, 811.-
503121/1; file on problems in Chile, RG 151, Box 2731, 544—Latin
America; Klein's memorandum, March 13, 1926, Box 927, 156—Pan
American Union.

disputes and thereby brought relations with Latin America more in line with the United States posture of official detachment from the problems of the world.[41]

[41] The evidence that the State Department considered itself solely responsible for these problems is as extensive as the department's files themselves. The evidence that the Commerce Department recognized this responsibility is in RG 151, Box 1652, 312—Petroleum, General; and Box 1654, 312—Petroleum, Argentina. Hoover tried to take over international radio accounting from the navy in 1923, but complications in the comptroller general's office delayed the transfer until fiscal 1925. By that time the State Department had achieved its objectives in communications and could step aside. See Box 2723, 544—General.

CHAPTER 4

Securing the Strategic Objectives:
Petroleum

Very few Americans saw any connection between petroleum deposits outside the country and the nation's security
when the United States entered the Great War. In less than
two years, the government made control over foreign oil
reserves adequate to the needs of the American navy and the
American economy one of its primary foreign-policy objectives. This sudden awareness was the product of painful wartime experience with the importance of fuel oil, together
with the chorus of prophecies that the underground reserves
of the United States were near exhaustion and an energetic
drive by the British government to secure access to a moiety
of the world's oil reserves. In a speech delivered shortly after
the Armistice, Lord Curzon declared, "The Allies floated to
victory on a wave of oil." He might as easily have said that
the Allies floated to victory on a wave of *American* oil. American refineries supplied 80 percent of Britain's petroleum
products from 1914 to 1916; in 1917, 92 percent. Just as
Allied petroleum requirements soared in 1917, the invaluable Russian source of supply was cut off, creating a fuel
emergency. The British and French threw themselves upon
the mercy of the Americans, begging them to save the Allies
from almost certain defeat. According to one story, Lord
Northcliffe delivered his government's message to the head
of Standard Oil of New Jersey:

He read it slowly twice, gave it back to me, saying, "If it can be done, it will be done." I said nothing whatever about price. Those people started in right there, and oil is pouring across the Atlantic with great strides and at a lower price than we have averaged over here. They could have squeezed millions out of our trouble if they had chosen. When I thanked them, they merely remarked, "It's our war as well as yours." [1]

This cooperation should not be romanticized. The American industry was driven to it by the constant threat of price controls by the federal government. The industry organized a Co-operative Committee on Petroleum which was made subordinate to the Council of National Defense. When the Council of National Defense became the War Industries Board, the industry group became the National Petroleum War Service Committee. By January 1918, it was under the Fuel Administration where it received the solicitous attentions of Mark Requa, who came over from the Food Administration, the man chosen by the industry to lead them out of the wilderness of excessive competition. Requa was primarily responsible for freeing the oil companies from fear of the antitrust laws for the duration of the war and helped precipitate a silent revolution in the federal government's relation to industry. In return for its services to the nation, the industry got the preservation of a substantial profit margin and the institution of a tax concession. From emphasis on competition and the dissolution of monopoly, public

---

[1] Herbert Feis, *Seen from E. A.* (New York, 1947), 94; Feis, "Petroleum and American Foreign Policy," *Commodity Policy Studies*, No. 3 (Stanford, Calif., 1944), 3–4; John A. DeNovo, "The Movement for an Aggressive American Oil Policy Abroad, 1918–1920," *American Historical Review*, LXI, 4 (July 1956), 854; H. F. Williamson *et al., The American Petroleum Industry: The Age of Energy, 1899–1959* (Evanston, Ill., 1963), 261; G. Roberts, *The Most Powerful Man in the World* (New York, 1938), 160; Gibb and Knowlton, *Resurgent Years,* 270; W. J. Kemnitzer, *Rebirth of Monopoly* (New York, 1938), 19; Gerald D. Nash, *United States Oil Policy, 1890–1964* (Pittsburgh, 1968), 20–36; Camilo Barcia Trelles, *El Imperialismo del Petróleo y La Paz Mundial* (Valladolid, 1925), 7–9.

policy now stressed cooperation and regulation of business practices.

The navy took the lead in urging a more aggressive petroleum policy overseas. It was obvious to students of Alfred Thayer Mahan that the security of the United States depended upon adequate supplies of fuel for the nation's fleet, supplies which would be secure in time of peace and in time of war. The navy even delayed conversion to oil because of doubts as to future supply. Domestic oil reserves were not enough; the United States must supplement its petroleum reserves by seeking foreign sources of supply. Until the United States had adequate reserves, the United States should not concede any advantage to any nation, even during war. Admiral William S. Sims, the navy's chief representative in London throughout the war, was convinced that the British were asking the United States to make great sacrifices to secure for themselves an adequate supply of petroleum, while they merely freed their own tonnage for the benefit of private companies. In private memoranda to the secretary of the navy, Sims accused the British of using valuable tonnage for the Anglo-Mexican and Anglo-Brazilian oil trade. This suspicion was so strong that it even made its way into official communications between the American navy and the British Admiralty, fed by the fact that the British and the Dutch had practiced exclusion within their empires for years. Aliens were barred from owning or operating oil properties; both governments participated directly in the ownership and control of major petroleum companies; and both acted to prevent the sale of property to foreigners.[2]

Sims got a sympathetic man at court when Mark Requa was made chief of the Petroleum Division of the Fuel Administration. Requa used the official statements of Sims and other naval officers to complement the constant complaints of American petroleum companies to convince the Depart-

---

[2] Report of General Board, Dec. 3, 1913, "Records of the General Board," File No. 429, Serial No. 215; SecNav to Sims, "For the Admiralty," Aug. 14, 1917, RG 45, Box 82, Subject File EF—Oil Situation; RG 59, 818.6363Am6/2, July 1, 1918; 818.6363Am6/4, June 15; 814.6363/1, Oct. 11; and 831.6375C23/.

ment of State and the president that the United States must act decisively to protect its petroleum supply. The final decision in petroleum, as in foreign loans, communications, and trade in general, held it more important to win the war than to launch an aggressive campaign to expand United States economic and commercial influence throughout the world. The war made American needs clear to all. For the duration, the petroleum companies and their champions in government had to bide their time. Once the fighting in Europe stopped, they renewed their efforts for an aggressive petroleum policy and did not rest until they secured for themselves and for the United States a dominant place in the worldwide struggle for petroleum. They were drawn by a fear of the exhaustion of America's domestic reserves that amounted almost to an obsession.

They tried to bring their case directly to the Paris Peace Conference. Requa urged Bernard Baruch to prevent oil lands in American hands from passing to foreign ownership; Admiral Sims warned of Europe's interest in petroleum and urged steps to prevent the state monopolies which would "have most prejudicial effect to America." Baruch converted these proposals to a general plan for an "open door" for oil exploitation and presented it to the peace conference. When it was rejected, he called upon the Treasury Department to withhold credits from any nation that would not give United States citizens equal opportunity to exploit its petroleum resources. This suggestion was not followed. Paul Foley, the navy's petroleum expert on duty with the Shipping Board, proposed in April that the United States government take advantage of its temporary superiority in tanker tonnage to guarantee adequate supplies for the navy. Corollary to this was the navy plan to close the domestic oil reserves to exploitation, to expand imports, and to increase navy storage and tanker facilities. The Wilson administration adopted the navy proposals for the domestic reserves, but the shipping proposal was politically impossible.[3]

[3] Postponing action in the Latin American Division memoranda by J. H. Stabler, Apr. 14, 1917, RG 59, 831.6375/4; and by Glenn Stewart,

The aggressive policy of the British government was extremely disturbing to the American government and exacerbated relations between the former allies. United States oil companies were afraid that their efforts to acquire foreign sources of supply were fatally late, and they were frightened by claims of British officials that Great Britain controlled all fields outside the United States and 50 percent of the world's oil reserves. Alarm was tinctured with indignation because the United States had helped Great Britain during the war. The stiff attitude of the British and French in the negotiations over the tankers belonging to the German subsidiary of Standard Oil and over the Rumanian oil properties owned by Standard Oil before the war increased the suspicion that powerful international forces were aligned against American commercial interests. This gave new life to Baruch's plan for worldwide reciprocity. In August 1919, the navy submitted a report to the State Department advocating reciprocity, and a month later the American Petroleum Institute, spokesman for the industry, supported this policy. Industry representatives stated their case at the 1920 conventions of the American Petroleum Institute and the International Chamber of Commerce. In 1920, the American Institute of Mining and Metallurgical Engineers added their vote for this policy.[4]

Nov. 7, 810.6363/–. Fear of exhausted reserves in Nash, *American Oil Policy,* 43–9; SecCom Alexander to Senator Reed Smoot, July 15, 1920, RG 151, Box 1652, 312—General Oils, Mineral; Captain A. W. Marshall to Opnav, Aug. 12, 1920, RG 45, Box 82—Oil Situation. Peace conference action in Sims to Opnav for Colby, Garfield, Requa, Franklin, and Bedford, Dec. 5, 1918; Requa to Baruch, Feb. 2, 1919, Foley to Opnav, Apr. 18, 1919, and Captain A. W. Marshall to Opnav, Aug. 12, 1920, RG 45, Box 82—Oil Situation; Baruch to Hurley, Apr. 21, 1919, RG 59, 800.51/146; Polk diary, Jan. 25 and 28, 1919; Gerig, *Open Door and the Mandates System,* 81; Levin, *Woodrow Wilson and World Politics,* chap. 1.

[4] DeNovo, "Movement for an Aggressive Oil Policy," 857–62; Ludwell Denny, *America Conquers Britain* (New York, 1930), 186; Denny, *We Fight for Oil* (New York, 1928), 3–4; J. A. Spender, *Weetman Pearson, First Viscount Cowdray* (London, 1930), 202–3; E. H. Davenport and Sidney R. Cooke, *The Oil Trusts and Anglo-American Relations* (New York, 1924), 1–90; Stanley K. Hornbeck, "The Struggle for Petroleum," *The Annals,* Supplement to 112 (Mar. 1924); Anton

While the implications of reciprocity were being discussed within the government, the Department of State proceeded to collect detailed information on petroleum resources throughout the world. In May 1919, the department instructed consuls in the Caribbean area to submit detailed reports on petroleum regulations, resources, concessions, and other conditions in their districts. While these were still coming in, the Petroleum Subcommittee of the Economic Liaison Committee recommended that American diplomatic representatives give special attention to helping American oil interests. This action led to a more general circular instruction to all diplomatic and consular officers, August 6, 1919, calling for detailed reports "regarding all matters of interest affecting the mineral oil industry." The instruction also authorized American representatives to lend "all legitimate aid" to reliable American interests. The replies to these circulars went into a loose-leaf digest kept in the Foreign Trade Adviser's Office and was then made available to the Bureau of Foreign and Domestic Commerce and the Geological Survey.[5]

To insure the effectiveness of any pressure on foreign companies and governments, the Department of State joined with the Department of Commerce and the attorney general's office to lobby in Congress for the General Leasing Act of 1920, which provided for retaliatory discrimination against United States citizens and for permission to use existing antitrust legislation to prevent British takeover and control of American companies by means of holding companies. The Commerce Department at first sought to coordinate the petroleum policies of the various government departments; the State Department coldly rejected the overture and moved quickly and with effect to assert its control over every aspect of the international petroleum situation that was not entirely domestic in scope and implications. It asked representatives

Mohr, *The Oil War*, (New York, 1926); Louis Fischer, *Oil Imperialism* (New York, 1926); Pierre l'Espagnol de la Tramerye, *The World Struggle for Oil* (New York, 1924), 97–198; Feis, *Petroleum Policy;* Gibb and Knowlton, 266–73; RG 59, 800.6363/11, 87, 89, and 95.

    [5] Consular instruction no. 672, May 31, RG 59, 800.6363/2a; subcommittee report, July, 811.6363/45; *Foreign Relations*, 1919, I, 167.

of the petroleum industry for an expression of opinion "regarding any action by this Government, or by a foreign government, which you believe would be especially appropriate and beneficial in the case of some specific cause of injury to your business in a foreign country." The same month (May 1920), the department informed an American oil company that it was ready at all times "to give consideration to difficulties in which American firms may find themselves as a result of foreign legislation." Emboldened by this indication of growing support, the oil men urged their views on the department. The results of the survey were submitted to Congress as the Polk Report. Senator Phelan of California used the report to prepare a bill calling for the formation of a government oil corporation to compete on equal terms with the British government-controlled companies enjoying great success in the Middle East and Latin America. The bill never was passed. Congress held it in reserve as a last-ditch possibility should all other measures fail to gain the objective of equal access to petroleum resources.[6]

The Department of State wanted American petroleum interests to understand that it realized the importance of the questions involved. It assured them that the United States government would go as far as it properly could in their support. For their own part, the companies pointed out that they would hesitate to extend their foreign holdings without assurances from the department of a stronger policy. They insisted that they could not compete with British oil companies without State Department cooperation. Much as the Department of State wanted to see American-controlled oil reserves all over the world, it would not assume responsibility for advocating specific programs for American companies. During the remainder of the Wilson administration,

[6] Commerce Department memorandum, May 9, 1920; and Frost to H. G. Brock, acting director of the Bureau of Foreign and Domestic Commerce, RG 151, Box 1652, 312—General Oils, Mineral; H. Dotterer to George S. Brady, trade commissioner in Buenos Aires, Nov. 16, Box 1654, 312—Argentina Oils, Mineral; circular of May 5, RG 59, 800.6363/-125a; letter to Southern Oil and Transport Corporation of New York, May 6, 810.6363/3; *Cong. Rec.*, 66th Cong., 2nd Sess., Senate Resolution No. 354.

it limited its role to providing information, giving assurances of goodwill, and making representations in favor of reciprocal treatment for American nationals. This was not enough to assuage the apprehension of the oil men. They, like other business leaders, were uncertain over the immediate course of federal policies during demobilization. They were anxious to continue cooperating with the government, and in March 1919, they established the American Petroleum Institute to preserve what A. C. Bedford of Standard Oil (New Jersey) referred to as a "different and entirely new spirit of understanding between the various elements of the petroleum industry."

By 1920, the department, eager to keep in step with American petroleum interests, invited oil men to policy-making sessions. Petroleum policy in the department was placed in the hands of Assistant Secretary Van Santvord Merle-Smith and of petroleum expert A. C. Millspaugh. These two men dealt with petroleum throughout the world and with the closely related problems of American rights in the mandated territories, especially Mesopotamia. Whenever a question of policy arose concerning Latin America, they called in William R. Manning of the Latin American Division. Generally, they subordinated local issues to larger policy questions. Trade Adviser Wesley Frost opposed linking petroleum to mandates and did not consider the "open door" adequate to protect American interests. He also argued that the United States should assume a stronger stance in Latin America than elsewhere and should assume greater responsibility in the fight for petroleum in the Western Hemisphere than in any other area. Frost persisted in defending his point of view and was transferred to Marseilles as consul, leaving Millspaugh completely in charge of petroleum questions in the Trade Adviser's Office.[7]

[7] Nash, 38–41; statements by E. H. Sadler in conferences with Merle-Smith, Aug. 3, 1920, and Jan. 12, 1921; Wesley Frost to Assistant Secretary Adee, Mar. 23, 1920; Frost to Van H. Manning, director of the Bureau of Research, American Petroleum Institute, Nov. 27, RG 59, 800.6363/162, 238, 120, 205a; trade adviser's memorandum by Millspaugh, Sept. 9, 1919, 467.11St25/36. DeNovo, "Movement for an Aggressive Oil Policy," 874, argues that the oil men had "successfully

Everywhere they looked, in 1920, department officials were amazed at the avidity of the British in reaching out to every possible oil area. American oil interests were obstructed at every turn by some company under the aegis of the British government. The British were entrenched in the Netherlands East Indies, India, Burma, the Near East, and Rumania and were trying to gain access to the fields of Central and South America. The department decided that the best way to weaken British hegemony would be to adopt a policy of insisting upon reciprocity and the "open door." In the Western Hemisphere, the Wilson administration was at first willing to try stronger measures.

The United States government made it known that it would not look with favor upon granting oil concessions to foreigners in the neighborhood of the Panama Canal. Beyond the strategic zone around the canal, the department would give no aid to companies with only minority American participation and actively opposed monopolistic concessions to aliens. To make this policy effective, the department had to learn which companies operating in Latin America were British controlled and what concessions they held. On the basis of this information, American diplomatic representatives were instructed specifically to withhold support from known British interests and to report on the activity of British oil companies.[8]

---

waged the campaign to convince the American public and its Washington policy-makers of the identity of the national interest and the commercial petroleum interests." He implies that the department acted only under pressure. I do not get this impression from the documents. The department was willing to support the oil companies because it believed that their advancement was in the national interest. The discussion of the petroleum question which led to the conviction that something had to be done, began immediately after the war, before the "publicity campaign" had a chance to get very far. In addition, the two men whom DeNovo credits with having led the campaign were largely discounted by the petroleum specialists within the department. See A. C. Millspaugh to Assistant Secretary Dearing, May 10, 1921, 800.6363/328. The internal policy debate is in the memorandum, Aug. 13, 1920, and Frost to Manning, Nov. 27; RG 59, 800.6363/237 and 205a.

[8] Special instructions to Latin America, Mar. 1921, RG 59, 800.6363/-240b. For an example of opposition to monopolistic concessions in

The end product of petroleum policy-making during the Wilson administration was incorporated in a lengthy memorandum prepared by Millspaugh in consultation with Merle-Smith in February 1921 for the incoming administration. Merle-Smith remained in office for a few days after Harding's inauguration to smooth the transition between administrations. His main task was to submit this memorandum to Charles Evans Hughes and brief the new secretary on the oil situation. In his memorandum, Millspaugh traced the causes of the government's interest in the petroleum question and summarized conditions in every major producing, or potentially productive, state. He used the General Leasing Act of 1920 as the basis for the policy of reciprocity and outlined the department's position as follows:

(A) that discrimination against American citizens with respect to participation in oil development in foreign countries is contrary to the principle of reciprocity and is likely to result in a movement for retaliation by this country;

(B) that equal treatment should be accorded to nationals of all countries in mandated territories;

(C) that monopolization is economically and politically undesirable and that the United States does not cherish for itself or encourage on the part of its nationals any monopolistic designs.[9]

After dealing with conditions in certain countries which required the attention of the department, Millspaugh spelled out the conclusion which was the result of two years of discussion in the department: that the various outstanding oil questions should be treated comprehensively as aspects of a world problem and that it was desirable, in order to improve the situation, to reach a constructive understanding with the British government. Merle-Smith and Secretary Colby

---

Latin America, see instructions to embassy in Buenos Aires, Sept. 15, 1920, 835.6363/28.

[9] Memorandum on the general petroleum situation, Feb. 1921, RG 59, 800.6363/325.

concurred on both points. They were less anxious to accept Millspaugh's proposal to eliminate discrimination against aliens in the Philippines and to eliminate obstructions to British concessions in the Panama Canal Zone because such actions were inconsistent with American policy and detrimental to the achievement of reciprocity. The British persisted in refusing to give an inch in the Near East without receiving some concessions in the Western Hemisphere, so that Hughes was forced to modify the department's policy in keeping with Millspaugh's suggestion.

At first, the Department of State, under Colby and Hughes, shied away from applying this general policy to specific problems in Latin America because of the persistent feeling that the area was a sphere of American special interest. Similar conclusions with respect to cable policy and financial policy were reached in the same way. In each of these important subjects, the Department of State conducted an internal debate over policy and decided that the United States government should have one general policy to cover exigencies all over the world. As specific cases arose in Latin America, it was decided, in each of the three strategic commodities, that Latin America was a region of special interest for the United States and that an exception to the general policy was necessary. In all three, when the basic strategic objectives of the United States had been achieved, the Department of State reasserted its general policies and determined once again that there would be no exceptions because of geographic area.

Oil and politics were closely connected during Warren G. Harding's brief stay in the White House. His secretary of the interior, Albert Fall of New Mexico, had been chairman of the Senate Subcommittee on Mexican Affairs and, as a senator, had played an active role in American relations with Mexico and Colombia, where oil was an important factor. Under Fall's guidance, Harding brought the long-pending Thomson-Urrutia Treaty with Colombia before the cabinet on March 8, just four days after his inauguration. He submitted the treaty to the Senate, but it was not ratified for over a year. At the same cabinet meeting at which Harding brought up the Colombian treaty, Fall asked for a decision on a general oil policy. He advocated leasing government reserves to private companies. In foreign policy, he favored a plan to partition the world into British and American oil zones, reserving the Western Hemisphere as a preferred field for Americans. Hughes submitted this view to his staff, and they rejected it. Arthur C. Millspaugh was still the department's petroleum expert, and he had not changed his views since writing the policy memorandum of February 1921, for the Wilson administration. His presence and influence meant continuation of Democratic oil policy—at least for a while.[10]

Using the Millspaugh memorandum of February 1921 as a starting point, Hughes began the department's third survey of facts and figures since the war. He asked oil men and diplomatic representatives for their views on all petroleum questions and, in April, instructed Millspaugh to draft a general agreement with Great Britain covering all petroleum questions. It appears from this that Hughes was proceeding slowly and logically along the lines laid down by the preceding administration.[11]

A month after he had begun a discussion aiming at a definition of petroleum policy, his plans were upset by Secretary of Commerce Hoover's calling a meeting of prominent petroleum leaders to consider ways to combat British oil monopolies in the Near East and the East Indies. Thus, Hoover obstructed the Department of State's attempt to supervise overseas petroleum activities just as he was to thwart Hughes's plan for a comprehensive loan policy later in the year. Millspaugh wanted the secretary to attend the meeting in the Commerce Department and to take along the rough draft of the agreement with Great Britain, which was nearly ready. He contended that negotiations with Great Britain must not be limited to the problem of oil but must cover the international situation as a whole and that such an interna-

[10] John D. Hicks, *Republican Ascendancy*, 30; Burt Noggle, *Teapot Dome: Oil and Politics in the 1920's* (Baton Rouge, 1962), passim; trade adviser's memorandum by Millspaugh, Apr. 23, 1921, RG 59, 800.6363/12.

[11] Letter, Apr. 6, 1921; Diplomatic Serial No. 55, Aug. 26, RG 59, 800.6363/243 and 13a.

tional agreement must be formulated with due regard for the
national interest and not merely for the special interests of
the oil companies. It must be "a constructive effort to deal
politically with a troublesome international economic question" and not merely "another instrument in the struggle for
oil control." The foreign trade adviser, W. W. Cumberland,
supported Millspaugh's position, adding his own sense of out-
rage that the Department of Commerce, which had "hitherto
taken little part in formulating petroleum policies and has
little or no technical information," should intervene in a
matter that was the rightful province of the Department of
State.[12]

Hughes and Millspaugh attended the meeting in Hoover's
office. It was inconclusive. The oil men could not agree on
techniques of cooperation overseas, and the two cabinet officials could not agree on a division of responsibility within
the government. The Department of State had little cause
to worry about its role in petroleum ventures overseas. Whenever Americans sought petroleum concessions from a foreign
government, they came to the department for aid, and they
generally followed the department's advice. For example, in
Mexico they complied with department policy even though
their own position suffered. The Mexican government offered to buy Mexican bonds from the oil men at par in payment of back taxes which were in dispute in 1921 and a major source of friction between the two countries. The oil men
would buy bonds on the New York market at a greatly de-
preciated rate and then sell them to the Mexican government
at par. Thomas W. Lamont opposed the move on behalf of
the International Committee of Bankers on the grounds that
it would defraud the bondholders and compromise the bankers' bargaining position with the Mexican government. The
department forced the oil men to accept this decision because
it had made living up to international obligations a basic requirement for recognition. The following year, the oil men
were asked to lend the Mexican government $25 million to
be repaid out of reduced tax assessments. Once again, the

[12] Memoranda, May 12, 1921, RG 59, 800.6363/329.

department was unwilling to give such support to an unrecognized regime, and the oil men, reluctant to go against the expressed wishes of the Department of State, gave up the scheme. It was in their interest at this time (1920–22) to keep in the department's good graces.[13]

At the meeting in Hoover's office, both Hoover and Hughes had advised the oil men to fight for control of foreign oil reserves, particularly in the Middle East. By publicly advocating action by the oil companies, the Republicans went a step further than the Democrats in assuming responsibility for the actions of private petroleum interests. By November 1921, the oil men were ready to look into the situation, and Hughes promised them full support. The State Department never tried to monopolize overseas petroleum questions; it solicited the cooperation of other departments.[14]

This May 1921 meeting actually marked the end of the coincidence of the national interest and the interest of the oil companies. The latter were more concerned with access

[13] *Foreign Relations,* 1921, II, 499–505; 1922, II, 696–97. This was a continuation of the policy followed during the Wilson administration, when the department assured the companies that it would protect American property from confiscation, but rejected the oil men's contention that Mexican efforts to "denounce American claims and to refuse drilling permits on various technicalities, constituted confiscation." See Daniels, *Years of War,* 248; Frederic N. Watriss, legal representative of the Association of Mexican Producers, to Polk, June 27, 1919, Polk papers; *Foreign Relations,* 1919, I, 591–613; 1920, III, 217–26; Carr diary, Apr. 7, 1920.

[14] Charles W. Hamilton, *Americans and Oil in the Middle East* (Houston 1962), 83; Feis, *Diplomacy of the Dollar,* 48–60; Ludwell Denny, *America Conquers Britain,* 186; Fletcher to Hoover, Apr. 12, 1921, RG 151, Box 1652, 312–General; Denby to Hughes, Apr. 21, and May 5, 1921, RG 80, 13668-929 and 928; Denby to Harding, Aug. 13, RG 45, Box 82–Oil Situation. An example of the energetic State Department support for private companies abroad is the work of Minister Maginnis and Chargé N. R. Peck for Standard Oil in Bolivia, Aug. through Dec. 1921, RG 59, 824.6363/15–28. Millspaugh took revenge on Hoover for upsetting his hold over petroleum policy when he was financial adviser to the Persian government, a few years later. Hoover was boosting the Sinclair Oil Company to join the British in exploiting Mesopotamian oil. Millspaugh favored the Standard Oil Company and got the Department of State to back him. Standard ultimately headed an American "group" which was given a share in the Turkish Petroleum Company.

to oil fields than with principles of policy, whereas the Department of State tried to remain true to the "open door"
and to reciprocity. In June 1922, the British and the French
offered the American oil group a 24 percent participation in
the Mosul oil concession. Hughes was torn between his desire to see Americans share in the Middle East oil development and his apprehension of a monopolistic concession. He
agreed to its participation on condition that the American
group include any other American company that wanted to
participate.[15]

Before the British would offer the Americans a share in
Mosul oil, they insisted that the United States alter its policy
toward non-American concessions in the Western Hemisphere. The Department of State was forced to agree and began moving slowly toward the consistent petroleum policy
that Millspaugh had recommended at the end of the Wilson
administration: opposition to all monopolistic concessions,
equal opportunity for all interests, and reciprocity of treatment for all nationals in every part of the world. It would
appear that in doing so, the Department of State was willing
to sacrifice certain advantages in the Western Hemisphere to
achieve other worldwide goals. The change in policy came
gradually, was never announced generally, and was applied to
individual situations as they arose. Consequently, diplomats
in the field sometimes fell behind the department. The minister to Guatemala continued to work for the exclusion of
European oil interests until February 1923, when the department told him:

> It is not the policy of the Department to seek any spe-
> cially favored position in any Latin American country
> with regard to the acquisition of petroleum concessions.
> . . . The Department desires to be of assistance in every
> proper way to reputable American companies seeking
> such concession, but it would not accord with the De-
> partment's policy of equal opportunity to suggest to the

[15] Feis, *Dollar Diplomacy*, 53–57; John A. DeNovo, *American Interests and Policies in the Middle East, 1900–1939* (Minneapolis, 1963),
167–68. The final American share was 23.75 percent.

Government of Guatemala any law which would discriminate unfairly against the citizens of any other country.[16]

This new, aloof attitude was possible because United States relations with Great Britain had improved. American and British companies opened direct negotiations for division of the spoils in the Near East.

By the end of the Harding administration, pessimism in the oil situation had turned to optimism. New oil reserves were discovered in the United States, putting an end to fears of impending shortage. By 1925, American companies had secured a foothold in the Middle East and had begun to tap the enormous resources in Venezuela. Furthermore, the British had become less aggressive in their pursuit of petroleum reserves, and by 1925 cooperation between American and British interests had become prevalent in Asia, Latin America, and the Middle East. The oil companies found they no longer needed the State Department. The department continued to propound reciprocity and the "open door" long after those policies had ceased to serve their original purpose in advancing American interests. In the rare instances in which the department did protest violations of American rights, its actions were halfhearted and were taken only after lengthy internal debate. The national interest no longer demanded slavish protection of American oil companies, and the department was determined not to compromise its policy. If the companies did not come up to the standards set by the policy, they would go without diplomatic support. The case studies that follow demonstrate the way in which the Department of State formulated petroleum policy—as a response to specific situations. In each case, the nation's security require-

[16] Hughes to Geissler, Feb. 21, 1923, RG 59, 814.6363/51. On changing attitudes toward Great Britain, see *Boston Evening Transcript*, Mar. 19, 1923, 12:3; speeches in Congress by Senators McKellar and Lodge, Jan. 6, 1921 and Apr. 12, 1921, *Cong. Rec.*, 1047 and 159–68; debate in the Senate, Apr. 19, 1921, *Cong. Rec.*, 433; report by Commercial Attaché Jackson, Mexico City, Apr. 28, 1921, RG 151, Box 1661, 312—Mexico; DeNovo, *American Interests in the Middle East*, 184; Harrison to Phillips, Nov. 6, 1922, Harrison papers.

ments, growing out of United States experience during World War I, defined the limits of policy. The Mexican case is omitted because petroleum policy there was too intimately connected with domestic politics and with other aspects of foreign policy to warrant treatment in isolation. With the passage of time, the department came to understand the worldwide implications of American petroleum needs and gradually worked out a petroleum policy for Latin America that was consistent with its petroleum policy elsewhere in the world and with the broader policy of the "open door." [17]

CASE STUDY No. 1. OIL IN COSTA RICA

The struggle for petroleum in Costa Rica centered around concessions held by John M. Amory and Son and by Lincoln G. Valentine, one British and the other American. The British and American governments made representations persistently and energetically on their behalf, and the Costa Rican Congress and Executive fought bitterly over both concessions. Both proved to be worthless.

The Department of State became interested in the Costa Rican petroleum situation during the war, as part of the general concern to have petroleum reserves under United States control. A Latin American Division memorandum of November 1917 noted the existence of a "monopolistic" oil concession first obtained by Dr. Leo J. Greulich of New York City, in 1915, and later taken over by the Costa Rican Oil Corporation of Delaware, controlled by Henry Ford Sinclair. Dr. Greulich enjoyed a most unsavory reputation because of his German affiliations, and his associates Lincoln G. Valentine and Washington S. Valentine were in bad odor with the department because of their revolutionary adventures. The department had refused to support Greulich and the Valentines in securing ratification of their so-called Pinto-Greulich concession. In 1917, the department urged Sinclair

[17] Diplomatic Serial No. 180, Mar. 6, 1923, RG 59, 810.6363/16a; instructions to Consul F. C. Chabot (Caracas), Apr. 25, 831.6363/172; solicitor's memorandum, Jan. 3, 1925, 824.6363/50; Nash, 53–66.

to reorganize his Costa Rican Oil Company so as to eliminate Greulich and the Valentines.[18]

The British firm of S. Pearson and Sons had tried to buy the Pinto-Greulich concession in 1915, but the Valentines had preferred to deal with Sinclair. Operating through New York stockbrokers, John M. Amory and Son, in May 1918 the Pearson interests secured a concession to explore and exploit oil resources in the provinces of Costa Rica not covered by the Greulich concession. Valentine immediately brought Amory's English connections to the attention of Stewart Johnson, the American chargé in San José. Johnson passed on the information to the department, conceding only that the Amory concession "possibly" was an English enterprise. Acting on the basis of Valentine's evidence, the department cabled Johnson that it was the policy of the United States government that only approved Americans should own oil concessions in the neighborhood of the Panama Canal. Since the Amory concession did not appear to meet this requirement, Johnson was instructed to do everything possible to carry out this policy and defeat the concession. The instructions arrived too late for Johnson to prevent the Costa Rican Congress from making the Amory concession the law of the land, but he did make the policy of the United States known to the Costa Rican government.[19]

The Latin American Division was anxious to wrest the Amory concession from the British but lacked the means to do so. The solicitor and the foreign trade adviser served as dampers on the division's enthusiasm. The first requirement was to win the war. Under orders from the department, Chargé Johnson was defending the Sinclair interests against attacks by the unrecognized Tinoco administration. The Sin-

[18] Memorandum by Glenn Stewart, Nov. 7, 1917, RG 59, 810.6363/–; ONI report, Nov. 21, 1918, 818.6363Am6/25; "Memorandum on the validity of the so-called Valentine oil concession in Costa Rica now owned by the Sinclair Consolidated Oil Corporation," June 22, 1920, 818.6363/45.

[19] Stewart Johnson's cable, June 6 and his dispatch, June 15, 1918, enclosing a letter from Lincoln Valentine, RG 59, 818.6363Am6/1 and 4; instructions of July 1, 1918, 818.6363Am6/2.

clair concession bordered on lands of the United Fruit Company at several points. The latter was afraid that drilling on the Sinclair side of their mutual border would drain all the oil from the United Fruit lands. Minor Keith, then president of United Fruit, joined with Amory to oppose Sinclair in the Costa Rican courts and Congress.

Tinoco was thrown out of office before the Amory concession could be exploited. The interim government was anxious to win favor in the United States and offered to annul the Amory concession, if so requested by the United States government. Stewart Johnson had returned to the department and was serving as Central American desk officer when this offer was made. He wanted the department to approve and support American interests which might be granted the concession by the existing government. The solicitor took the position that the department had not announced it would withhold recognition of commercial transactions with Tinoco and so could not do so now that his government had been overthrown. Legally, the solicitor had the last word. However, Acting Secretary Polk wanted to push the British out of Costa Rica. Following his solicitor's advice, the instructions he sent to the chargé did not request bluntly that the concession be annulled. They pointed out that the United States government opposed the concession as well as all other business transactions of the Tinoco regime. There is little doubt that the attitude of the United States was largely responsible for the subsequent difficulties of the Amory concession. Both petroleum concessions came under careful scrutiny as soon as the interim government in Costa Rica was replaced by a constitutional regime. The Amory concession was suspended in 1920 pending an investigation, and in May 1920 the Committee on Public Works submitted to the Costa Rican Congress a report which held that the Pinto-Greulich concession was not a law of the land. Without waiting to receive a complaint, the department wired Sinclair to inquire whether he wished the government to protest. Naturally, he did. The department informed the chargé that the Sinclair Consolidated Oil Company was a "responsible American concern of standing" and that "any action of the authorities in

Costa Rica looking to cancellation would be a source of concern and a subject of inquiry." [20] Having first committed itself, the department then turned to the solicitor for some support for its position. The latter obligingly upheld the validity of the original Pinto-Greulich concession and the legality of the transfer to Sinclair.

The department continued its support of Sinclair and its opposition to Amory despite strong pressure to the contrary. The United Fruit Company, in cooperation with Standard Oil Company of California, made strong representations against Sinclair, while a member of Congress defended the American qualities of the Amory concession. The department became more cautious in its approach when the British government interposed itself in the dispute. The first public notice of the British interest in the Amory concession was a formal complaint in its behalf by the British minister to Panama and Costa Rica, Percy Bennett. The department's first concession to the British was to refuse to support Americans with claims to territory within the Amory grant. After Bennett's activities had been confirmed by a report from Consul Chase, the department retreated still further. It cautioned Chase to "exercise extreme discretion in discussing the Amory Concessions" and to cease acting as informal adviser to the Costa Rican government. When the American position became known to the British, they intensified their efforts on behalf of the Amory concession. The department had gone as far as it would go. It refused a British request for active support.[21]

Department personnel in charge of the Costa Rican oil question remained the same when the administrations changed in Washington, and they continued the policy that had been formulated under the Democratic administration—

[20] RG 59, 818.6363Am6/29, 34, and 35; 818.6363/30 and 45.

[21] The United Fruit protest is in Lester Woolsey's letter of July 11, 1920; the department's reply is in the solicitor's memorandum by J. R. Baker, July 14, 1920, RG 59, 818.6363/93. Amory's interests were represented by George S. Graham, a prominent Philadelphia attorney and a Republican member of the House of Representatives. His correspondence with the department is 818.6363Am6/41 and 102. On Bennett, see 818.6363/90, and 818.6363Am6/42.

support for the Sinclair concession and tacit opposition to the British interests. As Hughes increased the pressure on Great Britain for an American share in the Mesopotamian fields, the department's stand in Costa Rica became more and more embarrassing. The British linked the two issues and refused to yield to the Americans in Mosul without a concession by the Americans in Central America. Millspaugh and Welles held out in 1921 against compromise. Millspaugh argued that the United States was merely being true to its policy of opposition to the Tinoco regime by refusing to recognize the validity of any of its acts. Welles recommended that the department oppose the British plan for arbitration of the dispute on the grounds that the Costa Rican courts were quite competent to deal with it.[22]

Hughes succumbed to British pressure. Undoubtedly, a factor in his decision had been the enormous disparity between the value of the oil in the areas in question. Sinclair had not been able to produce oil in commercial quantities in Costa Rica, whereas the Mosul field promised to be gigantic. What is more, the Americans interested in Mosul appear to have been far more influential than Henry Ford Sinclair or Lincoln G. Valentine.

In July 1921, the department withdrew its objection to arbitration as a solution for the dispute between Amory and the Costa Rican government. By the end of the year, the Costa Rican Congress accepted this solution. Costa Rica requested the chief justice of the Supreme Court of the United States to arbitrate the case, and Britain agreed. The department did its best to remain aloof from this dispute after 1921. It even refused information to the Costa Rican government for fear that it would appear to be assisting that government in preparing its case. The solicitor pointed out that, if the Amory concession were reinstalled, the United States would have no rights or claims against the Amory group in regard to their Nicaraguan Canal claims, and the secretary decided to do nothing about it. The arbitrator

[22] Memoranda by Millspaugh, Apr. 4, and Welles, May 11, 1921, RG 59, 818.6363Am6/80 and 86.

upheld the action of the Costa Rican government in annulling the Amory concession.[23]

As if to compensate for backing down before British pressure on the Amory concession, the department stiffened its position in favor of the Sinclair concession. When the new American minister to Costa Rica requested department instructions in May 1922 on the fight between the company and the Costa Rican government, he was directed to give firm support to the company. Costa Rica contended that the concession was null and void because of the improper transfer of ownership by the original concessionaires and because of failure to exploit the concession within the time provided by the contract. The department denied both allegations and protested the continued "harassment" of the company. Although the complaints against the company were arbitrable in accordance with the terms of the contract, the department held they "should not be further pursued." If the Costa Rican government persisted in its dissatisfaction with the progress made by the company in exploiting petroleum deposits, it should resort to procedures prescribed by the concession contract. In a scarcely veiled threat, the note called upon the Costa Rican government to stop impeding the company in order that "the two Governments may be spared the inconvenience which attends measures looking to the recovery of indemnity for losses sustained as a result of unwarranted interferences by the authorities of one Government in the enjoyment of legal rights possessed by the citizens of another." [24] Two years later, when Sinclair ended his operations and left the country, thereby forfeiting the concession,

[23] Instructions, July 19, 818.6363Am6/167; Latin American Division memoranda by Munro, Dec. 16, 1921 and July 30, 1923, 818.6363Am6/-115 and 160; 818.6363Am6/153.

[24] Minister Roy Tasco Davis to SS, May 24, 1922, and the department's instructions of June 13, 818.6363/120. Munro and Millspaugh had decided to increase the department's support for Sinclair, even before Davis requested instructions, May 16, 818.6363/130. They turned to the solicitor for legal support, got a neutral memorandum by a clerk in the office, June 7, 818.6363/129, and handed it right back with a request for a strong note protesting the action of the Costa Rican government, 818.6363/130; 818.6363/120.

the Costa Rican government canceled the contract without meeting any opposition from the department. Both of the concessions over which so many angry words were spent proved worthless.

CASE STUDY No. 2. OIL IN COLOMBIA

The Department of State faced two petroleum problems in United States relations with Colombia: the ratification of the Thomson-Urrutia Treaty of 1914 and the threat of nationalization by the Colombian government. British encroachments, so evident in Costa Rica and in Venezuela, were not a factor in Colombia. The Pearson interests had tried unsuccessfully to negotiate a monopolistic concession with the Colombian government in 1913. Beyond making known its opposition, it is not clear what role the department played in the rejection of this concession. By 1918, United States interests controlled the only concession of any consequence.[25]

After the war in Europe ended, President Wilson resubmitted to the Senate the treaty with Colombia designed to heal the breach caused by the Panama secession of 1903. Senators Fall, Lodge, and McCumber led the opposition. They objected to the inclusion of an apology by the United States for its part in the Panama revolt. They wanted to use the treaty as a lever to obtain a supplementary trade agreement with Colombia. The public debate outraged Colombians who resented the arrogance with which Americans discussed another sovereign nation. For a while, Wilson and Lansing opposed any changes in the treaty, but they soon became preoccupied with the Versailles negotiations and conceded the initiative to the Republican-dominated Foreign Relations Committee. Senators Fall and Lodge began to deal directly with the drafting officers in the department and with the minister to Colombia, Hoffman Philip. Philip thought

[25] Memorandum by J. V. Stinson, Oct. 4, 1928, RG 59, 810.6363/36. In 1921, the department went to great lengths to deny it had exerted any pressure on the Colombian government. Veatch to Harrison, Apr. 12, Harrison papers; confidential instructions to Ambassador Harvey (London), Sept. 19, 821.6363/160.

the treaty should precede any commercial agreement. He told the senators that the treaty could not be used as a lever for oil concessions; rather, that delay would only do irreparable damage to American interests in Colombia.[26]

Just as the treaty reached the floor of the Senate in June 1919, the president of Colombia decreed all petroleum rights reserved to the government, even those in privately owned property. The Senate immediately returned the treaty to the Foreign Relations Committee, demanding additional guarantees of American property rights. The department was willing to make representations before the Colombian government to gain the Senate's demands, but Minister Philip held to his view that the treaty should be passed on its own merits. The Senate refused to consider the treaty without settling the petroleum question.[27]

The congressional protests had their effect. The Colombian Supreme Court declared the decree unconstitutional, and the Colombian Congress passed a drastically changed law of hydrocarbons in December 1919. Despite the improvements in the Colombian attitude, the Senate, for reasons of domestic politics, refused to act on the treaty during the remainder of the Wilson administration. The department requested action almost continually, but it accomplished no more than keeping senators informed on conditions in Colombia.

When Minister Philip returned to the United States for consultation at the beginning of the Harding administration, he was given responsibility for convincing the Senate to

[26] On the treaty see Watt Stewart, "The Ratification of the Thomson-Urrutia Treaty," *The Southwestern Political and Social Science Quarterly*, X, 14 (Mar. 1930); I. J. Cox, "The Colombian Treaty—Retrospect and Prospect," *Journal of International Relations*, XI, 4 (1921); *Foreign Relations*, 1919, I, 726–95; 1920, I, 823–27; 1921, I, 638–45; Francisco J. Urrutia, letters to the *Washington Post* (unpublished), dated Jan. 25 and Feb. 7, 1916.

[27] The Senate's views are in letters from Fall to Boaz Long, then in charge of Colombian affairs in the department, Oct. 8 and 11, 1919, RG 59, 821.6363/74–76; instructions of Aug. 13, 1919, 821.6363/58 contains the department's position; Philip's views are Aug. 12, 711.21/-479 and Oct. 28, 1920, 821.6363/128. See John W. Belt to John Barrett, Aug. 29, 1919, Barrett papers; Gibb and Knowlton, 376–78; Anderson diary, June 30 and July 31, 1919.

accept the Colombian treaty. After two years of warning the
oil industry and Congress that delay on the treaty would
endanger American interests, Philip was successful. Lodge,
Fall (then secretary of the interior), and McCumber now
supported the treaty, and the oil men badgered the Senate
with requests for ratification. They used Philip's argument
that the treaty was essential to maintain the American position in Colombia. Latin Americans were convinced that this
change of heart was due to the influence of the oil companies.
Fall, Lodge, and Secretary of the Navy Edwin Denby still held
out for a prior supplementary agreement for the protection
of American rights, but Philip won the department's petroleum expert to his point of view, and together they convinced
the secretary of state that the treaty should come first. Philip's
policy had bridged the differences between the two administrations. The Senate ratified the treaty on April 20, 1921,
and the ratifications were exchanged the following March.

The Department of State had been so fearful of the possibility of having American properties nationalized that it had
given no thought to whether the 1919 Colombian law of
hydrocarbons fulfilled the principles of the "open door" or
of reciprocity. When these principles became central to
American petroleum policy in 1922, the Economic Adviser's
Office reviewed the Colombian law and found that it did not
discriminate between foreign nationals or between natives
and foreigners. He concluded that there was nothing in the
Colombia law detrimental to American interests.[28]

It was not until 1927 that British interests made a serious
attempt to win an oil concession in Colombia. The British
government supported the bid, and the Department of State
acquiesced, even though it contained certain monopolistic
provisions which obviously ran counter to the declared policy
of the United States. The crisis in petroleum had passed by
that time, and the Department of State was not so rigorous

[28] Speeches by Lodge (quoting letters from Fall), McCumber, and
Reed, in Rippy, *Capitalists and Colombia,* 114–17; Denby to SS, Mar.
18, and reply, drafted by Philip, Mar. 26, 821.6363/137; E. Taylor
Parks, *Colombia and the United States, 1765–1934* (Durham, N. C.,
1935); economic adviser's memorandum, Nov. 12, 1922, 821.6363/261;
Barcia Trelles, *Imperialismo del Petróleo,* 154, 159–66.

as it had been in defense of the "open door," or so fretful about European concessions near the Panama Canal.

CASE STUDY No. 3. OIL IN GUATEMALA

The Department of State had the same problem with Guatemalan petroleum that it had with Guatemalan banking and trade: it was impossible to interest reputable Americans in the business. Just before the Armistice, the department heard a rumor that the Pearson interests were trying to secure an oil concession in Guatemala. The department informed Minister Leavall, in October 1918, that "it is most important that only American oil interests receive the concessions in Guatemala."

The move was enough to block the British oil men for the time being, but it did not help any Americans. The only American on the scene was a representative of the Bancroft-Thrall Contracting Company, "General" Lee Christmas, an adventurer and soldier of fortune, whose record in Central America did not recommend him to the Latin American Division or the American minister. In July 1920, the Washington representative of the Bancroft-Thrall Company persuaded Undersecretary Norman Davis to support its Guatemala project. Davis was unaware of Christmas's record and consequently saw no objection. Without consulting the Latin American Division, he ordered the Diplomatic Bureau to draft instructions for Minister Benton McMillan to help the Bancroft-Thrall concession. When shown his error, he allowed Dana G. Munro to add a confidential paragraph to the instructions, July 1920, warning Minister McMillan not to give Christmas any "personal endorsement" likely to be used by him in his political activities and to exercise extreme caution in dealing with the oil interests.[29]

The State Department, meanwhile, tried to interest other, more reputable oil men in the Guatemalan situation. Both the Wilson and the Harding administrations conferred in

[29] Instructions to Leavall, Oct. 11, 1918, RG 59, 814.6363/1; Latin American Division memoranda, by Munro, July 2 and 6, 1920, 814.-6363/5.

Washington with leaders in the oil industry, with the purpose of coaxing them into Central America. The petroleum expert, Millspaugh, and John H. Murray of the Latin American Division conducted these meetings, which continued through 1920 and 1921.

At one of the sessions, the oil men pointed out that the Guatemalan mining code did not deal adequately with nonmetalliferous minerals. The Guatemalan minister was called in and was convinced of the need to frame a new law. Department experts helped to draft one. With the new Colombian law as a basis, they proceeded in keeping with the criticisms of American petroleum interests. The Guatemalan minister promised that preference would be given to American concessions over those sought by the nationals of any other country. This did not help the negotiations, for as far as the United States was concerned, the major issue was a clause guaranteeing equal and reciprocal rights for the nationals of each country doing business in the other. At first, the Guatemalan government refused to accept such a clause, and the negotiations dragged on without change through the end of the Wilson administration and into the Harding administration. In 1922, Guatemala broke under American insistence and inserted the required reciprocity clause, but it was another year before Guatemala agreed to permit United States citizens to own stock in Guatemalan corporations looking for oil or to allow United States corporations to own parts of Guatemalan corporations holding oil concessions. This final acknowledgment by the Guatemalan government was secured by persistent diplomatic representations, not through the reciprocity clause which the Americans had written into the Guatemalan law of hydrocarbons.[30]

The Guatemalan reciprocity clause was one of the State Department's last attempts to prevent British petroleum interests from securing concessions in Central America. The British had been stopped in 1918 by the department's ener-

[30] Trade adviser's memorandum, Mar. 21, and Latin American Division memorandum, Mar. 24, 1921, 814.6363/18 and 31; memorandum by Sumner Welles, Mar. 21, 814.001C11/–; Latin American Division memorandum by J. V. Stinson, Dec. 22, 1928, 810.6363/36.

getic representations, but nothing had been done to keep them from making additional attempts. The British government excluded all aliens from ownership of oil lands within the empire, and complete reciprocity would naturally exclude British citizens from Guatemalan concessions. Although the reciprocity clause was by no means ironclad, the British were uneasy under this threat to their interests. As formerly in Costa Rica, the British government used the Mosul oil situation to force concessions from the United States.

The decision to deviate from the policy of reciprocity (February 1923) was taken without informing Minister Geissler, causing him no little embarrassment. He had suggested an amendment to the law of hydrocarbons which would exclude all nonreciprocating Europeans, in keeping with what he understood to be American policy. He was somewhat confused by the department's instructions that it was not policy to seek any "specifically favored position" on behalf of American petroleum companies and that suggesting an amendment to the Guatemalan government would not accord with the policy of "equal opportunity." Fortunately, Geissler's excessive zeal caused no damage. No British interests sought concessions during Hughes's term of office. Only a handful of concessions, and they amounted to nothing, were signed with Americans.[31]

The State Department eventually lost all interest in Guatemalan oil. When Minister Geissler returned home on leave, he urged the department to recruit American oil companies to enter Guatemala. The chief of the Latin American Division merely referred him to the Department of Commerce. When pressed into service by the British, in 1926, the department showed itself true to the "open door" policy. It called upon the Guatemalan government to alter the interpretation of the reciprocity clause so as to allow aliens from a nonreciprocating country to control oil concessions. In order to placate the British and to maintain an "open door" in Central American petroleum concessions, the Department of State

[31] Instructions to Geissler, Feb. 21, 1923, and Latin American Division memorandum, Sept. 8, 1925, 814.6363/51 and 84; Stinson's memo, 810.-6363/36.

seemed willing to compromise the principle of reciprocity. This was further than the department had been willing to go in support of British interests in Costa Rica. Undoubtedly, the department acquiesced in this diminution of American influence in Guatemala because of the greater importance of oil reserves elsewhere and because it was confident that British incursions no longer posed a threat to the nation's security. The United States could protect its interests in Guatemala without monopolizing oil concessions there.

CASE STUDY No. 4. OIL IN VENEZUELA

Competition for concessions in Venezuela began during World War I. The Richmond Levering Company was the first to request the aid of the State Department. Levering complained, in 1917, that President Juan Vicente Gómez had granted to the Caribbean Petroleum Company a concession which overlapped one of his own. Levering said he was less concerned with the threat to his concession than he was with the fact that the Caribbean Petroleum Company was owned by Royal Dutch Shell and was, therefore, under the control of the British government. Although it was the policy of the United States government at that time to oppose European control of petroleum resources near the Panama Canal, the department did not act on Levering's complaint, pleading a lack of sufficient information about the company in question. The surprising thing is that the Latin American Division did not even trouble to request a report on the ownership of the Caribbean Petroleum Company. The department declared that it would not act except "where a manifest denial of justice can be clearly proven as a basis for a diplomatic claim." [32]

Shortly after granting the concession to the Caribbean Petroleum Company, Gómez changed his mind and began proceedings to annul it. As it was nominally an American company, the company's representative in Venezuela asked Minister McGoodwin for diplomatic support. Ignorant of the

[32] Latin American Division memorandum, Apr. 6, 1917, 831.6363/14; dispatch from Minister McGoodwin, Mar. 11, and department's instructions, Mar. 14, 831.6375C23/1.

company's British ties, McGoodwin cabled the department that he was inclined to grant the company's request even though he had heard rumors that it was British controlled. This was the move for which the department had been waiting. It instructed McGoodwin to delay making representations until the ownership of the company could be determined and then it asked for an intelligence report on the company. The intelligence report showed that the Caribbean Petroleum Company was under the joint control of the Colon Development Company and the General Asphalt Company of Philadelphia, but that the latter's interest was only 25 percent. The Colon Company was, in turn, controlled by the Burlington Investment Company, the holding company which operated the Royal Dutch Shell.[33]

At the same time, the Carib Syndicate, an American company owned by Henry L. Doherty and a group of Wall Street bankers led by J. P. Morgan and Company requested diplomatic intervention on behalf of their interests, which were also under attack by the Venezuelan government. The same intelligence report showed that Carib owned a 25 percent interest in another concession held directly by the Colon Development Company. Both General Asphalt and the Carib Syndicate asked the department to save the concessions in which they were interested. Richmond Levering and several other American companies vigorously opposed giving any aid to either the Caribbean Petroleum Company or the Colon Development Company because they had claims of their own to territory within the two large concessions. The department wanted the Colon concession canceled, but, when it was, in 1920, the Carib Syndicate appealed to the department for protection of its equity in the concession. The department instructed Minister McGoodwin to protest the threat to Carib's rights, which were acquired in good faith, but made no mention of what its position was with regard to the Colon Development Company.[34]

[33] McGoodwin's dispatch, Oct. 29, 1918, department's instructions, Nov. 26, 831.6375C23/7; 831.6375C23/10 and 11, have correspondence on the intelligence report.
[34] 831.6363/33.

The resolution of this tangled situation was left to the new secretary of state. By 1921, Washington had accepted the fact that the Colon Development Company and the Caribbean Petroleum Company were under British control and, therefore, should not receive United States support. On the other hand, bona fide American companies had purchased minority interests in several British holdings and demanded State Department representations to save their investments from Venezuelan expropriation. As soon as Hughes became secretary of state, the Carib Syndicate, an American group, asked him for stronger support than the department had offered them hitherto. Without consulting his petroleum expert or the Latin American Division, he instructed the solicitor to cable the Caracas legation to lend its support to the Carib Syndicate. When McGoodwin reported on his representations, the Latin American Division complained angrily to the solicitor and the assistant secretary that the minister's actions had supported the Colon claims at the same time. This confusion contributed to a department decision not to support any British-controlled companies. Only companies in which Americans held a majority control would qualify for representations by a representative of the United States government. McGoodwin was informed of this decision in May 1921 and was instructed to check with the department before acting, when in doubt as to the ownership of a particular company.[35]

The policy held for nearly a year. It was undermined by the growing cooperation between American and British oil interests that followed the agreement over Mosul oil. In April 1922, the Standard Oil Company of New Jersey obtained an option on one-third of the Colon concession, then held by the British Controlled Oilfields. In the next month, American oil companies and their supporters, including Senators Pepper and Lodge, withdrew their opposition to British pres-

[35] Latin American Division memorandum, Apr. 27; solicitor's memorandum, May 2, 831.6363/93 and 94; McGoodwin's report, Apr. 12, and instructions of May 16, 831.6375C23/15. These instructions referred specifically to the Colon Development Company, and to British firms in general. They were extended to the Caribbean Petroleum Company in Dec. 3, 831.6375C23/19.

ence in Venezuela and swung around to the defense of the Carib Syndicate and the General Asphalt Company of Philadelphia, which held minority interests in concessions of the Colon Development Company and the Caribbean Petroleum Company, respectively.

The drafting officers in the Latin American Division, the Economic Adviser's Office, and the Solicitor's Office, who had followed the situation in Venezuela for several years, opposed lending support of any kind to the American companies because of the advantage it would mean for British oil interests. The secretary decided to yield to political pressure; but junior officers persuaded him to give no more than token support. The minister was advised to "discreetly support" representations made by the British and Dutch governments with a view to hastening a decision by the Venezuelan courts in the pending case of the Caribbean Petroleum Company concession. The instructions included a warning that the representations must not deal with the company's case but only with its attempt to gain justice in the local courts. In this way, the department's policy against giving aid to British interests was maintained in letter, if not in spirit. It will be noted, however, that the department carefully refrained from making representations against British firms, as had been the policy in the hemisphere only two years earlier.[36]

The department did change its position, finally, a year later, when the Standard Oil Company requested support for its efforts to prevent the Venezuelan government from canceling their option to the Colon Development concession. It had been annulled in 1920, and the British and Dutch governments had been struggling thence for the revalidation of the entire concession. The department's first instructions in the matter were ambiguous, and the American minister restricted his efforts to a single interview with the minister of development, and the secretary general restricted his to one with the president. Standard Oil continued to press the department, which soon gave in and instructed the minister

[36] Instructions to Minister Willis C. Cook, Sept. 25, 1922, 831.6375C-23/29a; debate over policy is in memoranda of July 18, Sept. 2, 21, and 22, 831.6375C23/34 and 35.

to place himself completely at the disposal of the company's representative in Venezuela. With the good offices of the United States government, Standard Oil retained its rights to the Colon concession.[37]

Once the American companies felt secure in Venezuela, they turned their backs on the Department of State. For its part, the department remained true to the principles of equal opportunity. In 1924, certain German interests were rumored to have secured an option to the national petroleum reserves held by the National Petroleum Company of Venezuela, which was controlled by President Gómez. This amounted to a monopoly on all lands not actually exploited by the companies with previous concessions and was a violation of Venezuelan law. The department instructed Chargé Frederick Charles Chabot to register a complaint if he found that American interests were endangered by the option. Instead of cooperating with the department, the American oil companies made a great rush for concessions in the national reserve. Chabot was not competent to deal with the situation. The department specifically instructed him to give no support to illegal or monopolistic concessions, American or otherwise. Despite this warning, he continued to provide representatives of the American companies with an entrée to President Gómez and his cabinet and led the Venezuelan government to feel that the United States would support its nationals in every instance. In May 1924, the department restricted his activities to delivering notes sent to him.[38]

The American oil companies felt sufficiently confident in Venezuela to ignore the desires of the Department of State. Not only would they not cooperate with their government but they would not cooperate with one another. "Violent internecine strife" among the many American companies prevented American interests from obtaining important concessions. Because of a sandbar across the mouth of Lake Maracaibo, where nearly all of the productive wells were located,

[37] Memoranda by Harrison, July 20, 1923, and Oct. 25, Harrison papers; instructions to Cook, Sept. 19, 1923, and Oct. 28, 831.6363/142.

[38] Chabot incident is 831.6363/160, 172, 176, 181, 235; and Phillips diary, Dec. 12, 1923.

the American oil companies were forced to sell their entire product to the Shell Transport Company, which could carry the petroleum in light tankers over the bar to its refinery on the nearby Dutch island of Curaçao. The Americans would not cooperate to solve their transportation problem. First, each company tried to obtain a concession to build a port on the Paraguaná Peninsula, just outside the sandbar. Then, an independent American, William F. Buckley, obtained an exclusive concession to build a port on the peninsula and to transport petroleum from the fields, across the bar, to the port. He was to receive a tax payment on every barrel of oil he exported. The American petroleum companies managed to join forces long enough to protest the Buckley concession. They succeeded in delaying action by the Venezuelan Congress but not in arousing the department. It considered the matter one of competing American interests, which did not call for diplomatic intervention.[39]

By coincidence, just after Buckley had obtained his port concession, James J. Shirley, a representative of the United Dredging Company, came forward with a plan for clearing a channel through the bar across the mouth of Lake Maracaibo. After the oil companies succeeded in delaying the Buckley concession, Shirley returned to the United States to present his plan to the department. He wanted it to send a secret agent to Venezuela to persuade President Gómez to grant a contract for a channel through the Maracaibo bar. Shirley presented his case in such a clumsy fashion, however, that the officers in the Latin American Division refused to have anything to do with him.[40]

At the end of the Harding-Coolidge administration, the impasse had not been resolved. The State Department wanted very much to solve the transporatation problem in Lake

[39] Consular reports by Harry J. Anslinger, La Guaira, June 9, and July 3, 1924, 831.6363C73/orig. and 4; 831.156L33/5 and 11; Chabot's July 5, 831.6363C73/3.

[40] Chabot's June 18, 1924, 831.156/22. Shirley had been the representative of the All America Cables and the Equitable Trust in Latin America and had been fired from both positions. Latin American Division memorandum, Dec. 19, 1924, and Apr. 6, 1925, by Manning, and by Francis White, May 6 and 12, 1925, 831.156/28, 36, 45, and 46.

Maracaibo, in order to protect the petroleum produced by American companies for the American market. The economic adviser tried to convince the Latin American Division to step into the situation and effect some cooperation between the American companies. Francis White and William R. Manning, who were in charge of Venezuelan affairs for the division, would not intervene in favor of any particular interest. Their hands were tied, they said, until some American oil company registered a specific complaint with them about the conditions in the oil field. It was not until Hughes was out of office that the department's position changed. White and Manning were still in charge of Venezuelan affairs, and they continued to reject Shirley's plan, but Secretary of State Frank B. Kellogg stepped in and instructed the American minister to take a hand in the dispute between the various interests. First, the department brought pressure to bear on Standard Oil to temper its campaign against the Buckley concession and to give his port plan a fair chance in the Venezuelan Congress. Next, they instructed Minister Willis Cook to use his good offices to secure the cooperation of the American oil companies in solving the crucial transportation problem.[41]

This action was taken under Kellogg. During the Harding-Coolidge administration, after the oil companies had rejected the department's policy, the Department of State would have nothing to do with the American oil interests, unless one of them protested a denial of justice by the Venezuelan government. After 1923, the department assumed a far more detached position with regard to American interests than it had previously done. In banking, cables, and petroleum, the department seemed to wash its hands of involvement in the affairs of American business abroad, except in the rare cases provided for by international law of violations of rights or of the denial of justice.

Thus, in the period from 1918 to 1925 the Department of State had swung from active support for virtually all American efforts to secure petroleum concessions in Latin America

[41] Economic adviser's memorandum by Culbertson, May 29, 1925, 831.156L33/37; instructions, June 4, 831.156/38.

and hostile opposition to British interests to a passive stance in the struggle for petroleum in the hemisphere. The initial policy was the result of lessons learned during World War I about the importance of petroleum, of prophecies that domestic oil reserves soon would be exhausted, and of fear that Great Britain was about to win the lion's share of the world's oil reserves. The United States government at the end of the war was acutely sensitive to the possibility of a British oil monopoly because it seemed part and parcel of a broad commercial war between the two nations, especially in Latin America. The Department of State ordered its diplomatic representatives in Latin America to oppose all British encroachments in the hemisphere and, wherever possible, to support the aspirations of legitimate American interests.

This clear, aggressive policy was modified first by the absence of bona fide American interests worthy of support, as in Costa Rica, and by the confusing tangle of American, British, and Dutch investments, as in Venezuela. The policy was modified further as it became clear that the important struggle for oil was taking place not in Latin America but in the Near East, where the United States did not have clear strategic superiority. To strengthen the claims of American petroleum interests in the Near East and elsewhere, and to increase the effectiveness of the United States government's support for those interests, the Department of State moved gradually toward a single, consistent petroleum policy based upon the twin axioms of reciprocity and equal opportunity, or the "open door." Latin America became less vital as a special sphere of United States interest in the postwar struggle for petroleum, for a variety of reasons. The dire prophecies about American domestic petroleum reserves proved incorrect; the search for petroleum in several Latin American countries proved fruitless; and private companies, so eager to cooperate with the government in 1918 and 1919, had learned how to cooperate with their British competitors and were no longer interested in meeting the State Department's rigorous standards for cooperation. By 1925, the companies did not need the department, and the department did not need the companies, so the department could safely stick to its "open door" policy even when this policy ran counter to private American interests. Finally, Latin America declined in importance to the United States because the United States now had vital strategic interests all over the world. This was part of the impact of World War I: to make Latin American policy subordinate to the expanded needs of American security and consistent with American policy in other areas of the world.

CHAPTER 5

Securing the Strategic Objectives: Capital

Bank loans were used as an instrument of American foreign policy before World War I, especially in the Caribbean, where they were needed to preserve the financial responsibility of unstable nations and prevent European intervention. The discussion in 1915 of a policy with regard to loans to the Allies convinced President Wilson and his advisers that capital was vital to the nation's security, in that a shortage would cripple its military posture. As soon as the United States entered the war, the government took steps to control all available savings. Secretary of the Treasury McAdoo asked all those who contemplated issuing new securities to communicate with him so that he might pass on whether the issue of such securities was compatible with the public interest. Within a few months, the job of overseeing the capital market passed to the Federal Reserve Bank, which set up a Capital Issues Committee for that purpose. The Treasury Department thus arrogated to itself responsibility for funding the war effort and for disposition of the capital resources of the United States.[1]

[1] Address by Frederic H. Curtiss, chairman, Federal Reserve Bank of Boston, and chairman of Subcommittee on Capital Issues, Federal Reserve District No. 1, "The Capital Issues Committee of the Federal Reserve Board," Mar. 23, 1919, in the Paul M. Warburg papers, Yale University.

It was evident that the control of capital funds affected the foreign relations of the United States, especially in the question of loans to foreign governments. Secretary of State Lansing suggested that the Treasury Department consult with the State Department in cases where political or strategic considerations played a part in the negotiations, and McAdoo acceded to this suggestion in May 1917. Prior to this, Gordon Auchincloss had maintained unofficial ties with an *ad hoc* committee of New York investment bankers. Except in special cases, the State Department confined itself to expressions of opinion on the political aspects of the proposed loans and explicitly disavowed any opinion on their financial aspects. When neutral nations submitted requests for financial support through the Department of State, these were immediately passed on to the Treasury Department for evaluation as financial propositions. If these were not compatible with the greater needs of the United States government, the Treasury Department did not hesitate to veto the proposals.[2]

The Treasury Department considered all loans to foreign governments a single problem to be dealt with by one comprehensive policy. Officials in the State Department objected to this. They felt that Latin America required a special loan policy, one which would take into consideration the special sphere of United States influence in the hemisphere. In March 1918, Professor Jeremiah W. Jenks embodied this thinking in a memorandum, "Financial Assistance to Certain Latin American Countries," which was in part an extension to the entire hemisphere of an earlier dollar diplomacy and in part an adaptation of Secretary Bryan's plan for United States government loans to unstable countries in the Caribbean. It was intended as a first step in postwar policy planning. Jenks dealt with each country in the Caribbean, itemizing its financial weaknesses and suggesting what would be required to put it in sound condition. He proposed adding a section to the pending Fourth Liberty Loan Act to guarantee bonds, prin-

[2] Phillips diary, May 29, 1917; SS to Assist SecTreas R. C. Leffingwell, Mar. 14, 1918, RG 39, Box 21, Country File—Brazil; SecTreas to SS, Oct. 2, Box 20, Country File—Bolivia.

cipal, and interest, which each country would use to refund its outstanding external debt held in Europe. With this guarantee, American bankers would take the bonds and absorb the entire cost of the refunding. The government's influence would thus secure the success of the necessary financial reforms in each country without cost to the United States. Jenks argued that private bankers could not (or would not) make the loans without the government's permission. With that permission, they would be willing to make investments of considerable amounts if they could be sure that the government's support would be permanent.[3]

Before bringing Jenks's plan to the attention of the Treasury Department, Latin American hands in the State Department added two new elements. They proposed to extend the plan to cover all of Central and South America and to permit foreign countries to pay back a part of their war loans from the United States with Central American securities held by them. Undersecretary Polk outlined the department's position in his letter transmitting the plan to the Treasury Department:

> The Department of State believes that the acquisition of the above mentioned obligations of the Latin American countries would be of the greatest benefit to the United States and that the many complications which have occurred in the past, due to European holdings of these bonds, would be permanently eliminated. The political advantage of the ownership of these obligations by the Government of the United States is thought to be material in view of the fact that such ownership would tend to place the control of the financial affairs of the Western Hemisphere in the hands of the American Government thus rendering very unlikely a recurrence of the distressing complications which have arisen in the past between Europe and Latin American countries.[4]

[3] RG 59, 811.51/2058. An earlier version of the plan is in McAdoo to SS, Aug. 23, 1915, 833.51/160; SecCom to SS, Dec. 1914, 820.51/orig.

[4] Polk to the SecTreas, Apr. 3; Leffingwell to Polk, Apr. 8, 1918, RG 39, Box 203, Country File—South America.

The Jenks memorandum said nothing about government ownership; Polk mistook the government's guarantee for ownership. Polk's letter arrived at the Treasury Department too late to influence the drafting of legislation for the Fourth Liberty Loan. Undeterred, the State Department used the Jenks plan to formulate specific development plans for individual countries in Central America. Its purpose was to eliminate the influence of European capital and to neutralize the internal causes of instability.

The first completed was the plan for Guatemala. Guatemala long had been in a chronic state of financial instability. The country had defaulted many times on its external debt with consequent embarrassment to the United States. The government of Guatemala had appealed to the Department of State for aid in consolidating its foreign and domestic debts and in reforming its monetary system. It also needed financial help to repair damages suffered in the earthquake of 1917. The State Department plan called for official help to private American citizens to set up a corporation, whose various stockholders would represent the major American interests in Guatemala and would found a National Bank of Issue in Guatemala. The corporation would be the sole channel for the placement of all national loans and the instrument for the reform of the Guatemalan financial system. The plan also suggested a Guatemalan custodian of enemy property who would supervise the transfer of German property to American interests. The Guatemalan government would float a $30 million loan through the American corporation and guarantee the loan with the customs receipts which would then be controlled by the corporation. The custodian of enemy property would invest through the National Bank all the German monies he controlled in the proposed loan, thus providing the funds upon which the currency would be secured and Guatemala rebuilt. This proposal went to the Treasury Department on June 1, 1918 and received more encouragement than the general plan in the Jenks memorandum. Assistant Secretary of the Treasury Leo Stanton Rowe agreed that Guatemala deserved special consideration and implied that the Treasury Department would allow the corporation to float the bonds indicated. He reminded the State Department that the United States could not lend money directly to Guatemala or furnish that government with the means of undertaking any large internal improvements. This struck at the heart of the plan and left the major issues unsettled.[5]

In August 1918, when new Liberty Loan legislation was pending, Jenks went personally before the top officials of the Treasury Department to urge approval of his plan. The latter remained adamant that authority to purchase Central American bonds should not form part of the essential bond-issue legislation. Furthermore, and much more to the point, they were opposed to any loans "other than for advances made to aid in the national security and defense and for the prosecution of the war." No such commitment of American financial strength was possible without the *quid pro quo* of a "Platt Amendment" in the loan agreement. Since the negotiation of a "Platt Amendment" form of control over the finances and government of a sovereign nation was clearly a political question, the Treasury Department refused to discuss the matter further and showed irritation at being asked "to pull the State Department's chestnuts out of the fire." That settled the matter for the duration of the war. So long as the Treasury Department controlled the loan policy of the United States, no advances would be made by the United States government and no private advances would be condoned that did not contribute directly to the prosecution of the war. The commercial and political advantages to be gained from the financial commitments in the Jenks plan were subordinated to the larger financial goals of the Treasury Department and had to wait until after the war to be reconsidered. The same order of priorities prevailed throughout the war in other financial issues between the United States and the other nations of the hemisphere. The Treasury Department conceived of the national security narrowly, in terms of the war effort. The State Department had a broader

[5] Max Winkler, *Foreign Bonds: An Autopsy* (Philadelphia, 1933), 41–44; Latin American Division memorandum by Glenn Stewart, May 3, 1918, RG 59, 814.51/271.

view of national security, and, after the war, when the State Department moved to assert its control over foreign loans, it applied its broader conception to the entire hemisphere. It is worth noting that Assistant Secretary of the Treasury Rowe approved of the Jenks plan, but the issue was decided by Assistant Secretaries Leffingwell, Rathbone, and Strauss. Rowe pushed the plan from his post on the American Section of the International High Commission; later, when he became chief of the Latin American Division of the Department of State, he was instrumental in urging similar programs for Nicaragua and Guatemala.[6]

The State Department won control of international loans after the war because the Treasury Department abdicated its responsibility. The haste and insistence with which the Treasury Department discontinued its policy of supplying government credit contributed to the disorganized quality of demobilization. Officials in the Treasury Department were convinced that "private investments made outside of the United States, rather than an indefinite extension of credits payable in dollars," was the best solution to the problem of European recovery. There was considerable pressure on the government to set free the money market. Secretary of the Treasury Carter Glass, who replaced McAdoo after the Armistice, tried to hold together the War Loan Organization until the Victory Loan was floated. Despite his efforts, the Capital Issues Committee suspended its operations on the last day of December, and only a month later the Money Committee of the New York Stock Exchange stopped functioning. It must be noted that Treasury Department officials did not deem it inconsistent to push the sale of the Victory Loan while urging the United States government to remove itself from the European money market.[7]

In his message to Congress of December 2, 1918, President

[6] Draft of a letter by Assistant Secretary of the Treasury Albert Rathbone, Aug. 17, intended for SS but not sent; Treasury Department memorandum by Albert Strauss, Aug. 21, RG 39, Box 203, Country File—South America; Latin American Division memoranda by Hallett Johnson, Sept. 5 and 6, RG 59, 813.51/–; and the memorandum by Glenn Stewart, Sept. 4, 811.51/2057.

[7] Norman Davis to Anson Burchard, Nov. 10, 1919, Davis papers.

Wilson made it clear that the policy of his administration toward demobilization was readjustment rather than reconstruction. He told Congress that the American people neither needed nor wanted to be "coached and led." The government should merely mediate the natural process of readjustment. The domestic policy of "readjustment" was inextricably bound up with the government's policy with regard to the reconstruction of Europe, and the Treasury Department adopted the same "hands-off" policy for both. This policy grew out of a resolute refusal to consider any proposal for the cancellation of inter-Allied war debts. Secretary Glass told the Paris Peace Conference that he was "utterly opposed" to direct action by the United States government in the reconstruction of Europe. His policy, which was continued by David Houston, Wilson's third treasury secretary, was to "restore private initiative and remove governmental control." [8]

Notwithstanding his preferences, Glass recognized the urgent need for temporary relief loans to Europe, and in his brief period at the Treasury Department, the United States government made loans to European governments of $2.5 billion. This activity of the government, in the face of its stated policy to the contrary, upset the private money market in the United States and gave Europeans the unwarranted hope that they could expect the United States government to help them out of their difficulties. As a result, investment bankers in the United States were uncertain as to the role of their government and were unwilling to finance Latin America or Europe's trade and development until Washington took a clear stand on the question of private and public loans. Wall Street wanted to be set free completely or to be led firmly by the government. A member of J. P. Morgan and Company told an official of the government in 1919 that the demand for capital from abroad was intense and they were

[8] *Foreign Relations*, 1918, ix–xix; Norman Davis to Ray Stannard Baker, July 26, 1922, Davis papers; Crosby to McAdoo, Dec. 4, and McAdoo to Crosby, Dec. 7, 1918, RG 59, 800.51/122. Glass's policy is in the letter dated Nov. 14, 1919, 811.51/2414b; Houston's can be found most conveniently in Soule, *Prosperity Decade*, 257–58, and in Houston to Colby, Mar. 27, 1920, 817.51/1204.

"really awaiting the determination of some definite policy by the Government. Until the Government's attitude toward foreign investment is more fully known than it is at present, I think there is going to be reluctance on the part of responsible people to make foreign investments." [9]

Most of the financial experts in the Treasury Department wanted the government immediately to begin a stiff retrenchment policy at home, while continuing to play an aggressive role in reestablishing international trade and credit. So long as France and Britain insisted upon exorbitant reparations from Germany, the only way the United States could deal effectively with the problems of international finance would be to participate in discussions and arrangements with the European nations. The attitude of the public and the Senate made this impossible. Europe could not trade with the United States without credit, and that credit could not be made available unless the government was willing to commit its resources to the reconstruction of Europe. The Treasury Department refused to allow the government to become associated with any moves to strengthen European credit because such moves had the fatal defect of reviving hope of a comprehensive plan for having someone else pay Europe's debts, a hope doomed to certain disappointment. Because of this, Leffingwell told Warburg, in February 1920, the world must continue to move "without any concerted financial or economic leadership." Until European finances were put in order, most American banking houses were reluctant to consider the need for capital of Latin American nations. [10]

The financial community in the United States accepted the lack of definition in policy for nearly a year after the Armistice. Then, restlessly, they began to demand some guidance

[9] Morrow to Philip B. Kennedy, director of Bureau of Foreign and Domestic Commerce, Oct. 14, 1919, Morrow papers.

[10] An active financial policy is urged in Paul Warburg to John W. Davis, July 1, and Norman Davis, Nov. 26, 1919; Leffingwell to Warburg, Feb. 11, 1920, Warburg papers; Leffingwell to Wilson, Aug. 13, 1919, RG 56, Box 89; and Leffingwell to Rathbone, Dec. 10, Box 197. Official policy is in Norman Davis to Warburg, Jan. 7, 1920; and Glass to Warburg, Jan. 28; and the report of the SecTreas, 1919, Warburg papers.

by the government. Small businessmen engaged in the export trade deluged the Commerce Department with requests for aid in financing their export trade. They had plenty of orders but were too small to provide their customers with adequate credit, and the latter did not have the liquid assets to pay for their merchandise in cash. All the Commerce Department could do was refer the businessmen to financial houses in the East which might be interested in financing their trade, and enclose a statement indicating just how far the government had removed itself from responsibility for the export trade of the country:

> What part the United States Government is to take in making advances to European countries must, in the last analysis, be determined by Congress. Normally, these matters of financing foreign sales would be left to private enterprise. We are expecting that our bankers . . . will be able to arrange some practical plan for extending needed credits.[11]

The bankers, of whom so much was expected, were faced with an enormous problem of educating the public to buy foreign securities. Several New York houses formed the Foreign Bond and Share Company in an attempt to cope with the problems of financing export trade and selling foreign paper to the American public. On every possible occasion, bankers took the opportunity to convince the public that foreign government bonds were safe, readily marketable, paid high interest rates, and were a definite aid to foreign trade. By July 1919, the big New York bankers were convinced that they must act on their own in Europe. They formed a national syndicate to finance European trade and sent Fred I. Kent and Paul M. Warburg to Europe to open negotiations with the heads of the European central banks and the major private bankers of the Continent. The business end of the talks went smoothly until they ran afoul of the omnipresent issue of debts and reparations. At the request of the Euro-

[11] R. S. MacElwee to the firm of Rice and Hutchins, Boston, May 31, 1919, RG 151, Box 2956, 640—General.

peans, the American representatives at the monetary conference asked the United States government to comment on their
proposals. As before, the government refused to become
associated with any plan to finance European reconstruction;
such schemes "must be placed upon a clean-cut business
basis that will appeal to the American investor without
assurances from our Government."[12]

In one last effort to influence the president, forty-seven of
the country's most prominent lawyers, bankers, and economists petitioned the White House at the end of January 1920
for government action on foreign loans. They got a polite
response which promised them nothing. The petition did
seem to clear the air and convince the financial community
that the Treasury Department was not going to take the lead
in financing European construction and would not obstruct
private efforts to do so. The Edge Act, the McLean Act, and
the War Finance Corporation provided some help to private
interests and encouraged them to go on in their efforts.[13]

As the Treasury Department withdrew from the loan market, the Department of State came forward to express its
interest in the details of international finance, particularly
with reference to Latin America. The State Department was
interested in finance for two reasons: it felt loans were one
way of increasing foreign trade and investment; and it felt
the Treasury Department's "hands-off" policy was not relevant to "the exceptional situation which exists in regard to
[certain] Latin American countries towards which this Government has assumed special responsibilities because of the
control it has established over certain phases of their
finances." Department officials felt that the wartime supervision over and support for loans to foreign governments had
to be perpetuated in some form in order to promote Ameri-

[12] RG 151, Box 2956 and Box 2957, 640—General, has material on
the Foreign Bond and Share Company. On campaign to educate the
public, see the speech by Leffingwell before the Bond Club of New
York, Jan. 28, 1921, RG 56, Box 6, and the articles by William S. Kies,
Thomas W. Lamont, Hastings Lyon, Arthur J. Rosenthal, and James
Sheldon in *The Annals,* 88 (Mar. 1920); Hoover to Warburg, Jan. 10,
1920, Warburg papers.
[13] RG 59, 800.51/179.

can economic influence in Latin America. They said a special loan policy was required along the lines of the one suggested by Secretaries McAdoo and Redfield before the war or of the one contained in the Jenks memorandum of March 1918. In spite of the Treasury Department's opposition, the Jenks plan served as the basis for the State Department's postwar policy on loans to Latin America. The plan faithfully expressed the department's objectives of reforming financial systems in the Caribbean and of extending American economic influence in the hemisphere while eliminating European influence. As the Treasury Department had decided that it would no longer supervise foreign loans, the State Department put itself forward as the government department to be informed of the international projects of American bankers. When corresponding with bankers, it was careful to adopt the same formula used by the Treasury Department during the war, refusing to comment upon the financial aspects of a bond issue. It added that it was "prepared to give all possible and proper diplomatic support to any legitimate enterprise . . . to which its citizens are parties." [14]

The Departments of State and Commerce threw themselves into the job of placing United States loans in Latin America with fierce energy. At times it looked as if representatives of the United States government were working for finders' fees: they served as drummers for specific loans or business situations; they persuaded reluctant bankers to take a particular issue, as one from the Argentine province of Santa Fe and another for the national railroad in Chile. In trying to sell the Santa Fe project to various bankers in New York, Boston, New Orleans, and Chicago, officials of the Commerce Department emphasized that "trade follows the loan" and that "fair loans build good will." Later in 1919, in connection with a loan to the Argentine province of Córdoba, the Commerce Department told a banking house:

[14] Colby to Houston, Apr. 8, 1920, RG 59, 817.51/1204; Acting SS to Curtis, Mallet-Prevost, and Colt, counsel for Imbrie and Company, leaders of a syndicate to take a $10-million bond issue by Rio de Janeiro, May 1919; and SS to Leffingwell, Mar. 14, 1918, RG 39, Box 21—Brazil.

It is unnecessary for us to emphasize the importance of American houses investing in South American securities at this time, for there are now opportunities for American financial interests to pave the way for a very profitable business in the year to come. We hope, therefore, that you will give this matter your earnest consideration; that further investigation will be made, and that the security and terms offered may be found acceptable to all parties concerned.[15]

During the negotiations for a Chilean loan, the State Department made it explicit that it "hopes that [the] loan referred to may be placed in the United States." It had the same concern for loans all over Latin America, the expression of which was the best way to convince bankers of the department's abiding interest in their affairs.

The Treasury Department frowned upon such active interest, and, at the end of 1919, when continued export of gold put a serious crimp in the reserves of Federal Reserve Banks, it moved to discourage foreign lending except in cases of dire need. Europe was such a case; Latin America was not. Secretary Houston told Secretary of Commerce Alexander that the "Treasury would be very sorry to see loans negotiated by Latin American countries here." The exchange situation went from bad to worse in 1920, and it soon became next to impossible for Latin Americans to do business in the United States because the dollar was at such a premium. It was a situation in which a favorable balance of trade was most unfavorable for the United States. There was a price inflation in Latin America. United States banks were asked to provide progressively larger sums in credit for commodities held in storage. When the banks moved to secure their position, the market crumbled, leaving Latin American primary products in a vulnerable position. The difficulties of exchange also

[15] Memorandum by J. K. Towles, Feb. 1919; MacElwee to the William A. Reed Company, Dec. 26, RG 151, Box 2958, 640—Argentina. Instructions to Ambassador Shea, May 13, RG 59, 825.51/110; John W. Belt to John Barrett, Feb. 13, Barrett papers; Stimson to SS, Feb. 18, RG 59, 835.516/23.

filled warehouses and steamships in Latin American ports with United States exports on which Latin American buyers would not take delivery. If they did, the buyers contended, they would face losses forcing them into bankruptcy. In turn, the North American exporters were unable to get payment for their shipments and faced the same danger. For this reason, when the Treasury Department came forward with intergovernmental credit schemes to counter the unequal exchange situation, the State Department rejected them on the grounds that they looked to the United States side only; they would embarrass future trade with Latin America and would make difficult United States investments in Latin America. The State Department preferred to lift the United States out of its depression by stimulating exports to Latin America and by finding markets in the United States for the raw materials of Latin America. The furthest the State Department would go to compromise with the Treasury Department policy on loans to Latin America was to inform the representatives of Latin American nations that money was expensive in the United States and that it would be to their advantage to wait until the market eased.[16]

The decision to place Latin American loan policy apart from the general policy as announced by the secretary of the treasury was made, finally, at the beginning of 1920, when the president's illness and changes in the highest positions in the department made resolution of important issues extremely difficult. The decision was made on the basis of suggestions by junior drafting officers in the Latin American Division and in the Office of the Foreign Trade Adviser. It grew out of

[16] Houston to Alexander, Feb. 28, 1920, RG 151, Box 1968, 640—Latin America; memorandum for the secretary by Leffingwell, Jan. 15, RG 39, Box 203, Country File—South America; Fitzgibbon, *Cuba*, 167; speech by John Barrett at the Pan American Division of the Advertising Clubs of the World, "The Critical Pan American Commercial Situation," Nov. 1920, Barrett papers; Chargé E. Wadsworth to SS, Nov. 16, 1920, RG 59, 835.516/58; Albert Strauss to Norman Davis, Dec. 8, 1920, and trade adviser's memorandum, Jan. 26, 1921, 835.5151/3. The campaign to stimulate trade to offset exchange difficulties is the general instruction, consular, no. 765, Dec. 16, 1920, 164.2/126a; Norman Davis memorandum of conversation with Brazilian ambassador, Aug. 10, Davis papers; File "Argentina," May 17, RG 151, Box 2958, 640—Argentina.

a discussion over the department's role in the negotiations between Nicaragua and American bankers on marketing Nicaraguan bonds. The new chief of the Latin American Division, Leo Stanton Rowe, who had joined the department late in 1919 after serving as assistant secretary of the treasury and as secretary general of the American Section of the Inter-American High Commission, convinced Acting Secretary Polk and, later, Secretary Colby to accept the decisions as part of the department's loan policy.[17]

The State Department impressed its views on government loan policy in Latin America even as Secretaries Glass and Houston were declaring the government's intention to remove itself from the international money market. The Economic Liaison Committee, which the State Department controlled, dictated the terms of the agenda for the Second Pan American Financial Conference, to be held at Washington in January 1920. Rowe was secretary general of the American Section of the Inter-American High Commission when the agenda was being drawn up in 1919, and he was sympathetic to the State Department's objectives in Latin America. He allowed the foreign trade adviser to make the agenda into an expanded version of the Jenks memorandum, covering all of Latin America and outlining each country's financial needs.

Paul Warburg had tried unsuccessfully to use the International High Commission as the instrument to get his plan for a peace finance corporation through the Treasury Department. Secretary Glass merely pointed out that such legislation would be impossible to get through Congress. Because of its special interest in Latin America, the United States Section of the International High Commission was willing to be used by the State Department to launch a campaign of public education to help create a market for Latin American securities. Such a market was indispensable for the success of any scheme growing out of the Jenks memorandum. Rowe approved the State Department plan to provide some agency, which, "by giving an added sense of security to American

[17] Latin American Division memorandum by Rowe, Mar. 23, 1920, RG 59, 817.51/1198; Munro, *Dollar Diplomacy*, 418.

bankers will strengthen the spirit of financial coöperation with the countries of Latin America." The High Commission, however, would not go that far.[18]

The need for a special agency or for an aggressive policy by the United States government to solicit loans for Latin America evaporated in 1921 as the United States economy began to come out of its brief, sharp depression. Governments in Latin America that had had to beg for money just a year earlier were now being begged to take money. It was most definitely a buyer's market. The main role for the State Department now was to keep track of financial activity. Because of the aggressive stance it had assumed in helping United States bankers and businessmen in the years immediately after the war, the latter were willing to turn to the State Department, rather than to the Treasury or Commerce Departments, for advice and support. It was imperative for the Department of State to keep abreast of financial activity because its primary concern was the national interest of the United States, and not all loans were in the national interest. It was necessary to block loans that were considered detrimental to the national interest. How they were to be blocked was worked out according to the requirements of each situation. By the end of the Wilson administration, the Department of State, in its determination to continue as a prerogative of peace what had been initiated by the Department of the Treasury as a necessity of war, and through its participation in private economic dealings with foreign governments, had already established the bases for a comprehensive loan policy. It remained for the next administration to give, by a system of priorities among objectives, a coherence to this policy.

The State Department had made it clear that it wanted to be informed in advance of loans to Latin American govern-

[18] Rowe to Lay, Mar. 11, 1919, RG 59, 810.51/915; minutes of the meeting of the United States Section of the International High Commission, Dec. 30, 1918 and Mar. 24, 1919, RG 43, Entry 208, Box 45. State Department correspondence on the financial conference is in RG 59, 810.51A.

ments, to have America replace Europe as Latin America's
banker, to insure political stability in the Caribbean by
strengthening the financial system of the countries in the
region, and to promote loans to Latin America as the best
means of increasing American trade and investment. The
department recognized its responsibilities in the Caribbean
and wanted to take on new ones in South America. There
was, however, never any public announcement of this attitude
toward government responsibility, with the result that, by
1921, there was a marked disparity between the behavior of
the Department of State in dealing with loans to Latin
America and its cautious public statements on the subject,
which were not appreciably different from the general loan
policy announced by the Treasury Department immediately
after the Armistice.

The Department of State said it would not pass judgment
on the financial soundness of loan projects, and yet it dictated
the terms of numerous American loans to Latin American
governments. It insisted officially that the initiative for cooperation between it and the bankers must come from the bankers, though on several occasions—with regard to South
America as well as Central America—it solicited the cooperation of bankers. Disclaimers to the contrary notwithstanding,
bankers took every indication of the department's interest
and involvement in financial affairs as a guarantee of protection for their operations. Spurred by the State Department's obvious interest, American bankers and businessmen
went forth to do business in every corner of the hemisphere.
The great magnitude of new United States economic activity
in Latin America posed no problem of itself; it answered the
needs of American economic well-being and of American
security. Gradually, however, it so increased the demands
upon the United States government for support and protection that the government often felt compelled, against its
will, to commit the prestige and power of the United States.
Such commitments embarrassed the simultaneous efforts of
the government to limit its political and military commitments in the Caribbean. Resolution of the tension between

economic expansion and political withdrawal was a problem for every administration during the 1920s.[19]

The debate over the proper role of the United States government in international finance is a model for the study of the gradual transformation of the Latin American policy of the United States. It includes the first clear public declaration on any aspect of postwar foreign policy pertaining to Latin America—the Statement on Loans, March 3, 1922. The Statement on Loans typifies the ambiguities of the Latin American policy after the war. It contains an unequivocal declaration that the United States government will not be responsible for the foreign activities of private lenders. However, the fact that it was issued, together with the demand that the government be informed of all foreign loans, testifies to the deep interest of the government in the foreign economic activity of United States citizens. The conflict between expanding financial influence and the desire to restrict the responsibilities of the government outside the United States is reflected in the Statement on Loans and in the financial policy of the United States. How this conflict was resolved is important to our understanding of postwar Latin American policy.

One of the by-products of the Great Crash and the depression that followed was a widespread feeling that the economy had been undermined by an orgy of speculation in the 1920s; that the banking community had spurred the speculation for

[19] An official disclaimer is "Interview between the Undersecretary and the Brazilian Ambassador," Aug. 10, 1920, and Davis to Harold Stanley of Guaranty Trust, Oct. 22, Davis papers; department's involvement with International Bankers Committee of Mexico is *Foreign Relations,* 1919, II, 644–49; 1920, III, 231–35; and Lamont to Davis, Oct. 24 and Nov. 19, 1920, Davis papers. An example of department's insistence that initiative come from bankers is Davis to SecTreas, Jan. 18, 1921, RG 59, 835.5151/4. Herbert Feis, *The Diplomacy of the Dollar—First Era, 1919–1932* (Baltimore, 1950), 6, says "It was in the summer of 1921 that the Government first decided to maintain a watch over the loan offerings made to the American public." I hope the foregoing shows clearly that the Department of State made known its desire to "watch over" loan offerings as early as 1919 and, more importantly, that this desire was a continuation of an involvement which had been initiated during the war by the Department of the Treasury.

its own profit; and that the government had lent its influence to nefarious conduct of the "money power." The fact that so many foreign private and public bond issues went into default after 1930 lent credence to this argument. The famous hearings of the Senate Banking Committee in 1931–32 placed an irremovable stigma upon Wall Street, much as the Nye Committee in 1934, 1935, and 1936 succeeded in stigmatizing the munitions makers as warmongers.

With the passage of time, it is hard to condemn the cupidity of the bankers without also criticizing the greed of their willing customers. As for the share of blame for the government, in foreign lending at any rate, it erred in its reticence rather than in giving its support indiscriminately to United States bankers. The vast majority of foreign loans in the decade after 1918 were engineered without the cooperation of the United States government. More important, it is misleading to lump together all loans in the 1920s and to condemn them as unreasoning speculations. The foreign loan market went through several basic changes from 1918 to 1930. As we have pointed out, immediately after the war, bankers were hard pressed to sell foreign bonds to the investing public. After a brief experience with tight money in late 1919 and early 1920, the situation changed. The supply of funds in the hands of bankers increased steadily to an intermediate peak in 1924, fell off slightly, and then rose again to another, higher peak in 1929. After 1920, bankers devoted their energies to selling their money to borrowers, domestic and foreign. It was no longer necessary to appeal for funds. After 1925, investment capital was so plentiful and so eager to find employment that many bankers lost their customary caution.

There were vast differences between the money market at the beginning of the 1920s and that at the end of the decade. Only 6 percent of the foreign bond issues of 1920 went to borrowers who defaulted in the 1930s, while 63 percent of the issues of 1928 suffered the same fate. Of all loans issued in the five-year period 1920–24, only 17.5 percent went to borrowers who defaulted in the 1930s, while for the 1925–29 period, the ratio is 49.5 percent. Using a "default index" to measure the relative number of defaulted loans issued in any given year, the deterioration of credit through the decade is clear: 1920–23 = 34 percent; 1924–27 = 67 percent; 1918–30 = 68 percent. This suggests that, at the end of the 1920s, there may have been an excess of speculation which led to investment in poor-quality bonds and that there was a sharp deterioration in the quality of the foreign bonds marketed in the United States. Despite the marked tendency to relax standards in lending abroad, only two temporary, insignificant defaults occurred *during* the 1920s. The total number of foreign capital issues in the United States market for the period 1918–30 is given in Table 1. Of this total, nearly $2 billion was lent to 14 countries in Latin America, as shown in Table 2.

TABLE 1 [20]

TOTAL FOREIGN DOLLAR CAPITAL ISSUES, GOVERNMENT AND PRIVATE OFFERED IN THE UNITED STATES
(in millions of dollars)

Year	No. of Issues	Amount	Refund- ing to Americans	New Nominal Capital
1918	28	23.4	2.6	20.8
1919	65	771	379	392
1920	104	602.9	105.4	497.5
1921	116	692	69	623
1922	152	863	99	764
1923	76	497.5	77	419.5
1924	120	1,217	247.9	969.1
1925	164	1,316	239.7	1,076.3
1926	230	1,288	163	1,125
1927	265	1,577	240.6	1,336.4
1928	221	1,489	238	1,251
1929	148	705	34	671
1930	122	1,087.5	182.2	905.5

[20] Ilse Mintz, *Deterioration in the Quality of Foreign Bonds Issued in the United States, 1920–1930* (New York, 1951), 6 and 9; Jolliffe, *United States as a Financial Centre*.

TABLE 2 [21]

LONG-TERM DOLLAR ISSUES OF LATIN AMERICAN GOVERNMENT
BONDS MARKETED IN THE UNITED STATES, 1920–30
(in millions of dollars)

Cuba	99	Argentina	486.35
Panama	24.8	Brazil	424.53
Dominican Rep.	20	Chile	340.11
Salvador	16.5	Colombia	182.04
Haiti	16	Peru	129.50
Guatemala	9.97	Bolivia	68
Costa Rica	9.8	Uruguay	66.25
	Total	1,892.85	

Latin America was a bad risk compared with other areas of the world, although the credit of some countries within the hemisphere was as good as any nation's in the world. The Latin American default indexes for the two periods 1920–24 and 1925–29 were 55.2 percent and 79.4 percent, respectively, compared with the worldwide indexes for the same periods of 17.5 percent and 49.5 percent, respectively. More significant than these percentages is the fact that lending to risky areas increased markedly in the second period, that is, from 1925 to 1929, as demonstrated in Table 3.

TABLE 3 [22]

FOREIGN LOANS BY AREA AND PERIOD

	Amount in Millions of $		Percentage of the Total	
Area	1920–24	1925–29	1920–24	1925–29
Western Europe	1073	620	37.7	17.3
Latin America	529	1158	18.6	32.2
Others	1245	1813	43.7	51.5
Total	2847	3591	100.0	100.0

[21] Rippy, *Globe and Hemisphere*, 56. Rippy also provides tables which show how much of Latin America's bonds were in default at the end of 1934 and at the end of 1945, 62–64.

[22] Mintz, *Deterioration in the Quality of Foreign Bonds*, 52.

Just as there were disparities in the default index from area to area, and from country to country within any area, so were there wide disparities in the default index among different banking houses. The index ranged from a low of 13 percent to 100 percent at the top. Further, the houses which initiated the most loans had the fewest defaults, and those which entered the field late in the 1920s had the highest index of default. Evidently, when the more cautious bankers refrained from expanding their loans, their place was taken by more careless ones. As the latter did a larger share of total lending, the average quality of loans declined. The same pattern is true of loans to Latin America. The most reputable houses confined their activities to the safest loans and never demanded exorbitant rates of interest. On the other hand, companies that specialized in the risky loans to unstable Central American nations often commanded the greatest gross profit and raised the most disturbing political issues in their negotiations with the borrowing government for guarantees. Table 4 lists all major banking houses doing business with Latin America and gives how much money they lent and their gross profit. It is interesting that houses which did a great deal of business in the hemisphere and which had worldwide financial interests took the lowest gross profits. Morgan's and Kuhn, Loeb, for example, actually decreased their lending at the end of the decade. They were among the lowest in gross profits and default indexes.

It appears from the statistics in Tables 1–4 that the United States government policy of quiet surveillance of foreign lending was adequate in the period 1920–24 but became increasingly less so after 1924. That the State Department refused to alter its policy in the face of deteriorating standards for foreign loans indicates how strong was the inhibition against butting in. The State Department closed its eyes rather than accept the responsibilities that went along with involvement.

President Harding and his cabinet discussed loan policy at one of their first meetings. Secretary of the Treasury Andrew Mellon wanted foreign loans to be used as a means of getting the governments of Europe to pay their debts to the United

TABLE 4 [23]

GROSS PROFITS OF AMERICAN BANKERS ON
LATIN AMERICAN LOANS, 1920–30

Banking House	Par Value	Gross Profits	Average Gross Spread
Hallgarten & Co.	$ 253,495,500	$10,668,840	$ 4.21
Morgan & Co.	242,800,000	8,145,730	3.35
Dillon, Read	190,000,000	11,570,000	6.07
National City	167,912,000	6,898,930	4.11
Kuhn, Loeb	130,000,000	5,025,000	3.87
Blair [a]	127,072,000	8,808,360	6.93
Seligman	115,500,000	6,730,000	5.83
Chase Securities	109,060,000	3,906,700	3.68
Speyer	82,500,000	5,289,000	6.41
Lee, Higginson	49,750,000	2,705,750	5.43
Blythe, Witter [b]	45,000,000	3,771,250	8.38
Stifel-Nicholaus	29,000,000	2,435,000	8.40
First Nat. Corp.[c]	24,121,000	1,869,377	7.75
F. J. Lisman	16,500,000	1,875,000	11.36
Harriman	14,500,000	567,500	3.87
Harris, Forbes	5,443,000	475,440	8.00
Central Trust of Ill.	3,000,000	240,000	12.60
Equitable Trust	2,885,000	234,850	8.00
Marshall Field, etc.	2,500,000	315,000	8.14
Total	$1,612,038,500	$81,531,627	$ 5.06

[a] Blair issued $69,122,500 profit on which is unknown.

[b] Blythe issued $6,792,000 profit on which is unknown.

[c] First National issued $11,675,000 profit on which is unknown.

States. Secretary of Commerce Hoover was concerned with war debts, but his main interest lay elsewhere. He wanted the government to guard the private investor against bad loans by informing him of the borrower's ability to repay the debt. He also wanted to discourage loans that might be used for war or that might produce economic or political instability. Secretary Hughes wanted to shun the responsibility of passing judgment on the financial aspects of loans and avoid committing the department in advance to protect

[23] *Ibid.*, 67–70; Rippy, *Globe and Hemisphere*, 56.

any particular private interest. He doubted the usefulness of "discouraging" loans to countries outside the hemisphere. The cautious view of the Department of State was accepted by the cabinet, and the president asked his advisers to help him make the government's position known to the public.[24]

Mellon, Hughes, and Hoover met with the president and several prominent bankers in June 1921 to discuss loan policy. It was agreed at the meeting that the bankers, who spoke for "substantially all the people . . . who have anything to do with issuing foreign loans," would "keep the State Department fully informed of any and all negotiations for loans to foreign governments which may be undertaken by them." The sense of the meeting was that the bankers were to cooperate with the Department of State, ostensibly so that the department would be in a better position to assist them overseas. There was no indication that the Harding administration would recognize any distinction between general loan policy and Latin American loan policy. Hughes seemed to favor one consistent policy for the entire world just as he favored a single policy for cables. Mellon was willing to have the Department of State determine loan policy. The assistant secretary of the treasury responsible for foreign loans, Eliot Wadsworth, was a member of the "family" that lived at 1718 H Street, Northwest, and was on intimate terms with Assistant Secretary of State Leland Harrison. Wadsworth cooperated with Harrison by leaving the initiative in matters concerning foreign loans to the State Department. The rest of the Treasury Department seemed content to devote their energies to domestic tax problems. The Republicans riddled the Treasury Department with political appointees, much to the disgust of the conservative, apolitical "professionals" like Wadsworth and S. Parker Gilbert, who remained in the Treasury Department as Mellon's undersecretary after the change of administrations.[25]

[24] Feis, *Dollar Diplomacy*, 8–9; Brandes, *Herbert Hoover and Economic Diplomacy*.

[25] J. P. Morgan to Harding and Mortimer L. Schiff to Harding, June 6, 1921, both enclosed in Harding to Hughes, June 10, RG 59, 811.51/2981. Morgan spoke for the following banks: National City,

Secretary Hoover was not willing to leave foreign loans to the State Department. Without bothering to communicate his intentions to Hughes, Hoover organized a division in the Department of Commerce to consider foreign loans and asked the bankers, through the American Bankers Association, to consult with him in matters affecting commerce. The competition between the Commerce and State Departments confused the bankers, and they stopped informing anyone in the government of their activities. They complained that they did not understand the distinction between consultation and approval. To interrupt delicate loan negotiations in order to consult the State Department would give the borrower the impression that the United States government was going to pass on the merits of the loan. More to the point, the bankers insisted that they could not submit bids on a loan and then withdraw them unless they were to make it a condition precedent of the bid that "the issue in this country is approved by the State Department." Of course, the State Department refused to pass on the loans. It desired only "to be kept advised of such negotiations, in order to avoid any possible embarrassment with respect to the application of its general policies." At this point, some bankers openly admitted they did not understand the policy of the State Department.[26]

Dr. W. W. Cumberland, the financial expert in the Foreign Trade Adviser's Office, was disturbed by the "lack of clarity both in the Department and in the financial world in regard to the methods of giving effect to the understanding reached at [the White House conference in June]." He suggested, in September 1921, that this be corrected by a clear public statement of the State Department's attitude toward international loans, including specific suggestions as to how

Guaranty Trust, Bankers Trust, Kuhn, Loeb, and Co., Brown Brothers, Lee, Higginson and Co., Kidder, Peabody and Co., Dillon, Reed and Co., and Equitable Trust; Wadsworth to Dearing, Sept. 24, 1921, 800.51/300; Gilbert to Leffingwell, Apr. 6, 1922, RG 56, Box 6.

[26] Hoover to Hughes, Dec. 13, 1921, RG 59, 811.51/3044; Julius Klein to Scott R. Hayes, July 2, RG 151, Box 2963, 640—Foreign Loans, Colombia; Guaranty Trust to SS, Jan. 7, 1922, and Lee, Higginson and Co. to SS, Feb. 10, RG 59, 811.51/265 and 279.

bankers and the department might cooperate in a mutually advantageous fashion. Cumberland was the financial adviser in the department at the end of the Wilson administration and at the beginning of the Harding administration. He drafted nearly every important memorandum and letter on loan policy from March to September 1921, always emphasizing a cautious general loan policy and dismissing the need for special regional policies.

Hughes rejected the idea of immediately issuing a statement. He had experienced considerable trouble with a number of Latin American loan disputes, and he asked Cumberland to discuss the proposed statement with the Latin American Division so that it might be consistent with the "exceptional situation" in the hemisphere. This was the first indication since Hughes had taken office that loan policy might be more relevant to one geographic region than another. The secretary could not help but be aware of the policy that had guided United States financial relations with Latin America since the war; his hope was to formulate one policy that would eliminate the need for regional policies. He asked Morton Carrel of the Latin American Division to work with Cumberland to draft letters to Secretaries Mellon and Hoover outlining the State Department's loan policy. The letters were to reiterate the department's desire to be informed of loan negotiations and to impress upon both secretaries the need for some kind of public announcement to that effect. This was the first time under Hughes that a geographical division had taken part in the discussion of policy. Junior officers in the department favored a separate loan policy for Latin America. The economists in the Office of the Foreign Trade Adviser and the regional specialists in the Latin American Division had been responsible for the creation of the department's policy toward Central and South America after the war, and they argued in favor of continuing a special loan policy for the region in which they felt the United States had special interests.[27]

[27] Decision-making in: foreign trade adviser's memorandum by Cumberland, Sept. 6, 1921, and Assistant Secretary Dearing's memorandum, Sept. 24, 1921, RG 59, 811.51/2981; also 811.51/3104 and 800.51/244;

Carrel drafted letters in which he emphasized the importance of a clear loan policy to our relations with Latin America and implied that the department should accept the responsibility of supervising loans to foreign governments. This was no more than a restatement of the now-familiar attitude of the Latin American Division. Cumberland criticized Carrel's limited application of loan policy to Latin America and the implied suggestions of government control. He preferred to stress the worldwide application of policy and the importance of receiving full information on all loan transactions.

Carrel persisted in arguing that loan policy must be adapted to the special conditions of our relations with Latin America and was warmly supported by other officers in his division. Sumner Welles explicitly recommended a special loan policy for Latin America so that the State Department could continue to "exert as much influence as may be possible and proper" over loans to Latin American governments. Dana Munro, the Central American desk officer, wanted the department to make clear to the appropriate bankers that it would give them "proper support" in all their loan contracts. He pointed out to the secretary that this would not commit the department to any radically new policy as far as Central America was concerned because it had never declined to act in a case where a Central American government repudiated its obligations to American creditors. If the proposed announcement was to reflect the department's objectives in Latin America, Munro said, it should provide for department supervision over the proceeds of loans so that financial reforms could be assured, for the protection of worthy American interests so that European interests could be excluded, and for the promotion of American trade and investment so that American influence in the hemisphere could be extended.

None of this pleased Hughes. He was not prepared either to issue any blanket guarantee to American bankers doing business in Central America or to make any public state-

---

Cumberland to Dearing, Sept. 27, and Welles to Dearing, Oct. 6, 811.51/2981; Munro to Welles, Nov. 9, 813.51/5; Dearing to Fletcher, Jan. 17, 1922, 833.51/191.

ment judging in advance any bankers or any loans. On the contrary, he wanted to adopt a policy which would deny the department's responsibility for loan transactions, limit diplomatic intervention, and put an end to the special policy on loans to Latin America. It was obvious that this ideal general policy bore slight resemblance to the economic objectives of Latin American policy or to United States financial relations with Latin America. Hughes tried to take this into account by having Carrel work with Cumberland's successor, Arthur N. Young, to draft a public announcement on loans and letters to Mellon and Hoover explaining the announcement.

Their draft announcement was rambling and defensive and was robbed of its force by a tendency to suggest propositions conditionally. Carrel's influence was shown in the enumeration of a great many situations in which the department could be helpful if it had complete information on loan transactions. It was phrased so clumsily that it seemed to be a promise of support, and Dearing and Second Assistant Secretary of State Alvey A. Adee rewrote it. Their announcement was a brief and forceful assertion of the State Department's control over foreign policy and of the department's right to full information on all loan transactions. It avoided the clumsy implications of protection for loans but did indicate that the department would supervise or somehow control them. The letters to Mellon and Hoover asserted the State Department's responsibility for foreign affairs and the importance of its being fully informed of loans to foreign governments.[28]

Neither the proposed announcement nor the reasons for it pleased Hoover. He told Hughes that there was a purely economic aspect of American commerce "in which the State Department is not interested, but coming within the purview of [the Commerce] Department." He disapproved of the proposed announcement because he thought it would confuse the bankers who had been reporting to the Department of Commerce and would be used in their circulars to

<hr />

[28] The Carrel-Young draft is Dec. 2, 1921, RG 59, 811.51/3042A; the revised Adee-Dearing draft is Dec. 7, 1921, RG 59, 811.51/3042.

imply the government's responsibility for the political and
financial soundness of the bond issue. He curtly suggested
that the government would accomplish its objectives more
easily through an "informal negotiation" with bankers by
the Commerce Department.

In his reply, a rather cold and formal letter, Hughes assured Hoover that the State Department had no desire to
take on duties properly falling to the Commerce Department
and expressed doubt that the announcement would lead to
the assumption of any unwarranted responsibility for loan
transactions. Hoover called a meeting of the Executive Committee of the American Investment Bankers Association and
asked it to support the Department of Commerce. Hughes
did not enjoy arguing with Hoover. He was prepared in
December to sacrifice the public statement, but Dearing convinced him that it was vital in the application of general
policies. The issue now, in the opinion of the department,
was the control of foreign relations. Dearing felt that it was
more important to issue a statement on loans before the Department of Commerce did than to delay the statement until
it could be refined to satisfy the special needs of different
areas of the world.[29]

The final draft was written by Young and, with minor
changes, became the Statement on Loans of March 3, 1922.
It began with a rehearsal of the reasons for a public announcement. The bankers were reminded that the Department of State was charged with the conduct of foreign affairs
and that, "on account of the bearing of such [financial] operations upon the conduct of affairs," it was necessary for the
department to be advised of all details concerning loans
which the bankers contemplated floating for foreign governments. The announcement included four specific warnings
to bankers: the Department of State refused to accept responsibility for loan transactions or to pass upon their merits
as business propositions; it denied that it had the authority
or that it wanted to exercise control "with regard to the

[29] Hoover to Hughes, Dec. 13; Hughes to Hoover, Dec. 24; Mellon to
Hughes, Dec. 9, RG 59, 811.51/3044; Dearing to Fletcher, and Fletcher's
minute, Jan. 23, 1922, 800.51/306; 811.51/3106.

making of loans to foreign governments"; it affirmed that "the absence of a statement from the Department does not indicate either acquiescence or objection"; and it cautioned bankers against using any expression from the Department of State in any prospectus or contract. The statement closed with a plea for cooperation.[30]

In the years that followed, the department gradually settled upon five classes of objectionable loans which it would discountenance. Three of them are important for our purposes; loans for armaments, loans to unrecognized governments, and loans to foreign monopolies. By publicly denying responsibility for loan transactions and by accepting the restrictions on the department's involvement in private international financial affairs, Hughes committed himself to reject the special loan policy which had been used in relations with Latin America since the war. This was easier said than done. Giving special treatment to unstable nations near the Panama Canal was a deeply ingrained habit. The department still felt itself morally obligated to bankers who had come to the department for approval of their transactions and to certain governments whose financial stability was very important to the United States. For example, the department talked General Electric out of taking a Guatemalan bond issue with a British banking house and, on another occasion, dissuaded a group of bankers from taking Ecuadoran bonds which were insufficiently guaranteed. It kept a tight rein on the financial affairs of the Dominican Republic, out of a sense of responsibility for the dependent nation. As a result of official United States government concern, the Dominican Republic was able to borrow money on very favorable terms in 1922. The Dominican budget remained balanced so long as Americans had anything to do with it, and the Dominican Republic was the only nation in Latin America that had no defaults on its outstanding loans during the 1930s.

Hoover's prophecy proved to be correct: the bankers did use the department's approval on their bond circulars and

[30] *Foreign Relations,* 1922, II, 556–58.

took "no objection" to mean a favorable judgment on the
political and economic aspects of the bond issue. As conditions and prior commitments permitted, Hughes gradually
withdrew the Department of State from loan negotiations
between American bankers and Latin American governments,
continually trying to make policy in this one region of the
world consistent with policy in all other regions.[31]

The banks accepted the public statement with equanimity.
They were used to communicating with the government, and
the press release did not seem to change anything. More importantly, it did clear up whatever ambiguities bankers felt
existed in the government's policy. Most of the newspapers
in the country reported the statement as another "warning"
that the government wanted to be informed about foreign
loans. It was assumed by most papers that the government
was going to supervise the loans carefully and pass on them.

The banks did begin to inform the Department of State
of their loan activities after March 1922. As often as not,
however, the information was useless or irrelevant. Home
offices submitted fragmentary or premature reports from
their field representatives and never bothered to submit corrected reports of the final negotiations. The bankers generally telephoned or visited the assistant secretary, who immediately turned over the information to the economic
adviser, who in turn took it up with the appropriate geographical division and submitted a report to the assistant
secretary. That official then called the liaison officials in the
Departments of Commerce and the Treasury and communicated the final decision to the bankers.[32]

The disparity between the continuing involvement in
Latin American financial affairs and the restrictions in the
statement of March 3, 1922 continued to embarrass the Department of State. Nevertheless, it persistently reaffirmed that

[31] J. F. Dulles to SS, June 16, 1924, RG 59, 814.6463/19; Harrison's
memorandum, Feb. 14, Harrison papers; RG 80, 16870–315 and 16870–
710.

[32] *New York Times*, Mar. 4, 1922, 2:8; *New York Tribune*, Mar. 4,
16:7; *Washington Post*, Mar. 4, 13:8; *Boston Evening Transcript*, Mar.
3, 14:5; *Journal of Commerce and Commercial Bulletin*, Mar. 4, 1:3
and 6:2.

statement of policy in answer to inquiries about the relationships among the United States government, American bankers, and foreign governments. By the end of Hughes's term of office, it is fair to say that the general loan policy described more closely the department's activities in Latin America than it had in 1922, although this was due as much to the lack of cooperation from United States banks and to the Latin American antipathy to United States financial control as it was to any efforts by the Department of State. In the eyes of the department, the policy on loans was a reasonable combination of living up to prior responsibilities and of avoiding new ones, as is indicated in the following excerpt from a letter drafted in 1924, in response to a written inquiry from a college student:

> The payment of loans made by American bankers to Latin American governments is a matter governed by the contracts between the parties immediately interested, and the Government of the United States does not customarily take any action with regard to the payment of sums due under such contracts. . . . In certain instances where difficulties have arisen with regard to the payment of the loans this Government has been called upon to assist the American creditors either by the exercise of its friendly good offices or by making formal diplomatic representations.[33]

The draft was approved by White, Young, Carr, and Fletcher, signifying a complete review of policy.

The case studies that follow seek to describe the relationship between general loan policy and the problems encountered in dealing with loans to specific Latin American nations.

CASE STUDY No. 1. LOANS TO NICARAGUA

Financial relations between the United States and Nicaragua were based upon the Loan Agreement of 1913 and the

[33] Draft of a letter to Miss Alves Long of Saint Louis College Clubs, Dec. 12, 1924, RG 59, 810.51/1097.

Financial Plan of 1917. Under the Loan Agreement, Brown Brothers and Company and J. and W. Seligman and Company controlled the National Bank and the Pacific Railroad and had an option on all future financing. The State Department controlled the budget and disbursement of funds through the collector general of customs and through two American members of a three-man High Commission.

Nicaragua enjoyed a relative degree of financial stability and prosperity after the war. The American financial officials had supervised the accumulation of a large budgetary surplus, which President Emiliano Chamorro wanted to use to liquidate part of the Nicaraguan external debt. Just before the Armistice, Chamorro sent A. F. Lindberg, the resident American member of the High Commission, to the United States as financial agent of the government to borrow $4 million to refund the external debt and build an Atlantic coast extension for the railroad. Brown Brothers and Seligman would not take the refunding loan. They did, however, promise to consider the Atlantic coast railroad.[34]

The following year a former minister of finance went to New York with Collector General of Customs Clifford D. Ham to negotiate a loan for the new railroad. The bankers feared that the new line would take away business from the old Pacific line which they controlled. The Nicaraguans offered to eliminate this difficulty by buying back the Pacific Railroad. The railroad loan negotiations dragged on into 1920 and became part of the refunding loan project. The bankers worked out a refunding scheme with the Department of State in October 1919 and agreed to minor modifications in the plan of 1917. The department took over from the bankers the prerogative of nominating the receiver of Nicaraguan Customs. The bankers were delighted with this change, since added involvement by the State Department strengthened their position. The department accepted the added responsibility because of dissatisfaction with the bankers and out of a desire to reduce their power and independence. From a sense of moral obligation to Nicaragua as

[34] Munro, 388–417; report of the High Commission for 1918, n.d., RG 59, 817.51/1160.

well as to the bankers, it supported the High Commission and the Nicaraguan government against the bankers. The State Department was proud of its accomplishment in Nicaragua. Professor Jenks used the National Bank and the stable currency as models in his 1918 memorandum on Central American finance.[35]

While the refunding scheme was being considered, Nicaragua asked the department for support in creating a wider market in the United States for its guaranteed customs bonds. Proceeds from the sale of these bonds would be used to purchase Treasury certificates from the bankers and reduce their control over the Nicaraguan currency. The department gave its approval to this plan in March 1920 without consulting the Treasury Department. Second Assistant Secretary Adee refused to pass on the decision because it violated announced Treasury Department policy and required formal Treasury Department approval. Leo Rowe, chief of the Latin American Division and a former assistant secretary of the treasury, convinced Acting Secretary Polk and, later, Secretary Colby that the Treasury Department was "no longer exercising strict control over bond issues such as was necessary during the war" and that the "special relations" with Nicaragua called for a different policy for that country—and for others in Latin America—than for the rest of the world.[36]

United States responsibility for the financial condition of the Nicaraguan government was the basis for the crucial decision in 1920 to raise the special interests of the United States in the Western Hemisphere above the demands of general loan policy as formulated in the Department of the Treasury. It was not easy, therefore, for Secretary Hughes to restore the balance in favor of the general policy. At the end of the Wilson administration, Brown Brothers and J. and W. Seligman, who had served as Nicaragua's bankers, negotiated the Financial Plan of 1920, which provided for the construction of the much-needed Atlantic Railroad, the

[35] Latin American Division memorandum by H. Johnson, Oct. 18, 1919, RG 59, 817.51/1182; trade adviser's memorandum by Munro, Oct. 10, 817.51/1185; 817.51/1175.

[36] RG 59, 817.51/1198; Colby to Houston, Apr. 8, 1920, 817.51/1204.

purchase of the stock of the Pacific Railroad held by the bankers, and an increase in the Nicaraguan monthly budget allowance.[37]

Market conditions were not favorable in 1920 for the railroad-extension loan, and it was left for the incoming Republican administration. The first time Hughes interested himself in the matter, in May 1922, he tried to limit the department's responsibilities in Nicaragua and make the government's activities there consistent with the publicly declared general loan policy. He told bankers and the Nicaraguan government that the United States government could not give any guarantees for the railroad loan.

The loan negotiations got nowhere without the State Department's active participation. Rather than undo the years of constructive work in Nicaragua, Hughes gave up, for the moment, his attempt to modify the department's special Latin American loan policy, at least insofar as it was applied to Nicaragua. The department told the bankers in June that it would not select the route for the railroad or pick the engineers for the job but would pass on those chosen by the bankers.

The secretary's inclination to disengage the United States government from Nicaraguan financial affairs was reinforced by the Nicaraguan government's desire to be free of American influence. President Diego Chamorro took advantage of Hughes's attitude and of Nicaragua's continuing prosperity to undermine the authority of the High Commission and reduce the bankers' control over Nicaraguan finances. In 1923, he tried to remove Roscoe Hill, the American resident high commissioner. Hughes rejected Chamorro's demand and told the Nicaraguan minister at Washington that he objected to the tone and spirit of the message from the president of Nicaragua. Hughes wanted to withdraw from Nicaragua, but he refused to sacrifice the prestige of the United States. He stood by Hill until a compromise could be worked out that

[37] Munro, 416–17; trade adviser's memorandum by Munro, Feb. 21, 1920, RG 59, 817.51/1249; Assist SecTreas Davis to SS, May 20, 817.51/1251; Latin American Division memorandum by Welles, Oct. 1, 817.51/1240.

allowed the commissioner to retire gracefully, at the end of 1924.[38]

Chamorro's next step was to alter the internal-revenue structure of the country. The authority of the High Commission was established by statute, and elimination of a tax or creation of a new one reduced the area of its authority. When the State Department did not object to this, the Nicaraguan Congress increased the pressure, refusing to pass a new budget. This put the National Bank in difficulties since, as the disbursing agent for the government, it issued funds against specific budgetary provisions. Without a budget it could not issue checks. These and other measures struck the American chargé as a scheme "whereby the Financial Plan may be invalidated." The Nicaraguan government further reduced its debt to the bankers by retiring Treasury bills. As it did so, it slowly regained control over the National Bank and the Pacific Railroad.[39]

By the end of 1924, the High Commission no longer had effective control over Nicaraguan finances. The department decided to accept the new situation and the limitations on its own role—a state of affairs more appropriate to the official general loan policy than the earlier involvement. The department could not say that the new situation was of its own making. Munro recommended that the department work out an informal understanding with the Nicaraguan government as to the exact extent of the American financial control under the new conditions. He further recommended, and Hughes accepted, that the United States government give up control over Nicaragua's finances "except insofar as it is necessary to protect the contractual rights of Nicaragua's creditors." [40]

[38] SS to the bankers, May 17, 1922, and Latin American Division memorandum by Munro, June 28, RG 59, 817.51/1329; interview between SS and minister from Nicaragua, Mar. 15, 1923, Hughes papers; Latin American Division memoranda by Munro, Jan. 20, Feb. 23, Mar. 10 and 16, 1923, 817.51/1406, 1418, 1420, and 1442. Hill's graceful departure is planned in the instructions to Chargé Walter C. Thurston, Oct. 4, 1924, RG 59, 817.51/1517.

[39] Thurston's July 5, 1924, RG 59, 817.51/1504.

[40] Latin American Division memorandum by Munro, Sept. 30, 1924, with Hughes's approval appended on Oct. 3, RG 59, 817.51/1520.

With Munro's memorandum of September 1924, American relations with Nicaragua were brought more or less into line with general loan policy. Much of the credit for this success must go to the Nicaraguan government, which did everything it could to reduce the American bankers' control over Nicaraguan finances and to eliminate the conditions which provoked American intervention. Nicaraguan pressure forced Hughes to relinquish American control faster than the State Department would have wished. In the past, such pressure had led to increasing commitments of American power to maintain a given level of influence. Hughes accepted the diminution of American influence in Nicaragua rather than run the risk of increasing the commitment of American prestige, because he felt such a reduction would not threaten the nation's security. Hughes's successor, Frank B. Kellogg, was unable to maintain the delicate balance between influence and power which Hughes had struck, and American troops returned to Nicaragua in 1925.

CASE STUDY No. 2. LOANS TO GUATEMALA

Postwar negotiations with Guatemala began as a continuation of the State Department's wartime efforts to eliminate German influence. For nearly six months after the Armistice, the department tried to get President Estrada Cabrera to accept its plan for an American-controlled corporation to collect the customs and create a National Bank. After this period of nearly incessant representations in Washington and in Guatemala, Cabrera agreed to invite Professor Edwin W. Kemmerer to Guatemala to investigate and report on the country's financial condition. Kemmerer was a professor of economics at Princeton and one of the most famous "money doctors" of his day. He was a favorite with the Department of State. In the course of his career he served in Mexico, Guatemala, Colombia, Ecuador, Peru, Chile, Germany, Poland, South Africa, Turkey, and the Philippines. After spending three months of 1919 in Guatemala, Kemmerer submitted a lengthy report that covered every aspect of the nation's finances. Cabrera simply ignored the report. His successor,

Carlos Herrera, "lost" it until March 1921 and then turned it over to a congressional subcommittee, where it was pigeon-holed. Frustrated in its attempt to reform the currency through legislation, the department concentrated its energies on a refunding loan and a National Bank of Issue as the vehicle for reform.

When the war ended, the only American banking firm doing business in Guatemala was Lionel A. Stahl and Company, through its affiliate Schwartz and Company. Schwartz was Cabrera's personal banker and tried to use this connection after the war to take over German properties and set up a National Bank. Stahl repeatedly requested the State Department's aid for a bank project which he had drawn up in cooperation with the Mercantile Bank of the Americas. It was not deemed worthy of support because it was too vague in part and too onerous for Guatemala. Schwartz and Company had a bad reputation and eventually became the bête noire of the department. At this time, however, the department was not unwilling to lend the firm its support if the situation warranted, but it preferred not to and sought to interest other trade adviser, Sumner Welles wrote to the National City Bank, which declined to become involved. While the department was discussing the matter with the National City Bank, Schwartz enhanced his position by advancing the Guatemalan government sums to meet payments due on the external debt and to cover the deficits in the budget.[41]

The Guatemalan government did not want its National Bank controlled by Americans. In order to end the financial difficulties which caused the department's concern and provided the excuse for its interference, Guatemala tried to float a large loan without the department's advice, and without including any plan for financial reform which would give foreign bankers control over its economy. Schwartz could not provide sufficient capital for such a loan, and no reputable

[41] Gavin McNab to Polk, Apr. 12, 1919, RG 59, 814.516/1; Polk diary, July 8; instructions of Mar. 3, 1921, 814.51/320a; 814.516/11. The trade adviser was opposed to the Mercantile Bank project because it involved "a firm of Jews" (Schwartz and Company), Apr. 22, 1921, 814.516/22; memorandum, Mar. 15, 814.516/23; Welles to Farnham, June 15, 1921, 814.516/19.

American bank would express an interest in it without the State Department's approval. Herrera then tried to force the Electric Bond and Share Company and the International Railways of Central America to lend him the money by threatening them with confiscation. Both companies appealed to the department and received vigorous support.[42]

The initial representations did not end International Railways' troubles. Herrera refused to extend and then canceled the company's concession. In response to the company's complaint of May 1921, the solicitor found that the Guatemalan government had no legal grounds for canceling the concession and recommended that the department support the railroad. The Latin American Division urged a more circumspect approach. Unqualified support of the railroad company would cause much bitterness in Guatemala no matter what legal issues were involved. The important thing was to get the railroad finished. It would connect Salvador with the Atlantic and link Guatemala with Honduras and Nicaragua. Secretary Hughes accepted this evaluation and the proposed course of action that went with it. He decided to commit the department's influence to a compromise between the company and the Guatemalan government. Cooperation between the department and the counsel for the railroad was so close that the latter drafted instructions for the legation. Boaz Long, former ambassador to Cuba and a veteran diplomat, agreed to go to Guatemala as a special representative of the railroad. Although the American legation gave him "all proper assistance," he could not settle the dispute in the few months he was in Guatemala.[43]

There remained behind after Long, to continue the negotiations, John Bayard Pruyn, the railroad's counsel. He and American Minister Arthur Geissler reached an agreement with the Guatemalan government in 1923. They had to over-

[42] Latin American Division memorandum by S. Johnson, Sept. 12, 1921, RG 59, 814.51/332; the railroad's problems are May–Aug., 814.77/62–87.

[43] Latin American Division memorandum by Munro, Aug. 30, 1921, RG 59, 814.77/87; instructions to the Legation, Feb. 16, 1922, 814.77/94; Lansing and Woolsey to SS, Feb. 13, 814.77/95.

come the obstruction of Minor C. Keith, owner of the railroad, who insisted upon an exorbitant payment in damages.
Having committed its prestige in the dispute, the department
felt morally obligated to produce a settlement that would be
fair to Guatemala as well as to the railroad. Enlisting the help
of Keith's Washington lawyers, Lansing and Woolsey, the
department forced him to accept a compromise worked out
by Geissler and Dana Munro. The questions of a loan and a
National Bank of Issue were raised during the railroad negotiations. Keith, through Pruyn, offered to take a bond issue
to pay for the railroad extension, which would leave a portion
of the proceeds to balance the budget.[44]

While Pruyn was discussing the railroad settlement and
the bond issue in Guatemala City, representatives of the
Guatemalan government began conversations with Blair and
Company in New York. When the Pruyn-Keith negotiations
broke down temporarily in 1922, Blair managed to sign a
loan agreement with the Guatemalan minister of finance.
The Guatemalan Congress refused to ratify this and, as no
denial of justice was involved, the department decided not
to interfere. This decision was not based upon the recently
released loan statement of March 3, 1922. It was the result
of the department's dissatisfaction with the Blair project,
which did not include plans for a National Bank. That is to
say, the project did not fulfill the objectives of the special
policy for loans to Latin America. Blair promised to submit
proposals for a bank as soon as the loan was consummated,
but the department refused to consider the matter unless the
two went together, so Blair broke off the negotiations in
June 1922.[45]

The credit of the Guatemalan government was so bad that
no reputable American banking house would even negotiate
a loan without the State Department's tacit approval. The
approval hinged upon plans for American control of the cur-

[44] Latin American Division memorandum by Munro, May 5, 1923,
RG 59, 814.77/240. It was Munro's suggestion that the department
coerce Keith into accepting the compromise.
[45] RG 59, 814.51/346–367.

rency through a National Bank of Issue. Guatemala had not changed its attitude toward a foreign-controlled National Bank, and it continued to search for bankers who would not insist upon the State Department's cooperation. The only Americans who would deal with the Guatemalan government on this basis were Schwartz and Stahl. Neither Schwartz nor Stahl could take a large, long-term loan by himself, and whenever either tried to get backing in the United States, the department was able to stop him.

The State Department's official policy was to withhold comment on loan projects until it was informed fully in writing. It was so anxious to solve Guatemala's financial problems that it offered its assistance to Kelley, Drayton and Company before that firm had done more than indicate a vague interest in the financing. Spurred on by the department's initiative, Kelley, Drayton and Company sent its representative to Guatemala in April 1923. He soon learned that he would have to give Schwartz and Company a share of the loan in order to get anywhere at all with the Guatemalan government. The department did not approve, and the project was abandoned.[46]

The most serious attempt to establish a bank was made by a mysterious group of interests behind John Pruyn and Thomas F. Lee, both protégés of Minor Keith. They claimed to represent unnamed American interests in Guatemala which were trying to protect their investments and make extra money at the same time. After several months of fruitless effort on their own, Pruyn and Lee called in F. J. Lisman, a specialist in Central American financing. Lisman had been very uncooperative in negotiating a loan to Salvador, and the department would have nothing to do with him. Informing Lee of this decision, the department this time fell back on the formalities of the March 3, 1922 loan statement and denied that it had an obligation to help bankers obtain business. Here again, the decision was based upon antipathy to a particular banker and a particular project and not upon a

[46] RG 59, 814.516/33. Munro supported Geissler against Adee and Hughes in his efforts to secure American financing in Guatemala. Geissler and Munro dominated policy from 1922 to 1924.

desire to see United States relations with Guatemala fit the pattern of general policy.[47]

Thomas Lee was a young man of great ingenuity. He realized what lay behind the State Department's formal notice of objection and divined the true reasons for the lack of support. He dropped Lisman from his syndicate and engaged Edwin Kemmerer as a consultant. It is not surprising that the plan for a National Bank which Kemmerer formulated in July 1924 met the department's demands, since those demands were based upon the Latin American Division memoranda of 1918 and the Kemmerer Report of 1919. Six months or a year earlier, the department would have admitted its preference for the Kemmerer-Lee project and supported it before the Guatemalan government to the exclusion of all other American interests. Now, however, Secretary Hughes insisted that the department behave in accordance with general loan policy and favor no American interest over any other. This severe limitation on the department's special responsibility in Guatemala, which Hughes had been trying to effect for months, was prompted by Minister Geissler's undiplomatic antipathy to Schwartz and Stahl.[48]

Stahl had finally gotten backing for a loan in October 1923 from the Anglo and London Paris National Bank of San Francisco. The loan offer was so outrageous that the department refused to consider it. Munro said of it, "It is an American contract, although both parties are said to boast that it is made without the intervention of our State Department. The Guatemalan people will not so understand it and will hold the United States responsible for it. The American Government and people will not only in Guatemala, but throughout Latin America, be charged with exploiting the Government and people of Guatemala." In a mild attempt to restrict American involvement, the secretary decided that this deci-

---

[47] Phillips diary, Oct. 23, 1923, and Jan. 4, 1924; Geissler's Jan. 29, 1925, RG 59, 814.516/67; Lee to SS, Jan. 28, 814.51/496; Latin American Division memorandum by White, Mar. 5, 1924, 814.51/451.

[48] RG 59, 814.51/446–1/2; trade adviser's memorandum by Young, Oct. 10, 1924, RG 59, 814.51/461. The Geissler-Stahl episode is in: *Foreign Relations,* 1923, II, 381–84; 814.51An4/3 and 32; Munro's memorandum, Apr. 3, 1924, RG 59, 814.51/435.

sion should not be communicated to the Guatemalan government. Geissler was not accustomed to acting in so restrained a manner. He proceeded to exceed his instructions by advising the Guatemalan government against accepting the proposal and divulging the reason for the department's objection.

Hughes was considerably upset and nearly ordered Geissler to be severely reprimanded. Munro interceded in his behalf, so that the department's chastisement only reminded the minister that he was expected to remain neutral, favoring no American interest over any other. Geissler replied, in the form of an apology, that the government of Guatemala sought an early solution to its financial problems and was entirely dependent upon the judgment of the Department of State in the consideration of bank and loan projects, so that it was unfair to withhold that judgment. Hughes did not like this reasoning, but Munro and Geissler had forced the department's hand, and the secretary let their action stand. He was determined, however, that they should not so act again. Consequently, when the Kemmerer-Lee project came before the department, Hughes took charge of the correspondence himself and made certain that the limitations of the general loan policy were put into effect. Lee lost his backers at the end of 1924 and resorted to European capital. This displeased Geissler and the department, and Lee was forced to abandon his project in 1925.

In the brief period after March 1923 during which Hughes controlled the execution of loan policy in Guatemala, the threat of European influence was raised. Kidder, Peabody and Company told the State Department that they were considering taking a Guatemalan bond issue and establishing a National Bank with the help of the French firm of Bauer, Marchal and Company. The proposal was a sound one, and Munro saw in it the opportunity to settle Guatemala's financial problems. He subordinated his preference for American control over the National Bank and recommended that the department do nothing to stop the loan. Chief of the Latin American Division Francis White rejected this recommendation, giving the exclusion of Europeans priority over the bank. He said it would be "most desirable" to have American interests control any bank that collected Guatemalan customs receipts. The secretary preferred White's view and instructed the trade adviser to tell Geissler that the department "would not approve" the project and would not "extend any assistance to" Kidder, Peabody and Company so long as it was associated with European bankers. This was enough to end the negotiations.[49]

Apparently, then, general loan policy did not stand in the way of the department's opposition to European influence in the hemisphere. Geissler, violently opposed to any European influence in Guatemala, was happy to follow the department's instructions in this case. The minister felt himself personally committed to settling Guatemala's financial difficulties and was serving as an unofficial adviser to the government. In so doing, he failed to keep pace with changes in policy, and he continuously exceeded his instructions.

Minor Keith submitted another loan project in January 1925, to which the department showed no disapproval. Shortly thereafter, however, it offered strong objection when Keith began working with German interests to get a charter for a National Bank. The department had by now had enough of Guatemalan finances. It instructed Chargé Leon H. Ellis to refrain from committing himself to any group of bankers and to refrain from acting at all until a formal, detailed project had been submitted to the department.[50]

The Guatemalan currency difficulties were relieved by improvement in the international price of coffee, and the government was able to use local capital to meet the payments on the external debt. In 1926, it succeeded in founding a National Bank of Issue without foreign help. No American bank of importance was involved in the project, and the Department of State had nothing to do with framing the bank's charter.

[49] Instructions to Geissler, May 8, 1924, RG 59, 814.516/51; Munro's memorandum, Apr. 5, 814.516/59; trade adviser's memorandum by Young, Nov. 15, 814.51/475.
[50] Latin American Division memorandum by Munro, Mar. 21, 1925, and trade adviser's memorandum by Young, Apr. 8, RG 59, 814.51/505.

For five years, then, from 1918 to the end of 1923, the State Department had tried to force its ideas of financial reform on the Guatemalan government, only to be frustrated repeatedly by the reluctance of American bankers to risk their money in a bad market, by the determination of the Guatemalan government to prevent foreign control of its currency, and by the obstructiveness of an individual American firm. The persistent frustration and failure were factors in Secretary Hughes's determination to curb the enthusiasm in the department and in the field for a Latin American loan policy that violated the limitations of the statement of March 3, 1922, when, for a period of months in 1923 and again, in 1924, he took personal control of the execution of loan policy in Guatemala.

The United States thus achieved only minor successes with its loan policy in Guatemala. It prevented European bankers from gaining access to the Guatemalan securities market and stopped a number of loan projects which were unfavorable to Guatemala. In a related field—a dispute between the Guatemalan government and the International Railways of Central America—the department had achieved a compromise solution between the disputants which permitted the completion of a vital link in the Central American railroad system.

By 1926, Guatemala had solved many of its most critical financial problems, at least temporarily. There is no doubt that American interference and the department's ideas about proper financial reform had prevented or retarded Guatemalan efforts to improve the state of its own financial affairs. What few gains Guatemala did make before March 1925 owed less to cooperation from the United States than to a determination to prevent further American interference.

CASE STUDY No. 3. LOANS TO PERU

Before the war the Peruvian economy had been controlled by German merchants and British bankers. Toward the end of the hostilities, Peru severed relations with the Central Powers and confiscated many German-owned commercial and industrial properties. Postwar conditions seemed ideal for the investment of American capital: British bankers were not yet in a position to take any bond issues; many German properties were being sold on the open market; and in 1919 there began the long, stable reign of Augusto B. Leguía. The dictator attracted over $90 million in foreign loans to Peru, most of it intended for public improvements. Unlike Nicaragua and Guatemala, Peru saw investment follow loans.

The first important American interest to try to do business in Peru after the war was the Foundation Company, a general contracting and construction firm created by J. P. Morgan and Company, the Chase National Bank, and the First National Bank of New York. In 1919, the Foundation Company concluded a contract with Leguía which called for creating or improving the sanitary conditions in twenty-one cities at a cost of $50 million. The contract was contingent upon the successful flotation of a $15-million refunding loan. J. P. Morgan and Company left the financing to The Guaranty Trust, the Mercantile Bank of the Americas, and the National City Bank, with which it had exceptionally close relations. The market for foreign securities was unfavorable in 1919, so the bankers could not secure satisfactory conditions for the loan. Negotiations continued in 1920, slowed by the bankers' insistence on control of Peruvian finances through their own administrator of customs.

While negotiations with the Foundation Company and its bankers dragged on, Leguía cast about for some means of avoiding foreign control of his finances. He gave notice early in 1921 that he would transfer the gold guarantee deposit for the external debt from the National City Bank to the Bank of England. The exchange situation at the time would provide him with a $3-million paper profit. National City, through its representative, O. T. Crosby, former assistant secretary of the treasury, admitted that it could see no way to prevent the transfer, and the State Department solicitor reported to the secretary that there were no grounds for representations. Colby saw that this situation required firm action by the department, but he was unwilling to commit the incoming administration to such delicate negotiations, and the problem was passed over to the Harding administration.

Secretary Hughes picked up the full dossier on the affair and accepted Colby's evaluation and his suggestions on how to proceed. Without delay, the secretary decided that this "serious invasion into American banking prestige" warranted a stiff protest, with or without legal justification. This diplomatic intervention cowed Leguía temporarily, though he continued to use the threat of a transfer as an argument in favor of his refunding loan.

Hughes approved a compromise suggested by the Foundation Company, which provided for the appointment by the State Department of an official to serve as customs administrator and financial adviser to the Leguía government. The secretary of state was willing, in 1921, to have the department become involved in Peruvian financial affairs. With an American official in Peru, the bankers promised, "To make every effort to make it possible for American capital to become interested in Peru to the end that this country might occupy there the position formerly held by Germany and which England wants." [51] The post was given to the department's financial expert, Dr. W. W. Cumberland. He enjoyed the full support of the department during his term of office and performed his duties with skill. By the end of 1921, nothing stood in the way of the refunding loan except the current budgetary deficit which Leguía wanted to cover with a separate short-term loan. The bankers were willing to take this loan only if the department guaranteed it explicitly.

Both the bankers and the Peruvian government urged the State Department to take the responsibility for such a guarantee. Their request came just as the department was discussing the final draft of the Statement on Loans of March 3, 1922. An explicit guarantee to the bankers obviously would have violated the general loan policy, whereas refusal would

[51] Latin American Division memorandum by Murray, Apr. 9, 1921, and instructions to Minister Gonzales, Apr. 11, RG 59, 823.51/169; Latin American Division memorandum by Welles, with the undersecretary's approval, May 27, 1921, 823.51/203; and Latin American Division memorandum by Carrel, Aug. 20, 823.51A/3. The banker's position is in Joseph R. Swan of Guaranty Trust to SS, Sept. 22, 823.51/194.

undoubtedly have caused a breakdown in the loan negotiations and would probably have forced Leguía to get his funds from Great Britain. The department resolved this dilemma by pursuing an ambiguous course of action. It first explicitly declared itself free of all responsibility in the matter and then implicitly accepted responsibility by participating in the negotiations between Leguía and the bankers and by soliciting the interest of other bankers.

The response of the bankers to the State Department's expression of interest in 1921 was one of surprise and delight. They promised to renew negotiations and understood that the legation in Lima and the department "urged [their] participation in the loan proposed and . . . if [they] participated in this advance that State Department would use its good offices to see that [their] interests were properly protected." Assistant Secretary Dearing told them that the department considered the normal kind of diplomatic protection to be sufficient and tried to disabuse them of any hope for special protection. For their own part, the bankers pointed out that they were not particularly interested in the loan and would take it only if the department asked them to do so and if it virtually guaranteed their operations. They asked specifically if the department would go as far in Peru as it had in Nicaragua in backing up American bankers. Dearing felt that the circumstances in Nicaragua and Peru were very different and told the bankers that the department would not give "any guarantees of any kind." He added:

> [The Department] would be interested, of course, in having Peru's finances rehabilitated and having this take place with American assistance. . . . It [is] desirable for Americans to have as much a hand as possible in the development of Peru and its resources and for [the United States] to play the role in that and in all other South American countries which [its] interests . . . entitle [it] to play, but . . . it [is] not the Department's business to be giving guarantees or to be saying anything which

would indicate that it intended to apply any force in making South American government live up to their obligations to banks.[52]

While this stated the State Department's policy very clearly, it did not determine the department's relations with American bankers. The department considered the contract for the temporary loan, which Guaranty Trust proposed, to be too onerous. Chargé Frederick A. Sterling and Cumberland wanted the department to consult with other responsible banking firms about the plan. The department felt such action would be "highly improper" and yet was willing to negotiate with Guaranty Trust to alter the terms of the loan contract. The bankers took these negotiations as a token of the department's commitment to protect their interests.[53]

The temporary loan was consummated in July. Leguía spent the proceeds in less than a month and was still in need of money to balance his budget. Guaranty Trust held an option on all financing guaranteed by the customs receipts, but Leguía did not want to do business with that bank any longer. Chargé Sterling renewed his recommendation that the State Department interest other American banks in the big refunding loan. If the Americans did not move quickly, he warned, Leguía would break the option and go to British bankers. The prospect of Peru engaging in wildcat financing with British bankers was disturbing enough to cause the department to violate its policy with regard to taking the initiative in consulting other American banks. Officials in the department realized the implications of soliciting the participation of bankers in a particular piece of business, and the discussion of the issue involved every interested officer, from the Latin American Division to the secretary. The decision

[52] Identical letters to J. P. Morgan and Company, Guaranty Trust, National City Bank, and the Mercantile Bank of the Americas, Jan. 7, 1922, RG 59, 823.51/208. Dearing also called each of the bankers, Jan. 12, 823.51/220; 823.51/222 and 225; Dearing to Fletcher, Jan. 17, 833.51/191.

[53] Sterling's May 16, 1922, and the Latin American Division memorandum by Munro, June 28, RG 59, 823.51/253.

was made to contact Herbert Stabler, who was then with White, Weld and Company of New York.[54]

Introducing other American firms did not help the loan negotiations. The English banking house of Baring Brothers was able to float a small loan in December 1922 guaranteed by the guano receipts. The activities of the Foundation Company were restricted by the constant need to provide the Peruvian government with loan funds to pay the company for its services. So long as Guaranty Trust controlled the customs receipts with its option, it was difficult to get bankers to lend money to Peru. Peru was able to place only small bond issues in the early 1920s. The refunding project did not advance at all.[55]

The State Department's enthusiasm for interfering in Peruvian financial affairs ebbed markedly soon after White, Weld and Company had been introduced into the loan negotiations. None of the bankers seemed to be cooperative, and Leguía was now entirely unsympathetic to American supervision of his government's finances. Cumberland was eased out of his post as financial adviser and customs administrator in 1923 and was put into a figurehead position on the board of the Peruvian Federal Reserve Bank.[56]

As it had in Nicaragua and Guatemala, the State Department decided in 1923 to reduce its involvement in private loans to the Peruvian government and to make United States relations with Peru consistent with general loan policy. In 1924, when Equitable Trust asked for advice on a Peruvian bond issue to be guaranteed by the tobacco receipts, the department would not even take the question under consideration. Hughes had resolved to uphold the letter and the spirit of the official loan policy. The department did continue to

[54] Latin American Division memorandum by White, Nov. 16, 1922, RG 59, 823.51/294; Harrison's memorandum of Nov. 18, 823.51/295; Latin American Division memorandum by Willoughby, Dec. 2, 823.51/297.

[55] Chargé Post Wheeler (Great Britain) to SS, Dec. 15, 1922, RG 59, 823.51B23/–; legation's Jan. 28, 1924, 823.156/21; a British loan to pay for an Armstrong Vickers railroad contract is described in a letter from the Foundation Company, Dec. 27, 1923, 823.51/217a.

[56] Cumberland's Jan. 11, 1923, RG 59, 823.51A/6.

interfere to stop objectionable loans, as in the case of one by
Harriman and Company, which was to pay for destroyers
which the Merchant Shipbuilding Corporation wanted to
build for the Peruvian government. The department expressed its opposition even though Merchant Shipbuilding
threatened to get its funds in England.[57]

Even after Hughes had left office, the State Department
used his policy to guide its behavior. In 1925 White, Weld
and Company asked for diplomatic support in its competition with some British banking houses for a large loan. The
department declined to help. It would only request equal
treatment for American interests. It would not ask another
government to favor Americans over other nationals. This
was a significant change from the special Latin American loan
policy that had been followed, with minor exceptions, from
1918 to 1923, and which had provided for vigorous diplomatic support for American financial interests in order to
exclude all other powers. The equanimity with which the
department accepted the possibility of European influence
in Peru was never evident in United States relations with
Central American nations. Except for this difference, financial
relations with Peru followed the same pattern as relations
with Nicaragua and Guatemala; after 1923 they were brought
into line with the principles of general loan policy as expressed in the press release of March 3, 1922.[58]

Part of the United States economic legacy from the war
was the opportunity, offered by Europe's inability to control
its prewar capital markets, of extending American financial
influence in the hemisphere. This opportunity fitted into
United States foreign policy as part of the general conviction
that the government should assist in the economic penetration of Latin America and as a stimulus to the traditional
objectives of dollar diplomacy. The Department of State first
arrogated to itself the supervision of loans and then dealt

[57] Harrison's memorandum, Mar. 3, 1924, RG 59, 823.51/350; economic adviser's memorandum by Young, Oct. 11, 823.51H23/1.

[58] RG 59, 823.51/372. Blythe, Witter and Company, a member of
the Guaranty Trust–White, Weld syndicate, won the contract in 1926
without the State Department's aid, with the help of a significant commission to Leguía's son: 823.00/518; and Winkler, *Foreign Bonds*, 109.

with loans to Latin America in a manner which it considered consistent with the "exceptional situation" in the hemisphere, despite the fact that this manner conflicted with the Wilson administration's efforts to reduce United States commitments in the hemisphere. Secretary of State Charles Evans Hughes was opposed to a special loan policy for Latin America and was against taking on the responsibilities and commitments which this policy entailed. His efforts to formulate one consistent policy culminated in the declaration of policy in the press release of March 3, 1922. Insofar as Latin America was concerned, this general loan policy was not applied until 1923 and 1924, when it was instituted less as an unsolicited manifestation of the reluctance to intervene in Latin American affairs than as a recognition and acceptance of repeated failures of Latin American policy.

The Guatemalans and Nicaraguans at first had blunted the best-intentioned efforts of the United States government to reform their financial systems and then turned their efforts to regain control over their own finances so that they might reject United States advice. The Peruvian government at first encouraged United States involvement in its financial affairs but then blunted and finally rejected United States advances. While never for a moment seeking such an end to their efforts, the Department of State accepted these rebuffs or failures with a certain equanimity. It could do so because, by 1923, it was clear that the United States position in the hemisphere was secure, that the international bankers of the United States did not need the active support of the United States government to win business, and that the loss of any given contract or loan in no way weakened the financial dominance or the basic strategic security of the United States in the Western Hemisphere. The Department of State accepted rebuff with equanimity also because the consequences of the enforced inaction were more in keeping with the department's stated policy on loans and its general opposition to intervention than any active involvement in loan negotiations might be. So long as Hughes remained secretary of state, the department continued to execute a financial foreign policy more decorous than any since the Roosevelt corollary to the Monroe Doctrine in 1905.

CHAPTER 6

Securing the Strategic Objectives: Cables

During World War I, the importance to the national security of international communications links was made painfully clear by virtue of their inadequacy. Relations with foreign-owned cable monopolies in the Far East, Russia, and Latin America left a legacy of bitterness and frustration which hardened American policy after the war. Communications with Latin America, except for a line of All America Cables down the west coast of South America, were subject to British control. Dependence on British facilities, never an ideal condition, became increasingly irksome as trade competition with Great Britain intensified. With the outbreak of the war, it became an insufferable encumbrance. For example, because the British had broken American codes, a "top-secret" message to Argentina had to be sent down the All America company line through Mexico, down the west coast, and then over the Andes Mountains to Buenos Aires. No message could be sent to Rio de Janeiro over American facilities.

The lack of communications facilities under American control upset the entire war effort. Chandler Anderson complained that his work in the War Industries Board was constantly hampered by failures of communication between the board and its agents overseas; the navy was disturbed by the lack of facilities and, even more, by the lack of government control over existing facilities in the Western Hemisphere. It was common knowledge that the majority of radiotelegraph equipment in South America was of German manufacture. In Argentina, the German Telefunken Company kept the United States intelligence officers uneasy with its efforts to establish direct radio communication between Argentina and Germany.[1]

There were other irritations. American businessmen were convinced that the British government was utilizing its censorship facilities to promote British commercial interests. The British government had always been solicitous of the commercial advantage of its nationals in the South American market, and British cable companies reciprocated by giving their government access to all their cables. It is only fair to point out, however, that the United States government took over certain cable facilities during the war, and, where American cable companies predominated, the United States government enjoyed the same supervisory privileges as the British. At every turn, Americans ran into British cable monopolies. The entire east coast, with the single exception of old French and German cables direct to Africa and Europe, was controlled by the British Western Telegraph Company. Anti-British sentiment among American communications interests was so strong that as late as January 1917 they were willing to cooperate with German companies to circumvent British cable monopolies and to insure themselves against loss of traffic in the commercial war they felt certain would break out as soon as the guns ceased firing in Europe. The State Department did not discourage these efforts; it regarded monopoly concessions as "decidedly prejudicial to American interests." Even after the United States entered the war on the side of the Allies, its representatives in Latin America were instructed to encourage any purely American company and to exert their influence to thwart extension of British monopoly rights to communications facilities. The order of priorities

[1] Anderson diary, May 8, 1918; report of the General Board to SecNav, June 22, 1920, "Records of the General Board," File No. 419, Serial No. 968; RG 80, 12479A; report by Major A. T. Smith, Apr. 24, 1917, RG 38, ONI Register 2213, B-7-e.

was clear: control of communications was more important
than foreign trade.[2]

Inadequacy of facilities was an annoying corollary to dependence upon foreign cable monopolies. Several Latin
American countries were not served with cables from the
United States. Telegrams to Venezuela, for example, had to
be routed through Panama to Colombia, and then overland
to Caracas. Along the route they were subject to the vagaries
of local facilities and local political conditions. During the
war, cabled information would sometimes arrive later than
mailed dispatches, much to the vexation of many government
agencies. What impact could the Committee on Public Information hope to achieve with their carefully planned publicity material when it was quite likely to arrive after the
story had been broadcast in the local press? Postwar policy
in international communications was born of such wartime
experiences.[3]

The Department of State's first opportunity to give effect
to the desire for American-controlled communications facilities in the Western Hemisphere was in the struggle of All
America Cables for concessions in Argentina, Uruguay, and
Brazil through its subsidiary, the Central and South American Telegraph Company. In each country the Americans
were challenged by the British Western Telegraph Company,

[2] Elihu Root, Jr., counsel for All America Cables Incorporated, testi-
mony before a Senate subcommittee, 1921, in Leslie Bennett Tri-
bolet, *The International Aspects of Electrical Communications in the
Pacific Area* (Baltimore, 1929), 5; Phillips diary, Feb. 21, 1917; James
L. Merrill, president of the Central and South American Telegraph
Co. (a division of All America Cables), to SS, Jan. 15, RG 59, 833.73/17;
instructions to Minister Robert E. Jeffery (Uruguay), Feb. 8, 883.73/14.
SecNav to SS, Apr. 12, and attached foreign trade adviser's memorandum of same date by Julius G. Lay, 831.74/15; instructions to
Jeffery, Oct. 25, 833.73/21; SecNav to SS, May 21, RG 80, 12479A-297.
Jordan Herbert Stabler, chief of the Latin American Division, was in
charge of cable problems. He did his job so well that he left the department in 1919 to become a vice president of All America Cables.

[3] "Digest of Concessions and Contracts held by the Mexican Telegraph Company and the Central and South American Company under
which their cables are landed and operated in Foreign Countries," n.d.,
no signature, RG 59, 811.731/697; and F. J. Brown, *The Cable and
Wireless Communications of the World* (London, 1927); McGoodwin's,
May 16, 1919, RG 59, 103.91/1620; 103.93/1262 and 1278.

which owned interport cables in Brazil and cables from Brazil to Argentina, from Argentina to Uruguay, and from Brazil to Barbados. Ambassador F. J. Stimson began the drive by persuading the Argentine government that cables between Buenos Aires and Montevideo were not subject to the monopoly provisions of the British concession. He argued that whereas the Western Telegraph concession was for a submarine cable, one between Buenos Aires and Montevideo would be subriparian. This position coincided with the claims of the Argentine and Uruguayan governments that the river Plate was not part of the Atlantic Ocean but an internal river under their joint control. The Argentine government wanted to improve its communications with other nations and resented its dependence upon the British. The American company got a concession. Western Telegraph fought back and carried the defense of its monopoly privileges to the Argentine courts and Congress. The British government came to its support, protesting vigorously that the proposed concession to Central and South American Telegraph infringed upon the rights of Western Telegraph.[4]

The Department of State promoted the Buenos Aires–Montevideo cable project. It turned for support to Bernard Baruch and the War Industries Board to license sufficient materials, particularly copper, to enable the American cable company to build the new facility. Ironically, the All America Cables Company was under contract for all its new cables to the best cable manufacturing company in the world, the Telegraph Construction and Maintenance Company in London. In order to put through this commercial order for new cable, the War Industries Board had to convince its counterpart in Great Britain to permit the use of strategic materials for the manufacture of the cable and then to grant the necessary export licenses for it. The British government, then

[4] Stimson, *My United States*, 402; RG 59, 811.731/697, concession dated Oct. 22, 1918; *Foreign Relations*, 1919, I, 172; *La Nación*, Apr. 23, 1916, 3:5; *La Prensa*, Aug. 10, 1918, 9:5–6; Ministerio de Relaciones Exteriores [World War I Records], Caja 18, Legajo II, C, 1 and 17; *London Times*, Dec. 21, 1920, reprinting, with comment, an article on this subject by Mark Sullivan and included with many other documents of similar purport in RG 38, ONI Register 5132-B.

pressing its case before the Argentine government, was most reluctant to accede to the American wishes. When it came to a final decision, the policy of prosecuting the war before worrying about postwar trade conditions won in the struggle for communications facilities as it had in the question of financial dominance and as it did in every other area of conflict between the British and Americans in Latin America. Resolution of the struggle would have to wait until the end of the war, but officials in Washington would not forget quickly their experiences with British cable monopolies. Breaking the stranglehold of British and French exclusive cable privileges became an unchanging and unyielding United States goal from 1919 until it was achieved in 1923. The Department of Commerce and of the Army and the Navy shared with the State Department the belief that it was of vital importance to the United States, from the military and commercial points of view, to control communications between the United States and other countries. The departments urged that no effort be spared to aid American companies in their search for new facilities and new markets, and they agreed to leave coordination and execution of this policy in the hands of the Department of State, where it had been placed during the war by executive order.[5]

The Wilson administration attacked the problem of communications simultaneously on two levels. It sought a general international agreement at the Paris Peace Conference while it continued diplomatic negotiations with Great Britain and individual Latin American nations to end British monopolies in the Western Hemisphere. The essence of the United States position at the peace conference was commercial relations with no barriers: "Civilization depends upon open communication among nations and the economic stability of the world depends upon the open door." In order to provide adequate communications facilities, there must be

[5] Duncan to Auchincloss, Oct. 30, 1918, Auchincloss papers, Box 53, Folder 31; Department of Commerce memorandum, May 23, 1919, RG 151, Box 2721, 543—General; RG 59, 574D1/146; RG 80, 12479A-384 and 389; reports by Walter Rogers, Sept. 11, 1918, and Breckinridge Long, Jan. 25, 1919, RG 59, 574D1/188.

an end to monopolies and a concerted program of development in cables. Despite the very best efforts of the United States delegation, all Wilson could get from his colleagues on the Council of Five was an agreement to convoke a world conference on communications to settle the question of German cables and cable monopolies.[6]

The Department of State was given the job of preparing for the conference by making arrangements with foreign governments and by conducting an elaborate, formal review of communications policy within the United States government. Work on the domestic side was complicated in 1919 by Wilson's illness and then by his growing enmity toward Secretary of State Lansing. Even without such unnecessary difficulties, the problem was enormous. As Lansing explained to the president,

> No department of the Government has any particular jurisdiction over the subject of communications. The Navy has the wireless under its authority; the War Department has a cable and some telegraph lines which it operates; the Post Office Department is interested in various aspects of communications abroad as they mean very much to American commercial and financial enterprises; the Department of State, too, is particularly interested, not only as a practical measure of communication with our agents abroad, but as regards the general policy of the Government in the subject matter of communication.[7]

Wilson made no mention of the issue Lansing had raised; instead, he merely approved sending out invitations to the conference.

The original peace-conference plan called for a worldwide conference to which all nations would be invited. It was to be preceded by a preliminary conference among the five

[6] Report by E. E. Power on the International Cable Situation, Jan. 15, 1919, RG 59, 574D1/–; Creel to Wilson, Mar. 24, 1918, 103.91/1566; Norman Davis to R. S. Baker, July 26, 1922, Davis papers.

[7] Lansing to Wilson, Dec. 23, 1919; and Wilson to Lansing, Dec. 24, RG 59, 574.D1/13.

Great Powers at which the agenda for the full conference would be prepared, the German cables would be disposed of, and there would be an endeavor to agree upon a general policy in pursuance of the recommendation of the peace conference regarding international communications. The British and French did their best to delay the preliminary conference on the very sound premise that if the preliminary conference was delayed or not held, it would delay or force the abandonment of the plenary conference. Before a worldwide audience, Wilson's proposals for the elimination of communications barriers among nations would have an enthusiastic response. The British and French first refused to name their delegates, then found minor objections to the preliminary agenda, and then held up the departure of their delegates until they succeeded not only in postponing the preliminary conference from April 1920 to September and finally to November but also in indefinitely postponing the plenary conference. When the preliminary conference did meet, finally, it could not settle the issue of the German cables, which was left to drawn-out negotiations throughout the 1920s, but it did open all the major questions of world communications to public discussion and forced the United States government to make sure of its own ideas and policies on the subject.

While the British and French dragged their feet against a worldwide solution to the problem of communications, the Department of State went ahead with its campaign to end monopolies in the Western Hemisphere. Pressure on the British monopoly in Argentina and Brazil had been relaxed when it had become apparent that further efforts would embarrass prosecution of the war. Once the war had ended, however, the Central and South American Telegraph had the full, uncompromising cooperation of the Department of State. Ambassador Stimson was placed at the disposal of Jordan Herbert Stabler, the company's new representative to Argentina. The company had another friend at court in Frank Polk, a major stockholder in the Mackay Company, which controlled the Commercial Cable Company and was a close ally of the All America system. Although Polk refused to be associated with any dispute concerning Commercial Cable which came before the department, he had no such qualms where All America Cables was involved. The department negotiated with the Argentine ambassador at Washington, while Stimson and Stabler conferred with President Hipólito Irigoyen in Buenos Aires. The decree authorizing the Central and South American Telegraph Company concession was signed by President Irigoyen on December 18, 1919. The cable was operating within a month.[8]

The course of action in Uruguay was not so assured. To be of consequence, concessions for operating in Montevideo would have to wait for the approval of the Argentine end of the cable. Consequently, the company did not press for a specific concession. The department obligingly held back, remaining ready whenever requested to defend the company's rights. An appeal came in June 1919, when the Uruguayan government made plans for a word tax on all cable messages into or out of the country. All America called on the department for a protest. Minister Robert E. Jeffery obliged promptly but had little success. He was hindered by the company's representative, James J. Shirley, who considered the tax a totally nondiscriminatory, internal matter not calling for diplomatic intervention. The department was taken aback and informed the company that it considered further representations pointless. The company disagreed. It asked for continued support, disclaiming the opinions of Shirley, who had been dismissed. Stabler entered this perplexing situation fresh from his success in Buenos Aires. He requested immediate, strong representations by the Department of State. Rowe exerted pressure on the Uruguayan minister at Washington, but to no avail. Stabler retreated gracefully. After all, he had achieved his main objective. The All America system was slowly working its way up the east coast of South America.[9]

The most persistent monopoly of all was the Western Telegraph concession in Brazil. As the only convenient station

[8] *Foreign Relations,* 1919, I, 172–80; Polk to Lansing, Nov. 22, 1918, Polk papers.
[9] Information on Uruguayan cable is in RG 59, 833.721.

for cables across the South Atlantic, Brazil was the British company's firmest legal foothold, the keystone of its entire east coast monopoly and the biggest barrier to a United States-controlled communications network around South America. Here, as in Argentina and Uruguay, the Central and South American Telegraph Company had attempted to enter the area upon expiration of the original British monopolies in 1914. The Americans proposed to build cables from Buenos Aires to Rio de Janeiro and from Buenos Aires to Santos. Separate cables were necessary because the British company's monopoly in cables between Brazilian ports would be valid until 1933. Their plan was brought before the British company by the Brazilian government, in accordance with a clause in the interport concession acknowledging their rights of "preference under equality of conditions." In other words, the Western Telegraph could build similar lines under terms laid down by the American company. The British company first proposed modification in the terms and then suggested arbitrating the dispute. The Brazilian government rejected these proposals and granted a concession to Central and South American Telegraph. After a protracted legal battle, the concession was confirmed and was signed by the president of Brazil in 1917.[10]

It took two years to make the concession effective. Western Telegraph had been in Brazil for many years and had made many friends. Throughout the interim, minor officials in the Ministry of Transport and Communications refused to register the American concession, and officials in the Ministry of Finance refused to recognize the clause exempting the company from duty on its cable services. In 1919, this turn of events was brought directly to the attention of Acting Secretary of State Polk by Percy R. Pyne, a personal friend of Polk as well as a director of the company. Polk did not need much prodding. Complaints of anti-American discrimination by the British in the use of the Brazilian cable came to his desk from every department of the government. The issue had been under consideration within the Department

[10] Tribolet, *International Aspects of Electrical Communications,* 47; *Foreign Relations,* 1919, I, 45–46.

P. E. D. Nagle, International Communications and International Telegraph Convention, U. S. Bureau of Foreign and Domestic Commerce, Miscellaneous Series 121.

of State for some time, and opinion on it was unanimous and emphatic.[11]

Polk instructed Ambassador Edwin V. Morgan to raise the issue with the Brazilian government. The government of the United States, he said, "had a lively interest in this undertaking to facilitate and extend cable communications between our two countries." Morgan promptly transmitted the formal statement, adding a personal message from Polk to Foreign Minister Da Gama urging a speedy settlement. The ambassador's effectiveness was reduced by the peculiar nature of the circumstances. It was decidedly improper for him to make direct representations to the Tribunal de Contas, which was blocking the registration of the concession. He had to resort to Brazilian officials friendly to the cable company and to Frank Carney, the representative of the cable company. He complained to the department that his task was complicated by the obstructive tactics of Western Telegraph and asked for some assistance in curtailing the British company's activities. The embassy in London was instructed to bring the matter before the British Foreign Office, in the following strong language:

> The Western Telegraph Company has . . . far exceeded proper methods of commercial rivalry notably in opposing registration of the Central and South American company's contracts for cables from Brazil to Cuba and Argentina and opposing grant by Brazilian Government of concessions for cables to Uruguay. The Western Telegraph Company also grossly discriminates in rates charged on messages handled by the Central and South America Company.[12]

[11] Pyne to Polk, June 17, 1919, Polk papers; report by Commercial Attaché J. E. Philippi (Rio de Janeiro), July 7, RG 151, Box 2722, 543—Latin America; Latin American Division memorandum, June 16, Box 2731, 544—Latin America; SecNav to SS, Nov. 12, RG 80, 12479–362; Fletcher to Polk, May 14, Fletcher papers.

[12] *Foreign Relations,* 1919, I, 200, and 193–203; Tribolet, passim; subcommittee of the Committee on Interstate Commerce, *Hearings, Cable-Landing Licenses,* 66th Cong., 3rd Sess. (Washington, D.C., 1921); RG 80, 27014–20:98.

At this point, July–August 1919, Western Telegraph tried to come to terms with its competitor. As a first step it proposed a halt in the wasteful battle between the two companies. They could divide South American cable business evenly between them and utilize Western Union cable connections from Barbados to the United States mainland. If Central and South American Telegraph refused, Western Telegraph would join ranks with Western Union, run a cable from Brazil to Barbados and thence to Miami, and drive Central and South American Telegraph right out of the market by any "keen methods" available to them. Among these might be an exclusive traffic arrangement with Western Union. Since All America and its subsidiaries had no system of offices throughout the United States for collecting cables, such an arrangement could inflict a serious blow. Western Telegraph also threatened to join lines with Western Union at Panama and exclude All America subsidiaries from their cables.

When Central and South American Telegraph rejected the ultimatum, the British decided to hurt the American company by linking with Western Union through Barbados. The State Department supported Central and South American Telegraph. Word was allowed to leak out that "it might prove advisable to refuse permission to the Western company to land their cable at Miami," should they continue their "unduly aggressive and obstructive measures in Brazil and the Argentine." On October 24, 1919, the president of Brazil signed the concession for a cable from Brazil to Uruguay, and the State Department focused its attention entirely upon the Western Telegraph monopoly on cables from Brazil north to Barbados and on the British attempts, in cooperation with the American Western Union Company, to run a cable from Barbados to Miami.

The United States was determined that neither Western Telegraph nor Western Union should land a cable at Miami before the British company renounced its cable-monopoly privileges in the Americas. A force of marines guarded the causeway at Miami, and a navy cruiser kept a watchful eye over the movements of the cable-laying ship, even sending boarding parties periodically to make sure no attempt was made to link the Barbados cable with existing Miami cables. One such attempt was made, and a navy gunboat drove the ship out to sea and severed the cable. The attorney general, acting on orders from the president, refused to grant a license to Western Union because it was not in the best interests of the United States. The government maintained that the president had the power to control the issuance of cable-landing licenses in the absence of pertinent legislation. Western Union contested that right in court and lost. That the company should attempt to land a cable with or without the government's approval served to dramatize the importance of the issues at stake and enhanced the importance of the upcoming preliminary conference on communications.

Preparations for the conference proceeded in the old Interdepartmental Committee on Cable Communications. As the time for the conference drew near, it became imperative to turn the work over to a formal delegation to be nominated by the president and approved by the Senate. By this time, Colby had replaced Lansing as secretary of state, and Norman Davis had moved over to the State Department from the Treasury Department. These were two men in whom Wilson reposed complete faith, and he turned cables over to them. Postmaster General A. S. Burleson was made official head of the delegation, but the real leadership came from Davis and from Walter Rogers, who had worked with George Creel on the Committee on Public Information. The other important member of the delegation was Admiral William S. Benson, who had worked with Rogers on communications problems throughout the war and at the Paris Peace Conference.

At the first meeting of the American delegation, on June 22, 1920, it was decided to make the German cables the key item on the agenda and to settle that before going on to determine a program for the broader problems of world communication. Before the second meeting of the delegation could be held, Secretary of Commerce Alexander raised objections to its procedure and to the elimination of private companies from the sessions. The argument was settled by the president in favor of the State Department on the grounds that the matters to be discussed "were broad matters of international understanding and policy." Colby made every effort to patch up his differences with Alexander. He also went out of his way to curry favor with, and win the support of, Henry Cabot Lodge and the Senate Foreign Relations Committee. He kept Lodge informed at every stage of the preparations for the conference and urged him to communicate with the department whenever he chose. Relations with the Department of Commerce eased because Davis and Rogers became convinced in September that it was necessary to consult the private companies in order to strengthen their preparations for the conference and in order to maintain the close liaison necessary in the delicate negotiations with the Brazilian and British governments.[13]

By this time, the Department of State was so disturbed over the competition with Great Britain that it reversed the order of priorities for the conference agenda. At the meeting of September 15, 1920, the delegation decided that agreement on international communications should not be prejudiced by a discussion of the German cables. The lesson of the Miami cable-landing fight was that the German and the Miami problems would not be solved until a general agreement was reached on the elimination of monopolies. Until the central issue was settled, all others must wait.

Throughout the conference, the State Department exerted pressure on the British government to force Western Telegraph to back down. Although the British did not want any violence as a result of the dispute and did keep British ships from helping Western Union, they declined to take any action to settle the dispute on the grounds that it was a private

[13] Alexander to Colby, July 8, 1920, RG 59, 574D1/74; memorandum by Assistant Secretary of State Merle-Smith, Aug. 14, 574D1/105; Colby to Lodge, July 31, and Aug. 23, 574D1/131a; letters to all major cable companies Sept. 15, 574D1/139c-g. Minutes of the meetings of the United States delegation are in "Records of the United States Participation in International Conferences, Commissions, and Expositions." "Records of the Preliminary International Conference on Electrical Communications," 1920, National Archives, Record Group 43, Entry 66, Box 91.

matter for the companies to negotiate. For their part, Wilson and Colby refused to give an inch. When the conference failed to produce a general solution, they resolved to remain fixed in their policy and hand the entire issue over to the incoming Republican administration. It was the view of the United States that the dispute involved basic issues of international communications, which were the province of governments. At the very end of the Wilson administration, the United States explained its policy once again to the British government:

> the matter involved important government policies and at least the Western Union Company is not in a position to address directly any proposal to the Western Company without the approval of this Government. Since your answer indicates that the British Government has no longer its former interest in the situation, I presume no progress can be made by a further interchange of views. Without an agreement between the two governments on the larger questions of policy involved, and their concurrent support, it is not apparent to me how the companies could make any progress toward a settlement by direct negotiations.[14]

Of course, the preliminary conference did not settle the key issue or any of the other ancillary issues. They were left to hard, acrimonious negotiations between the United States government and the individual governments concerned in each case. But it did clarify the issues for the United States and gave the government a sure sense of the nation's strategic requirements in communications. By the end of the Wilson administration, the policy of support for legitimate American communication interests had been extended, by its own logic, to a broader policy of opposition to any kind of monopolistic concession anywhere. Although the incoming Republican administration was given an open file on the Western Union cable case and on the other unsettled issues—

[14] *Foreign Relations,* 1921, I, 826–27; 1920, II, 686–99; Colby to Wilson, July 17, 1920, Colby papers; RG 38, ONI Register 12743, B-10-g.

Yap, the Azores, German cables, and others—it did not disturb prevailing policy in communications. That had been formulated by the Democrats. By 1921, the government of the United States stood for reciprocity and against monopoly. What began in 1918 as a fight for concessions on the east coast of South America had become a worldwide policy for an "open door" in communications.

Relations between the cable companies and the government remained amicable so long as there was adequate coincidence of the private interests of the companies and the national interest. As the Department of State neared the strategic objective of the "open door" in communications, it became less willing to extend itself on behalf of the companies, and relations with the companies grew strained. When this occurred, the Commerce Department became the spokesman for the companies in government circles. Once the lack of communications facilities was corrected, the State Department willingly stepped aside and allowed the Commerce Department to assume the burdens of liaison with the cable companies. United States vulnerability in international communications had been eliminated.

Secretary of State Hughes dealt with cable problems at the outset of the Harding administration. The Miami cable-landing struggle had to be resolved; the disposition of the German cables remained unsettled. In fact, most of the items on the agenda of the preliminary conference on communications were unsettled, even the basic question of holding a regular worldwide conference on communications. It was necessary also to complete the transition from the emergency conditions of war to peacetime conditions in communications. This required a decision upon the proper role for the government in domestic and international communications.

Within the Department of State, Assistant Secretary Leland Harrison was given charge of cable issues throughout the world. His memoranda were written with the advice of the solicitor, Fred K. Nielsen. The geographical divisions were called upon for background information only; they played almost no role in the formulation of policy. The department continued Wilson's interdiction of monopolistic cable licenses and took up the fight against the Western Union cable-landing at Miami. It withheld public statement of cable policy until Congress had completed hearings on cable-landing licenses and had passed the Kellogg Bill empowering the president to grant cable licenses and to control their terms in the national interest. Congress passed the Kellogg Bill on May 20, 1921, and the president signed it on May 27.[15]

Coaxing the bill through Congress produced some dramatic moments. While first the Senate and then the House considered the bill drafted by the State Department, the Supreme Court had under consideration the request by the Western Union company that it be freed from the restraining order barring it from landing a cable at Miami. The order had been secured by the attorney general during the last weeks of the Wilson administration. It was assumed in Washington that the Supreme Court would decide against the government and find that the executive did not have authority to deny cable-landing licenses without being granted power to do so by the Congress. The Kellogg Bill was intended to provide the necessary power. If the Supreme Court handed down its decision before Congress passed the legislation, Western Union would be free to land its cable at Miami.

Happily for All America Cables, which opposed Western Union, its corporate interest coincided exactly with the objectives of the Department of State. To insure active prosecution of the case, All America Cables engaged Chandler Anderson, one of the most effective lobbyists in Washington. The very identification of State Department and All America Cables objectives raised suspicions in the House Committee on Foreign and Interstate Commerce. Several members of the committee thought the dispute was a matter of private concern in which the Democratic administration had played a malodorous role. The congressmen could not understand why the Department of State was so concerned over a cable from Miami to Barbados. They even impugned the character

[15] *Hearings, Cable-Landing Licenses.* The Kellogg Bill is S. 535, Public Law No. 8, 67th Cong.

of Solicitor Nielsen, who represented the department at the committee hearings. The suggestion that he was compromised in a matter of private commerce infuriated Nielsen. In no uncertain terms, he told an executive session of the committee,

> [This was no] mere business man's squabble . . . the interests of the American people in general were involved, and [the committee] should understand that when Mr. Hughes sent him up there it meant that the Department was in favor of the proposed legislation, but that Mr. Hughes did not propose to put himself in the position of demanding legislation, which rested in the discretion of Congress, and if they did not think it necessary to protect American rights, they must take the responsibility.[16]

This, together with his assertion that the dispute was part of Britain's campaign to gain control of the world's communications, had the desired effect. Within a few days the House passed the bill, with minor amendments in which the Senate quickly concurred. Once the president signed the bill, action by the Supreme Court was superfluous.

Emboldened by this success, the State Department intensified its campaign for an "open door" in cable licenses. At the preliminary conference on communications of 1920 the American delegation had attempted vainly to have an anti-monopoly resolution adopted. Now, the department attacked monopolies on three fronts: the Azores, China, and South America. Gradually, separate grievances were fused into a single brief against all monopolies until, at the end of 1921, the United States government announced its commitment to the "open door" in cables and its policy of opposition to all monopolies. The campaign extended to radiotelegraphy, as the department insisted that Americans retain control over

[16] Quoted in the Anderson diary, May 14, 1921; SS to SecNav, July 18, RG 80, 27014-20:136; memorandum by the foreign trade adviser, Apr. 2, RG 59, 574.D1/618.

the new Radio Corporation of South America, which was organized by an American-British-French consortium.[17]

The government's opposition to monopolies brought few cheers from American cable companies. Only in one area, South America, did they enjoy any special privileges. They feared lest the government sacrifice these for a principle without gaining adequate concessions from other nations. Events justified their apprehension. The United States gained access to the Yap Island cables in return for recognition of Japanese mandatory right to the island, but the United States remained shut out of China. In the Azores, the department's policy was circumvented by an independent agreement between British Western Telegraph and the American Commercial Cable Company to divide the market between them, and relations between the department and the cable companies deteriorated as a result. The latter had felt encouraged at the opening of the Harding administration. The president's message of April 12, 1921 referred to the country's "strategic commercial and political needs" in the field of radio communication and cables and advocated that "active encouragement should be given to the extension of the American-owned and operated cable and radio services." During the first months of 1921, the department continued to spring to the aid of American interests, sometimes with embarrassing haste, and Assistant Secretary Harrison supported the cable companies' contention that until there was a worldwide agreement to renounce monopolies, the government "should support American private interests in maintaining . . . those privileges which they now possess." Hughes ignored this advice in order to support the general principle of opposition to monopoly. After 1921, the depart-

[17] Harrison to Fletcher, July 6, draft memoranda of July 17 and 19, 1921, memorandum to Henry Fletcher, Dec. 21, folder marked "Cables," Harrison papers; Tribolet, 9 ff.; RG 59, 820.71. On formation of the Radio Corporation of America in competition with the British Marconi Company, see: Tribolet, 9; Laidler, *Concentration of Control in American Industry*, 105–6; "Memorandum on Radio Communications in the Pacific," No. 23, Dec. 15, 1932, *Institute of Pacific Relations;* Keith Clark, *International Communications—The American Attitude* (New York, 1931), 242–44; Freidel, *Ordeal*, 28.

ment restricted its interest in South American cables to obtaining Latin American acquiescence in the abdication of special privileges by American companies.[18]

The protracted and arduous negotiations between the British and the Americans over the Miami cable-landing dampened the State Department's enthusiasm. Mediations dragged on at the department through the fall of 1921 and into the winter of 1922, directed by Harrison with the aid of Solicitor Nielsen. Western Union and All America Cables submitted briefs in support of their positions, and the Department tried to effect a compromise. Finally, the companies agreed to surrender their special privileges in South America, and, as soon as the terms were carried out, the government consented to grant Western Union a license for the cable-landing at Miami. The navy continued to patrol the beaches of Miami to prevent violation of the compromise.[19]

On February 4 and 6, 1922, instructions were sent, *mutatis mutandis*, to all South American nations, advising them of the agreement and urging acceptance and cooperation. In addition, the chargé in Argentina was to see that Western Telegraph permitted All America Cables to enter Argentina, and the chargé in Peru was to guard the rights of All America Cables. On the west coast most of the countries acted promptly to accept All America Cable petitions to discontinue its exclusive privileges. Not so on the east coast. Brazil gave speedy consent, but Uruguay delayed a reply, and in Argentina the British company failed to carry out its part of the compromise. The department proceeded against these dilatory tactics, instructing the embassy in Buenos Aires to inform the Argentines that "This Government would be gratified if the Argentine Government could see its way clear to acquiesce in [the] waiver undertaken by [the] Western

[18] *Cable-Landing Licenses,* quoted in Tribolet, 49. The Yap situation is described in *ibid.,* 67; and "Memorandum on Cable Communications in the Pacific," No. 16, Sept. 1, 1932, *Institute on Pacific Relations. Foreign Relations,* 1921, I, xiii–xiv; Harrison to Fletcher, Dec. 21, 1921, Harrison papers; Anderson diary, Jan. 4 and 31, 1922.

[19] Folder marked "Cables" in the Harrison papers; *Foreign Relations,* 1922, I, 518–23 and 526; SS to SecNav, Mar. 9, RG 80, 27014-20:16 (also filed in RG 59, 811.73W52/55).

Company." Uruguay complied in May 1922, but Argentina
still hesitated. Ambassador John W. Riddle made "frequent
inquiries of the Argentine Government impressing upon
them the extreme urgency and importance of the matter."
Acquiescence finally came in August, but not before Secretary Hughes had been subjected to personal embarrassment.

The first hint of a change of heart in Buenos Aires came
early in August. The secretary, most anxious to settle the
issue before departing on his trip to Brazil, gave Argentina
a final prod on August 24, expressing his "personal concern."
On the eve of sailing he received a telegram from Ambassador
Riddle informing him of Argentina's formal acceptance of
Western Telegraph's waiver of privilege. Satisfied that this
message closed the transaction, Hughes signed the license for
the Western Union cable-landing and left it at the department for transmission to the president. Somehow, the news
reached J. H. Stabler, vice president of All America Cables,
who complained at once to the company's counsel in New
York, Elihu Root, Jr. The company considered the Argentine note (or what they knew of it) to be inadequate in certain technicalities, so that granting the license to Western
Union would be premature. Grenville Clark, Root's law
partner, went aboard the S.S. *Pan America* while it was still
in New York, entered Hughes's stateroom, and accused the
secretary of a "breach of faith." A rather strained discussion
ensued, but Clark persevered, winning a promise to hold up
the license until All America Cables could be satisfied that
the Argentine note met its objections. As it turned out, this
unusual intervention by a private interest in the conduct of
foreign relations delayed the license for only one day.[20]

Solution to the Miami cable-landing controversy was a
great relief to the State Department, but it was by no means
an end of its cable problems. The Kellogg Bill had tidied up
the legal requirements for cable-landing and had made the
department responsible for negotiating all licenses in order
to bring them into line with the provisions of the bill. The

[20] *Foreign Relations,* 1922, I, 528–29 and 535–38; RG 59, 833.73/45;
Anderson diary, 1922; Armour's, May 13, 833.73/49; Pusey, *Hughes,* II,
538–40.

solicitor drew up a model license, and Harrison set about extolling its excellence among the American companies. He seems to have initiated discussions with Root only, and these dragged on for more than a year. The companies, through Root, objected to the provision requiring department approval prior to conclusion of agreements with foreign firms holding monopoly privileges. They wanted to be free to work out an agreement and then seek department approval. They also objected to the "dead-head" clause, giving the United States most-favored-government rate privileges. The Mexican government was transmitting its messages free, and the companies feared that the United States government might, at some future date, demand the same discriminatory treatment.

Harrison pointed out that although it was not the State Department's aim to ask for a government rate that was less than half the commercial rate, the department would lay itself open to criticism "if it did not reserve to itself the right to treatment equal to that accorded by the Company to any foreign Government, although it may well not exercise that right." The department had its way. It had gone beyond any position the companies were willing to maintain. Henceforward, it would support American nationals in a fight against foreign monopolies only if its rigid requirements were met by American as well as by foreign concessions.[21]

With firm resolve, the State Department refused to compromise the principle of the "open door." By so doing, it sidestepped the basic issue of the government's role in the field of communications. The United States was one of the few countries in the world in which major lines of communications were controlled by private enterprise, which made it virtually impossible for Americans to participate in international conferences or to sign conventions on rules of behavior in the field of international communications. The United States government refused to represent the companies so long as it had no power over their operations.

The debate over the government's role in international communications was kept alive after the war by the military,

---

[21] Clark, 156–57; memoranda, Mar. 10 and 24, 1923, Harrison papers.

which believed the national interest required sufficient communications facilities in government hands to handle classi-
fied messages in peace or war. Both the navy and the army
were all the more vehement in support of their positions
because they had enjoyed unrestricted use of communications
during the recent war and continued to hold certain facilities
pending disposition by the government. To them, a sudden
return to laissez faire, advocated by the Harding administration and the companies, was an unwarranted sacrifice of
United States defense.

The debate was confused by the fact that in 1916 the Wilson administration had advocated government ownership of
radio facilities in the hemisphere. The war followed soon
after, and this policy was put into effect. The navy preferred
to continue government ownership rather than to sell out to
monopoly interests, and it blocked the transfer of certain
facilities to RCA because of the company's ties to the British
Marconi interests. After the war the government never renounced this policy, although it was not followed, and American companies complained that the ambiguity hampered
their efforts to extend their facilities abroad. In an internal
policy memorandum, Harrison said the department was opposed to government ownership of anything. He indicated
that getting definite action from the Interdepartmental Committee on Communications would require more energy than
it was worth and would divert attention from the primary
objective—destroying monopolies. Rather than confront the
issue of government ownership directly, the State Department
allowed it to slide and concentrated on breaking communications monopolies all over the world and on providing sufficient communications facilities to handle the commercial
and military requirements of the United States.[22]

All America Cables, having broken Western Telegraph's
domination over the east coast of South America, set about
extending its facilities in the hemisphere. Its next step was
the acquisition of a French company, Haiti Telegraph and

[22] Lansing and Woolsey to SS, Sept. 29, 1925; and SecNav to SS,
Oct. 29, 1925, RG 151, Box 2731, 544—Latin America; Freidel, *Ordeal*,
28; Harrison to Welles, May 18, 1921, RG 59, 574D1/431.

Cable, with rights in Haiti, Santo Domingo, Venezuela, and French Guiana. The concessions of this company carried certain exclusive privileges in Haiti and Venezuela. Hughes called James Merrill, the president of All America Cables, to the department and warned him that the United States government would attack the monopoly as soon as it became part of the All America system linking South America with the United States. To do otherwise would be "inconsistent with the Department's policy in South America." Merrill argued that the conflict of interests in Venezuela was unlike the earlier one with the Western Telegraph Company monopoly. He wanted to be assured of the government's protection against direct cable competition at the outset of All America's operations in Venezuela. Hughes was not convinced. Yet the company need not have protested so much. It used the department's position to secure advantageous terms from the French company. In its final stand on the Haiti Cable Company, the department took a less rigid attitude. All America Cables would be permitted to take over the French company's rights, but these rights might not be renewed. This minor concession was Harrison's doing. He still considered it more important to maintain a consistent worldwide cable policy than to enforce a strict ban on monopoly in South America. As a result of the department's effort, All America did submit the desired waivers, and Haiti, Santo Domingo, and Venezuela gave the desired acquiescence.[28]

That the State Department even listened to counterargument from the company was evidence of its concern to establish communications links between the United States and Venezuela that would be under United States control. Communications with Venezuela had been egregiously bad during the war, much to the disgust of the navy and the Committee on Public Information. Coincident with the negotiations between the State Department and All America, there was a report from Caracas that the German Telefunken Company was about to win a concession to establish a radio sys-

[28] Harrison to Hughes, May 28, June 29, and Dec. 13, 1923, Harrison papers.

tem in Venezuela. The State Department, the navy, and the Commerce Department agreed that it was important to have United States interests control the projected radio system. The State Department called upon the United States minister in Caracas to delay negotiations until United States firms had a chance to bid on the contract; the Department of Commerce took the matter to the private firms; and the navy helped by entering into negotiations with the Venezuelan navy for communications between the two countries in times of crisis. The Venezuelan navy could be expected to oppose a German-controlled radio network for military communications. All America Cables won the radio concession in 1925.[24]

All America was able to maintain a privileged position somewhat longer in Central America. Here, the company had never been anxious to exert itself on behalf of other American interests, although trade suffered from a lack of communications facilities. Americans in Guatemala had to resort to the department for pressure on the cable company to increase its services. All America Cables engaged in halfhearted conversations with the Guatemalan government until it learned that the United Fruit and its subsidiary, Tropical Radio, were thinking of buying the government's radio station. Suddenly energetic, the cable company resumed its talks with the government, and this time it succeeded in making arrangements for direct service from the capital to the coast.[25]

The final breakdown in cooperation between the State Department and American cable companies took place in 1922 and 1923 during a bitter battle with Portugal and Great Britain over cable-landing rights in the Azores. Commercial Cables and Western Union sought licenses to land cables in the islands. The British government, in behalf of Western Telegraph, complained that concessions to the Americans would violate rights of British citizens. After failing to pre-

[24] Instructions to Minister Cook, Mar. 1, 1923, RG 59, 831.74/82; Theodore Roosevelt, Jr., to SS, June 14, 1922, RG 80, 12479A-418:1; RG 59, 831.74/83; and RG 38, "Office of the Director of Naval Communications."

[25] In Consul Philip Holland's May 22, 1924, Minister Arthur H. Geissler's July 15, and Chargé Leon H. Ellis's, Nov. 7, RG 59, 814.73A115/15, 17, and 22.

vent the granting of concessions, it influenced the Portuguese legislature to encumber these with many onerous amendments. When Ambassador George B. Harvey complained about these maneuvers to the Foreign Office in June 1922, he was told, "as long as the American government continues to refuse to grant an operating permit for the line from Brazil to Florida via Barbados, this attitude is likely to continue." The British suggested that the companies get together on their own terms without government interference, promising to withdraw their objection upon the conclusion of an agreement. Hughes lodged a strong protest against British policy, pointing out the vast distinction between the United States taking action on its own soil and Great Britain dictating to the Portuguese government. United States representations to the British as well as to the Portuguese government continued through 1922 and 1923, with no success.[26]

The Department of Commerce was not satisfied with the State Department's efforts. United States trade with Europe depended upon rapid transatlantic communications. It was the view of Hoover's staff that "our whole European development is held up in the Azores." In their opinion, "neither that State Department nor the cable company has pushed the matter as far as it might have." The Commerce Department focused on the problem of establishing facilities adequate to the needs of United States trade.[27]

The American cable companies were in no mood to delay their expansion until the State Department had won its case against Great Britain. Contrary to the wishes of the department, Western Union and Commercial Cable entered into negotiations with Western Telegraph. To win over the Portuguese legislature, Commercial Cable offered to float a loan for Portugal in the American market. The department expressed its displeasure with the cable company's behavior by intimating that it would not be "over-zealous to sanction any Portuguese financial operations in America so long as Portugal held out so unjustifiably in the matter of granting the licenses." This did not deter Commercial Cable and the Ital-

---

[26] *Foreign Relations,* 1922, II, 360–61 and 383–91.
[27] RG 151, Box 2721, 543—Cables General.

ian cable company from admitting Western Telegraph to a
share in their proposed line from the United States through
the Azores to the Mediterranean. As soon as the British demands had been met, the Portuguese Parliament passed the
enabling legislation for the Commercial Cable and Western
Union concessions. These admitted only specified companies
for specified cables. The Department of State's insistence
upon equal treatment for all American interests in all situations was ignored. When the companies announced their
agreement, Minister Fred M. Dearing asked the department
whether he should continue his efforts with the Portuguese
on behalf of equal treatment for American interests and with
the British for an end of interference with American enterprises. He was instructed, rather petulantly, to refrain from
comment pending specific protest by an American company.
The government would no longer take the initiative in
protecting American cable interests. American firms, said
Hughes, "can accept less than equal treatment [if they wish
to, but they must] take the consequences."

So long as national interest coincided with their own, the
companies welcomed government intervention. Through
1921 the State Department wielded its powerful influence
in South America for the benefit of American companies,
enforcing its policy on the nations in the hemisphere, on
the intransigent British Western Telegraph Company, and
on American cable companies. But when the American
companies had achieved most of their objectives, they began
to chafe under government protection and struck out on their
own, undermining in the process the government's exertions
for the destruction of preferential and exclusive privileges
and the achievement of a worldwide "open-door" policy in
communications. This firm opposition to monopolistic concessions made the department a hindrance rather than a help
to American cable companies. The expansion of their facilities had reduced American dependence on foreign-controlled
cables, and they could now negotiate on an equal basis with
foreign companies almost anywhere in the world.[28]

[28] Fred M. Dearing to Harrison, Aug. 29, 1922; Frank L. Polk,
representing All America Cables and Commercial Cable to Harrison,
Jan. 12, and Dec. 1, Harrison papers; *Foreign Relations*, 1923, II, 305–6.

In 1923, the State Department, its patience worn out by the American companies' negative attitude and by their flouting of its policy, withdrew its support from the American companies except in the rare cases of denial of justice. The original objective of cable policy in Latin America had been achieved. By 1924, it was possible to send a message over American facilities to any country in the hemisphere. Once the basic objective was achieved, the State Department allowed the Commerce Department to take up the cudgels for United States communications interests abroad.[29]

The State Department had, as a result of the United States experience in the war, formulated clear objectives for its cable policy in Latin America. These were essentially strategic objectives. To the extent that these strategic objectives of the government coincided with the objectives of particular cable companies, the department was happy to support and even promote the interests of those companies. When the interests of the companies and the department did not coincide, the latter hewed rigidly to its predetermined objectives. Where the objectives of the government were not clear, as in general trade and investment policy, the department's behavior was not so consistent. There was a tendency, however, to restrict the support of the United States' commitments in the Western Hemisphere. In the vital areas of bank loans and petroleum, where the department's objectives were as clear as they were for cable policy, the formation and execution of policy followed the same pattern as in cable policy.

[29] For example, Hoover to SecNav, Nov. 21, 1923, RG 151, Box 2723, 544–General.

CHAPTER 7

Pointing the Way for a
Good Neighbor

When Charles Evans Hughes first entered the government, he had been content in most things to follow the path taken by the Wilson administration after the war. He accepted without question the strategic objectives defined by the Democrats in petroleum resources, bank loans, communications, and economic expansion; he followed through on Wilson's initial efforts to restrict the commitments of United States power in the Caribbean. His decisive, almost aggressive resolution of difficulties, so in keeping with his personality, was facilitated at the start of his administration by groundwork laid by his predecessors. As Hughes acquired experience in dealing with Latin America, he grew more confident. As he grew more confident, he grew more consistent. As he grew more consistent, he began to restate the principles of Latin American policy so that they would conform more closely to the basic precepts of Republican foreign policy.

Since the Republicans had rejected Wilsonian internationalism, it was logical to expect that their general pronouncements would depart in some respects from the policy that had received its first inspiration from Wilson and from Wilsonian supporters in the Department of State. The departures were largely rhetorical. They did not deflect the department from the course it set following the war. Continuities in Latin American policy were much more important than any discontinuities from one administration to the other. Hughes's basic problem was the same as Lansing's and Colby's: to formulate principles of policy flexible enough to protect America's hegemony in the hemisphere and the special situations in the Caribbean without producing the kind of involvement which had caused the United States to reduce several nations to protectorate status.

The secretary of state explained the basic principles of his policy, designed to govern relations with Latin America, in a series of formal speeches during 1923. Because the Republicans rejected Wilson's schemes for international organizations, Hughes made a point of correcting the Wilsonian interpretation of the Monroe Doctrine and Pan Americanism. Hughes saw in Pan Americanism elements of geographical propinquity, economic interdependence, and shared political values. He hoped Pan American cooperation would be achieved through the processes of reason, by discussion and mutual accommodation. The instruments of this cooperation would be meetings, conferences, and the various organizations created by the Pan American Union. The real accomplishments of these instruments, he told the American Bar Association in 1923, "are not to be found in any formal acts or statements but in the generation of helpful and friendly influences which draw people together through a better mutual understanding." Hughes simply denied that United States interventions contradicted the spirit of Pan Americanism. If the first pillar of Pan Americanism was independence, the second was stability. The United States was merely trying to create the conditions of stability and thus promote the foundations of Pan Americanism.[1]

Hughes subsequently offered an apologia for his policies at the Sixth Pan American Conference at Havana in 1928, justifying them by the demands of national security and by the practice of international law. After denying that the United States had any territorial ambitions in the hemisphere, he said:

[1] Hughes, "Observations on the Monroe Doctrine," *The Pathway of Peace* (New York, 1925), 113–41.

We simply wish peace and order and stability and recognition of honest rights properly acquired so that this hemisphere may not only be the hemisphere of peace but the hemisphere of international justice. . . . What are we to do when government breaks down and American citizens are in danger of their lives? Are we to stand by and see them butchered in the jungle because a Government in circumstances which it cannot control and for which it may not be responsible can no longer afford reasonable protection? . . . Now it is a principle of international law that in such a case a government is fully justified in taking action—I would call it inter-position of a temporary character—for the purpose of protecting the lives and property of its nationals. . . . Of course the United States cannot forgo its right to protect its citizens. . . . International law cannot be changed by resolutions of this conference. The rights of nations remain, but nations have duties as well as rights. . . .[2]

Hughes felt secure on grounds of international law. Even while speeding the withdrawal from the Caribbean protectorates, he insisted that law, order, and constitutional government follow in the wake of United States occupation. The rehabilitation of weak states must accompany the liquidation of imperialism so that they might be capable of self-government.

Hughes came closest to Wilson's thinking on Pan Americanism when he said that the Monroe Doctrine provided the basis for Pan American cooperation by establishing the independence and security of the American states. But he parted company with Wilson by going on to say that the Monroe Doctrine was a unilateral policy of the United States and that it would be used by the United States to prevent European encroachments in the Western Hemisphere. Hughes began to assert his interpretation of the Monroe Doctrine early in 1923. The first step was a memorandum, written at his re-

[2] Pusey, *Hughes,* 559–60; Hughes's speech before the Havana Chamber of Commerce, Feb. 4, 1928; Hughes to A. Lawrence Lowell, July 20, 1923, Hughes papers.

quest by Solicitor Charles C. Hyde, for the United States delegates to the Fifth Pan American Conference, to be held in Santiago, Chile. The memorandum, designed to anticipate problems that might arise at the conference and to offer tentative solutions to them, is notable for the absence of the spirit of cooperation.

> It is important to take note of the full extent of the claims of the United States under the Monroe Doctrine at the present time, and to observe the facts rather than the theories on which they rest. . . . It may be noted also that the United States is uninfluenced even by the willingness or desire of an American State to yield any transfer of its territory, or to permit any lodgement therein, or to submit to any form of political control or influence of a non-American State. Again, it seems important to bear in mind that in asserting the foregoing rights the United States has always been governed primarily by its own interests and that these concern in particular two distinct matters—(a) its own defense; and (b) its national prestige and distinctive position, rendering it as Secretary Olney declared in 1895 "practically sovereign on this continent." . . .
>
> The following suggestions are, therefore, submitted: In general, no arrangement should be entered into, or resolution concurred in, which could possibly be interpreted as curtailing in any way the full scope of the rights today asserted by the United States under the Monroe Doctrine. Thus there should be no opening for curtailment of those rights through acquiescence in any arrangement whereby an American State could at will accept even the slightest non-American control of its territory or independence. There should be no opening given to any non-American State through any Pan-American agreement to press for the slightest diminution of the rights now asserted by the United States. There should be no arrangement entered into, serving to encourage the League of Nations, to urge the United States to accept any restrictions of the rights now asserted by

it under the Monroe Doctrine. As to what could be appropriately accomplished by the Conference, subject to these limitations, no suggestion is offered.[3]

Hughes carried these sentiments to the public in his speech to the American Bar Association. Latin Americans were not impressed. They objected to the tone of benevolent paternalism that characterized Hughes's rhetoric, and they were bitterly disappointed with the United States attitude at Santiago. They wanted to make the Pan American movement a powerful political arm of equal, sovereign states. North Americans applauded Hughes's interpretation of the Monroe Doctrine, according greatest praise to what they understood as a promise to keep the United States out of European affairs. Only the *New York Times* editorialized about the inconsistency between United States protestations of brotherhood and interventions in the Caribbean.[4]

It was fitting that Hughes spent so much time in 1923 talking about the Monroe Doctrine. That year marked the centenary of President Monroe's message to Congress. By far the most important part of the centennial celebration was a major address on foreign policy which Hughes delivered to the Academy of Political and Social Science in Philadelphia, on November 30, 1923. He began by saying that the Monroe Doctrine was virtually unchanged from its original declaration. Then he surprised his audience by turning away from the doctrine with no more than an admission that it had value: "it simply states a principle of opposition to action by non-American powers." That night Hughes was not interested in defensive policies or opposition. He preferred to dwell on "affirmative policies relating to our own conduct in relation to other American states." He mentioned nine:

[3] Solicitor's memorandum, Feb. 24, 1923, RG 59, 710.11/586.

[4] Review of the Latin American press in the Samuel Guy Inman papers, LC. On press opinion in the United States: *Boston Evening Transcript,* Aug. 31, 1923, pt. I, 12:2; *Christian Science Monitor,* Aug. 31, 16:1; *New York Times,* Sept. 1, 10:2; C. E. Chapman, "A Monroe Doctrine Divided," *Political Science Quarterly,* 37 (1922), 75–82; Edward S. Corwin, "The Monroe Doctrine," *North American Review,* 218 (1923), 721–35.

First: recognition of the equality of the American Republics.

Second: respect for the territorial integrity of the Latin American Republics.

Third: support for the fundamental principle that states have duties as well as rights.

> Every State on being received into the family of nations accepts the obligations which are the essential conditions of international intercourse. Among these obligations is the duty of each State to respect the rights of citizens of other States which have been acquired within its jurisdiction in accordance with its laws. A confiscatory policy strikes not only at the interests of particular individuals but at the foundations of international intercourse, for it is only on the basis of the security of property validly possessed under the laws existing at the time of its acquisition that the conduct of activities in helpful cooperation are possible.

Fourth: assistance for promoting the stability of the Latin American Republics.

> In promoting stability we do not threaten independence, but seek to conserve it. We are not aiming at control, but endeavoring to establish self-control. We are not seeking to add to our territory or to impose our rule upon other peoples.

Fifth: establishment of a Pax Americana.

Sixth: encouragement for the limitation of armament.

Seventh: hope for mutually helpful cooperation.

Eighth: establishment of unconditional most-favored-nation treatment in customs matters.

> Not only does the Monroe Doctrine not mean that the United States has a policy of seeking in the Latin American Republics economic advantages denied to other countries but it is not the general policy of the United States to seek preferential rights.

Ninth: protection of certain special policies of the highest importance to the United States. Included in this category were the safety of the Panama Canal, peace in the Caribbean, stability in Cuba.[5]

The final impression left by his speech was that the policy of the United States called for independence of action; that the United States was prepared to cooperate with the other nations of the hemisphere; but that it insisted upon the recognition of certain special responsibilities which it exercised in the hemisphere. The third, fourth, fifth, and ninth policies seemed to outline the conditions under which the United States might intervene in the affairs of other nations in the hemisphere. Hughes, the careful advocate, thought it wise to include these. As secretary of state, he exerted a great deal of energy trying to avoid situations that required intervention, but he would not give up the right to intervene. In this manner, he acknowledged that the reluctance to become involved had not yet been elevated to the same level as the nine principles of action or policies. As with the speech to the American Bar Association, the press gave primary attention to the passages in which Hughes spoke of the independence of the United States and of the separation of the Western Hemisphere from Europe.[6]

Hughes denied that any one of his nine affirmative policies was not consistent with all of the others. He based this upon the propositions in international law that confiscatory acts

[5] Reprinted in *The Pathway of Peace,* 142–63.

[6] *New York Times,* Dec. 1, 1:8; Dec. 2, II, 6:3–4; *Boston Evening Transcript,* Dec. 1, pt. I, 4:3; *Atlanta Constitution,* Dec. 1, 1:1; *Christian Science Monitor,* Dec. 1, 1:7–8; *Washington Post,* Dec. 1, 1:2; Dec. 2, pt. II, 2:1–2. Using the distinction in Ernest R. May, "The Nature of Foreign Policy: The Calculated versus the Axiomatic," *Daedalus* (fall 1962), 651–67, nonintervention at this time was a calculated policy; preservation of stability in the Caribbean was an axiomatic policy which might take precedence in a crisis. It is suggestive, also, to analyze the disparities between American hegemony in the Caribbean and in South America in terms of the distinction between formal empire—control exercised in political or constitutional terms—and informal empire—control exercised in terms of influence gained through trade, investment, migration, or culture, as put forward in John Gallagher and Ronald Robinson, "The Imperialism of Free Trade," *The Economic History Review,* 2nd ser., VI (1953), 1–15.

were irresponsible and that instability in one country might jeopardize the safety of other countries. Unstable or irresponsible nations did not merit equal treatment. If his defense seemed harsh, Hughes felt the United States had softened it by sincere efforts to "liquidate imperialism" in the hemisphere. In Mexico and Cuba, this meant an effort to avoid formal intervention. In Haiti and the Dominican Republic, where the United States already had troops, it was an effort to end or at least reduce the existing intervention.

The greatest part of the Philadelphia speech dealt with political or juridical relations among nations. At least one of the nine policies, the eighth, dealt directly with economic matters. Hughes considered the Monroe Doctrine itself the guide for United States economic policy. The Monroe Doctrine was synonymous with the "open door" and its corollaries of equal opportunity and reciprocity, the main themes of United States economic foreign policy in Latin America. Assistant Secretary of State J. Butler Wright summarized United States economic foreign policy in 1925 with a quote from a speech by Hughes. He told the Foreign Trade Convention in Seattle: "Our policy rests on the conviction that given an equal opportunity abroad, fair and equal dealing, American businessmen can take care of themselves." Wright went on to state unequivocally that the Department of State would not claim exclusive advantages for American citizens abroad nor would it sponsor private interests. The policy of the United States government was to assure protection to legitimate American interests and to work for equal opportunity in foreign countries.

This policy was the result of seven years of experience with expanding United States influence in foreign markets. At the end of World War I, it became a part of official policy to encourage foreign trade and investment by United States citizens. Specifically, the government energetically sought to expand communications facilities under American control, to win control over foreign petroleum reserves, and to replace European bankers with United States bankers as arbiters of the Latin American money market. By 1925, these objectives had been achieved, and the Department of State could afford to assume a less aggressive position with regard to United States private interests abroad and to insist on no greater advantage for Americans than equal opportunity.

The United States achieved its major financial objective in Latin America almost at the moment it was formulated. Europe did not have the capital to regain its position of influence in Latin America. Americans supplanted European financial interests by default. Thereafter, the concern of the government was with the economic and not with the strategic aspects of bank loans. The State Department intended the Statement on Loans of March 3, 1922 as an informal and flexible check against the possibility that contemplated loan issues might run counter to some governmental policy or aim. As Americans secured their financial paramountcy in the hemisphere, the Department of State grew increasingly reluctant to be involved in loan negotiations. Time after time, it denied that it was the policy of the United States government to defend bankers in their negotiations with foreign governments or to provide unusual protection for United States investments abroad. The most the State Department would do, even in cases of obvious denial of justice, was to send a cable of inquiry and charge it to the bank or individual requesting aid. The principle behind the Statement on Loans remained fixed until the depression. Secretary of State Stimson explained loan policy in 1932 with virtually the same words Hughes used a decade earlier:

> The Department of State has not passed on the security or the merits of foreign loans . . . and the public has been made to understand that the department's action carried no implications as to government approval of loans. In fact, it may be said that no foreign loan has ever been made which purported to have the approval of the American Government as to the intrinsic value of the loan.[7]

[7] Quoted in Winkler, *Foreign Bonds,* 163–65; Anderson diary, Sept. 18, 1925, on loan to Argentina by Blair and Co.; Dec. 1925 and Sept. 1926, on loan to Yugoslavia; and Sept. 28, 1926, on loan to Rio de Janeiro.

As credit became easier during the 1920s, bankers did not bother to complain of the State Department's lack of interest in their activities. Nor did they make a great effort to comply with the spirit of the government's policy. By 1925, there was less contact between bankers and the State Department than there had been in 1918 or in 1921.

Relations between the Department of State and cable companies, banks, and petroleum companies doing business abroad formed similar patterns. In the quest for petroleum, cooperation between the public and private sectors was born of a profound fear that the United States was being squeezed out of the world petroleum market by a British plot and that United States domestic reserves were close to depletion. Anxiety in the United States reached a peak in 1923 when the Netherlands East Indies granted a concession to a subsidiary of the Shell Oil Company and the United States Congress retaliated by refusing a concession in public lands to another Shell subsidiary, the Roxana Petroleum Company. The bogey of imminent exhaustion of domestic reserves faded as new discoveries within the United States promised an ample oil supply in the foreseeable future. Suspicions of the existence of an oil monopoly from which the United States was excluded gradually grew dim, and the large international oil companies of all nationalities came together in a network of understandings. The policy of expansion begun after the war was too successful. By 1924, excess storage of crude oil drove prices down, and the industry had to work feverishly to liquidate the results of its overproduction. As the need for petroleum reserves outside the United States became less desperate, the Department of State became correspondingly less eager to defend the interests of American petroleum companies. The department seems to have retreated from its aggressive position by the end of 1922, even before the public anxiety and hostility had reached a peak.[8]

[8] Feis, *Petroleum and American Foreign Policy*, 11; *Boston Evening Transcript*, Mar. 19, 1923, 12:3; Apr. 17, 11:3; *New York Times,* Mar. 20, 23:3; Kemnitzer, *Rebirth of Monopoly*, 53; Edward Meade Earle, "Oil and American Policy," *The New Republic* (Aug. 20, 1924), 355; *Oil and Gas Journal*, vol. 23, no. 29 (Dec. 11, 1924), 28; no. 30 (Dec. 18), 24; no. 32 (Jan. 1, 1925), 20; no. 34 (Jan. 15), 24.

The United States reached the goal in communications last. The State Department broke the British monopoly over cables on the east coast of South America in 1921 and almost immediately withdrew from participation in the competition between British and American cable interests. Cooperation between the government and the private companies broke down as soon as the companies realized that the government was no longer willing to secure special privileges for them and would stand firmly on its policy of the "open door."

By 1923, securing the strategic objectives and loyalty to the "open door" had dulled the edge of the State Department's enthusiasm for using diplomatic pressure to advance the fortunes of private American interests. When the department adhered firmly to its principles, American cable companies, banks, and oil companies found that it was no longer in their interest to be ruled by the Department of State. They gave up the department's support in order to pursue policies of their own. The Department of State was, by March 1925, far more aloof from commercial affairs than it had been at any time since the war. Even in such previously important situations as a loan to Nicaragua, financial legislation in Cuba, and petroleum in Venezuela, the department confined its interposition to diplomatic representations against the denial of justice to American nationals. The disposition to avoid entanglements reached beyond the Caribbean and included commercial as well as political affairs. Each decision to remain neutral in a dispute between American nationals and Latin American governments was easier after 1923 because the way had been cleared for an American-controlled network of communications in the hemisphere, the fear of a petroleum shortage no longer disturbed Americans, the Latin American capital needs were being met in the United States, and Americans were taking a rapidly growing share of Latin American trade. By the same token, the desire to avoid intervention could more easily be accorded priority over the need to reform political conditions in unstable nations because the threat of European intervention and the danger to United States security had virtually disappeared and because the United States repeatedly failed to impose its will on one or another of the protectorates.

Despite the bitter Republican attacks on Wilson's foreign policy, no major changes in Latin American policy were made immediately after March 1921. One significant factor behind this was the continuity of personnel in the Latin American Division, the Office of the Foreign Trade Adviser, and the Solicitor's Office. Experienced drafting officers had a tendency to perpetuate preestablished patterns of action unless specifically ordered to change. Generally, the secretary and the assistant secretaries left even crucial decisions on policy to these men and followed their advice.

For the most part, changes in the conduct of foreign affairs immediately after March 1921 were attributable to the personality and style of Charles Evans Hughes. Hughes was far more direct than Colby or Lansing in negotiating the settlement of Central American boundary disputes and the resumption of relations with Mexico or in making representations in defense of American property rights. At first, he appeared more willing to commit the prestige of the government to the solution of commercial and political disputes. He sharpened the definition of the principles of reciprocity and the "open door" to guide the department in attaining its economic objectives. These served not only to justify the expansion of United States influence in the Western Hemisphere but also to set the requirements for government support in economic matters all over the world. Americans, as well as other nationals, were asked to satisfy these requirements.

In setting forth the Latin American policy of the United States in his major speeches of 1923, Secretary Hughes protested that the United States had no intention of compromising the sovereignty of any nation by intervention. At the same time, he made it clear that he felt, that in the Caribbean area, the United States had certain rights under international law and certain peculiar responsibilities which permitted or required the exertion of United States power in the hemisphere. At the Havana Conference in 1928, he referred to this form of intervention as "interposition of a temporary character." On the surface, this policy seems no different from the policy of every administration since Theodore Roosevelt. The difference was that the war and the struggle for the peace had generated considerable sentiment within the United States in opposition to the exercise of responsibility in world affairs and to imperialism in Latin America. Before he left office, Wilson had been anxious to place hemispheric relations on the same plane with the massive effort to save the world for democracy. He lost faith in the efficacy of foreign democracy and constitutionalism for the peoples of the Caribbean. All too often, the presence of United States troops and advisers had failed to produce the expected economic and political progress. In crisis after crisis, from 1918 to 1925, the Department of State conscientiously avoided assuming a position from which it could not retreat. At times, the drive to secure the strategic objectives in oil, bank loans, and cables made it difficult to exercise the necessary restraint, but once the objectives were achieved, economic policy reinforced the disposition to avoid foreign entanglements. Older, more traditional policy objectives, such as the effort to supervise the Cuban elections of 1920 or to impose financial reforms on Guatemala and Nicaragua, required diplomatic interference and constant pressure by the United States government, but generally, the pressure was not allowed to get out of control.

Hughes's tenure as secretary of state was not free of interventions. While he was in office, United States Marines landed in Honduras to restore order. This was his only major intervention, and its circumstances help to define Hughes's Latin American policy. For over a year, he refused to be drawn into the political debate raging in Honduras and bent every effort to keep the other Central American nations out. He even rejected two Honduran requests for mediation and an appeal from the American minister for a warship to protect American lives. Hughes approved the landing of troops in 1924 only after his naval advisers on the scene insisted it was necessary to prevent chaos and after his political advisers in Washington had convinced him that the breakdown of public order in Honduras would precipitate hostilities throughout

Central America, endanger the Panama Canal, and lead to unnecessary bloodshed.[9]

At the same time that he ordered marines ashore in Honduras, Hughes ordered the State Department's most prestigious Latin American expert, Sumner Welles, to Tegucigalpa to compose the differences among the various political factions and to call a general meeting of Central American leaders in an attempt to end the bickering among the small republics. His desire to keep the United States intervention within limits was demonstrated by the repeated instructions to the United States minister in Tegucigalpa and to the commander of the Special Squadron that "the sole purpose of the force sent is to protect American lives." The marines were withdrawn as soon as Welles had negotiated a settlement among the Honduran political leaders. When the agreement was violated, Hughes refused to do more than press verbally for adhesion to its terms.

Hughes gave another demonstration of his qualities during the difficulties following the Nicaraguan elections of 1924. Nicaragua was of special interest to the United States. The most desirable route for an alternate isthmian canal ran through Nicaraguan territory, and the United States had committed itself to the route in the Bryan-Chamorro Treaty. United States prestige had been committed to the stability of Nicaragua in 1913 by the placement of a legation guard of marines in the country and again in the reorganization of the nation's finances under the financial plans of 1917 and 1920.

The canal treaty, the financial plans, and the marines proved insufficient to create political stability in Nicaragua. Rather than permit its involvement in Nicaraguan affairs to increase, the policy of the United States after World War I was to work for order through moral suasion. Intervention was avoided. The strongest diplomatic measure employed was nonrecognition of unconstitutional governments. In 1920, the

---

[9] RG 80, 8480–98 traces the decision to intervene; *Foreign Relations,* 1923, II, 424–49; 1924, II, 300–24; George Navarrete, "The Latin American Policy of Charles Evans Hughes, 1921–1925," Ph.D. dissertation, University of California, Berkeley, 1968, 68–113.

United States withheld recognition from the revolutionary
government of Diego Chamorro until the latter had promised
to hold elections in 1924. The Nicaraguan opposition maintained that the United States was obligated to insure free
elections, just as it did in the Dominican Republic. Secretary
Colby denied this. Secretary Hughes followed the lead of his
predecessor by inducing Chamorro to invite Dr. Harold W.
Dodds, secretary of the National Municipal League, to re-
write the electoral laws of the nation. The Dodds mission
was prompted by the belief that a popularly elected government could maintain order and thus make it possible for the
United States to withdraw the legation guard, much as the
Crowder mission to Cuba had helped prevent intervention
there.[10]

President Chamorro died in 1923 and was succeeded by
Vice President Martínez. Martínez immediately began to
make a mockery out of Dr. Dodds's new electoral laws. First,
he announced that he would be a candidate for president in
the elections of 1924. This was an obvious violation of the
Nicaraguan constitution. United States Minister John Ramer
and the Nicaraguan opposition asked Secretary Hughes to
protest the Martínez candidacy. Hughes was reluctant to become more involved and took the position that the Nicaraguans were as capable of interpreting their constitution as
was any officer of the State Department. He admitted to
Ramer, in confidence, that he was dismayed by Martínez'
decision. In direct violation of his instructions, Ramer made
the secretary's views known to the Nicaraguan government.

Once his position had been exposed, Hughes decided to
stand by it. Martínez ultimately withdrew his candidacy, but
he substituted an official candidate, Carlos Solórzano, and
continued with his systematic destruction of the safeguards
against political manipulation which the electoral law had
tried to establish. The elections of October 5, 1924 were
notoriously fraudulent. As soon as they were over, Martínez
declared a state of siege, maintained strict military rule for
two weeks, suspended communications, and imprisoned many

[10] Juan B. Sacasa and S. Calderón to Colby, Dec. 24, and Colby to
Minister Jefferson, Dec. 15, 1920, RG 59, 817.00/2745 and 2758.

who might have expressed dissatisfaction with the Solórzano regime. The State Department informed the Nicaraguan government that the new administration would be recognized only if it promised to hold honest elections in 1928. This measure, as a deterrent against unconstitutional behavior, was no longer of any value. The Solórzano government freely gave the promises which it intended, just as freely, to ignore.

In accepting the promises and recognizing Solórzano, Hughes made a calculated decision that it was better to allow the resumption of orderly, although unconstitutional, government in Nicaragua than to prevent it and precipitate another civil war. He felt his primary responsibility was to peace in Central America in general and to the reduction of United States commitments in the area to a level in keeping with the nation's hemispheric concerns. If the new government were permitted to take office, the United States could proceed with the evacuation of the legation guard. If Hughes tried to exert greater pressure on the Nicaraguan government, the presence of the guard and the nature of the political opposition in Nicaragua would mean certain disorder and greater involvement for the United States. He contented himself with the promise of free elections in 1928 and an agreement to establish a national constabulary, never fooling himself that the desires for democratic government in Nicaragua had been fulfilled. This withdrawal from responsibility in the political sphere went hand in hand with the parallel withdrawal from responsibility for Nicaragua's financial affairs.

Partial intervention or diplomatic interposition employing threats was untenable unless the tendency to extend the intervention was kept firmly in check. Hughes provided that control so long as he remained in office. The United States legation guard left Nicaragua in August 1925. Within three months, Emiliano Chamorro, the disappointed candidate in 1924, began trouble by ousting his Liberal opponents. In May 1926, the Liberals struck back and removed Chamorro from office. On several occasions that year, United States Marines landed from their ships to neutralize the port of Bluefields. In January 1927, the marines reestablished the legation guard and spread their pacifying mission to the west coast. By February 1927, Rear Admiral Julian L. Latimer, commander of the Special Squadron, had ordered the entire railroad from Corinto to Managua neutralized, and the affair had become a full-scale intervention for the marines. Secretary of State Kellogg could not grasp the subtleties of Hughes's policy, nor had he the same energy in controlling the interventionist representatives of his government in the field.[11]

Hughes's careful balance of pressure and influence worked to perfection in United States relations with Mexico and collapsed as soon as he left office. Closer to the United States than any other Latin American nation, Mexico had always presented the most difficult problems for the Department of State because United States–Mexican relations so easily became part of domestic politics. Wilson and Colby had established the terms on which the United States would resume relations with the Obregón regime. Hughes adopted the same terms and reached an agreement with Mexico in 1923. The preliminary treaty between the two countries provided for recognition of the Mexican government and for bilateral negotiations on the many outstanding claims and disputes. While these negotiations dragged on for months without significant progress, Mexico seemed to backslide into the same kind of disorder that had nearly precipitated intervention in 1919. United States citizens were abducted; provincial governors expropriated bona fide American businesses; groups of local bandits terrorized the countryside; and the central government continued to threaten United States oil companies with confiscatory taxation. The tension between the two nations was excruciating, and the Mexican Division of the State Department urged the secretary to deal more sternly with the Mexicans. In a similar situation in 1919, Robert Lansing had acceded to the wishes of his Mexican Division

[11] *Foreign Relations,* 1924, II, 487–509; 1925, II, 618–46; 1926, II, 780–823; Greer, "Charles Evans Hughes and Nicaragua"; and "State Department Policy in Regard to the Nicaraguan Election of 1924," *HAHR,* 34 (1954); Floyd Cramer, *Our Neighbor Nicaragua* (New York, 1929); William Kamman, *A Search for Stability, United States Diplomacy Toward Nicaragua, 1925–1933* (Notre Dame, Ind., 1968); Neill Macauley, *The Sandino Affair* (Chicago, 1967); Navarrete, 115–43.

and had delivered an ultimatum to the Mexicans. Hughes spurned that course. So long as he was secretary of state, the United States maintained a proper attitude toward the internal affairs of Mexico. He gave every possible encouragement to the central government during the violent uprising of 1924 and angrily refused to use the disorder as an excuse to "set things right" south of the border. The diary of Chandler Anderson, who was spokesman for numerous interests in favor of intervention, reveals the frustration which advocates of a "hard line" felt in the face of the imperturbable secretary of state. Anderson kept up a constant barrage of protests on behalf of his clients. But Hughes stood fast and was able to hand over to his successor unbroken relations with Mexico.[12]

With Hughes out of office, the interventionists found they could make headway through Ambassador James R. Sheffield. Sheffield was no diplomat, and he had no sympathy for the group ruling Mexico. He restrained himself until Kellogg took office, and then he added his voice to the chorus calling for intervention. Kellogg made the mistake of giving his ambassador free rein. Sheffield proceeded to bring relations between the two nations to the verge of rupture. A final break was averted only at the cost of much ill will.

Hughes had tried to formulate a flexible policy to govern relations with the entire hemisphere, not just with the Caribbean protectorates; to justify the formal assumption of control over the internal affairs of unstable nations whenever such responsibilities could not be shunned; and to establish the guidelines for exerting the precise amount of influence necessary to protect America's new interests in the hemisphere without giving undue offense to Latin Americans.

[12] Memoranda by M. E. Hanna, July 7, 1922, Harrison papers; and Feb. 28, 1923, Fletcher papers; *Foreign Relations*, 1924, II, 428–38; Phillips diary, Mar. 14, 1924. Anderson diary, May 1922 through Mar. 1927, records protests of companies trying to do business in Mexico. Mexican point of view in A. Manero Suárez and J. Paniagua Arredondo, *Los Tratados de Bucareli*, 2 vols. (Mexico, 1958); Lorenzo Meyer, *México y los Estados Unidos en el Conflicto Petrolero (1917–1942)* (Mexico, 1968), chap. 5; Luis G. Zorrilla, *Historia de las Relaciones Entre Mexico y los Estados Unidos de America, 1800–1958*, 2 vols. (Mexico, 1966), chaps. 6 and 7.

After the war, the United States had to adjust to a new status in Latin America; it acted virtually without interference from European nations. As the State Department came to understand the nature of America's postwar hemispheric hegemony, and as the strategic objectives were secured, it had less cause to project itself into international disputes which threatened to entangle the nation. With Wilson's idealism and Hughes's firm leadership, the Department of State slowly learned to use the nation's power with greater subtlety—to strike a balance between pressure and influence so that it would not be necessary to assume formal control to secure policy objectives or to protect the nation's interests. As the United States assumed a predominant position in the hemisphere, Latin Americans reacted by trying to restrict United States political influence in order to maintain their independence. They fought for a stronger Pan American movement. Wilson was sympathetic to their efforts; Hughes was not. He defended America's independence of action. Although in matters of daily relations he would compromise a great deal, he would not be pushed, and he would not give up the theoretical basis for his actions.[13]

It must detract from Hughes's achievement that, having recognized the need to improve hemispheric relations, having accepted and extended Wilson's postwar antipathy to protectorates, and having perceived the end of the threat of European intervention in hemispheric affairs, Hughes did not proceed to declare unequivocally that nonintervention was a policy of the United States. The Department of State continued to reserve the right under international law to interpose the authority of the United States government in the affairs of other nations. It was not until 1936 at the Buenos Aires Conference that the United States formally renounced that right and acknowledged the juridical equality of all sov-

[13] L. Ethan Ellis, *Frank B. Kellogg and American Foreign Relations, 1925–1929* (New Brunswick, N. J., 1961), 23–37; and *Republican Foreign Policy, 1921–1933* (New Brunswick, N. J., 1968), 240; Navarrete, 284–326. Withdrawal from Cuba, Haiti, and the Dominican Republic discussed in Tulchin, "Dollar Diplomacy and Non-Intervention: The Latin American Policy of the United States, 1919–1924," Ph.D. dissertation, Harvard University, 1964; 1–32, and 59–86.

ereign states. Without such an explicit principle or axiom of policy, Hughes's example could only point the way for future leaders. Each administration had to learn for itself the sad lessons of intervention; each had to calculate anew the precise amount of power required to achieve its goals without being saddled with unwanted responsibilities. Kellogg learned from his experiences in Mexico and Nicaragua. Stimson learned faster because of Kellogg's mistakes and because of his own experiences in Nicaragua. It was easier for him to avoid entangling commitments, also, because of pressure from Japan and the Hoover administration's intense preoccupation with domestic affairs. Even the Roosevelt administration experimented with limited intervention in Cuba, only to pull up short of military occupation at the last moment. Finally, during the presidency of Franklin Roosevelt, the United States came to understand that in order to avoid intervention in the internal affairs of other nations, it was necessary to accept the Latin American interpretation of the rights of nations and the principle of equal sovereignty among nations. This acceptance by itself could not end international tensions, but it did provide the basis for mutual understanding and the hope for meaningful cooperation in the hemisphere.

A Note on Sources

I. MANUSCRIPT MATERIALS

The quantity of United States government records for the war period is staggering. Many organizations participated in the foreign relations of the United States and each left a mountain of paper as a legacy to scholars. The country files of the "General Records of the Department of State," National Archives Record Group 59, are the most important source, but on any major policy issue it is necessary to consult the files of other departments and boards deposited in the National Archives, and the private papers of important figures, housed in libraries across the country. The files of the War Trade Board, Record Group 182, are voluminous, well indexed, and easy to use, although information on Latin America is scattered through more than a hundred different boxes. They contain sufficient correspondence with the Shipping Board, the War Industries Board, and other government agencies to understand the relations of the United States with the neutral nations of Latin America as well as the administrative confusion which often embarrassed those relations.

To deal properly with the financial problems arising from the war, it is necessary to consult Record Group 56, the "General Records of the Department of the Treasury, Correspondence of the Secretary of the Treasury," or Record Group 39, the "General Records of the Department of the Treasury, Bureau of Accounts." The latter also is a useful supplement to the State Department records on loan negotiations with individual countries. Military records in the National Archives, unhappily, are not so accessible as the others. The "Records of the Department of the Navy" contain information not found elsewhere and warrant the extra

effort it takes to use them. The "Records of the General Board,"
deposited in the Old Naval Gun Factory, contain some interesting
war plans. The "Records of the Office of Naval Intelligence,"
Record Group 38; the "Collection of the Office of Naval Records
and Library," Record Group 45; and the "Correspondence of the
Secretary of the Navy," Record Group 80, are a rich supplement
to the State Department records to document the growing wartime concern over communications facilities, petroleum resources,
and bank loans in the hemisphere, as well as United States relations with its protectorates in the Caribbean. Only the most formal State Department communications concerning Latin America
are published in Department of State, *Papers Relating to the
Foreign Relations of the United States, 1861–* (Washington:
Government Printing Office, 1861–). For this reason the
unpublished records take on added importance.

The archival materials are easier to use for the period after
the war. The international activities of the War Trade Board
and other agencies passed to the Department of State. Furthermore, the Treasury Department seemed to lose interest in financial foreign policy after 1921, and there is very little of value
either in the secretary of the treasury's records or in the Bureau
of Accounts. As the Treasury Department retreated from the
limelight, Hoover brought the Commerce Department forward.
The "Records of the Bureau of Foreign and Domestic Commerce," Record Group 151, are just as important as the State
Department records for an understanding of the rivalry between
the two departments. The Commerce Department records con-
firm the findings in the State Department papers that the latter
controlled cable and petroleum policy, whereas the former
gradually assumed control over commercial and financial matters.
The fight over the International High Commission is in the
State Department records and the records of the commissions,
filed along with the "Records of the Preliminary Conference on
International Communications" in Record Group 43, "Records
of the United States Participation in International Conferences,
Commissions, and Expositions." The Navy Department records
are a very useful supplement to the State Department papers on
matters pertaining to petroleum, cables, competition with Great
Britain, policy toward the several Caribbean protectorates, and
gradual acceptance of a policy of nonintervention.

None of the prominent figures whose private papers are open to
scholars spent much time during the war worrying about Latin
America. The papers of John Barrett, in the Library of Congress, are an obvious exception, but Barrett was held in such low
esteem by government officials that his correspondence is useful
mainly for the insight it provides into Latin American thinking.

The Chandler P. Anderson diary, also in the Library of Congress, complements the official records of the negotiations with Chile over the shipment of nitrate of soda. The William Phillips diary, in the Houghton Library of Harvard University, has a few comments on governmental organization during the war, as does the Frank L. Polk diary, in the E. M. House Collection, Yale University. Also in the House Collection, the papers of Gordon Auchincloss contain important memoranda on intragovernmental cooperation. Auchincloss was Undersecretary Polk's representative on many wartime liaison committees.

Many different private manuscript collections have information on individual postwar problems. The Anderson diary covers many Central American boundary disputes because Anderson represented several of the countries in Washington. The papers of Norman H. Davis, in the Library of Congress, contain vital correspondence on the changes in United States policy toward Cuba. The papers of Henry P. Fletcher, also in the Library of Congress, are good for Mexican policy. Polk's papers contain a fairly complete file on United States relations with Costa Rica and some interesting material on Mexico and the Dominican Republic.

Formulating policy after the war was complicated by difficulties within the Department of State and differences between Wilson and Secretary Lansing. Breckinridge Long and Wilbur J. Carr kept diaries, now in the Library of Congress, in which they note fairly objective versions of the breakdown within the department. Polk's diary comments on the administrative chaos through which the department suffered before Colby was appointed. The papers of Robert Lansing, in the Library of Congress, which are generally disappointing, contain some private memoranda which reveal that the secretary understood the president's enmity for him, but waited for the right moment to resign. The papers of Bainbridge Colby and of Woodrow Wilson, in the Library of Congress, contain the correspondence between Colby and the president in which the decisions were made to change policy, and are of use in demonstrating Wilson's control over his secretary of state. The papers of Paul M. Warburg, in the Yale University Library, supplement the Treasury and State Department records on financial policy. Warburg exchanged views with nearly every man of importance in the world of finance.

The difficult period of transition between two different political administrations can be followed in the papers of several professional diplomats. The diaries and correspondence of such men as Wilbur J. Carr, Henry P. Fletcher, Leland Harrison, in the Library of Congress, and of William Phillips, also explain the "family feeling" that existed in the diplomatic corps and demonstrate how continuity of personnel was so important in the continuity of policy. Harrison and Fletcher were central figures in the "family" of bachelors that lived in 1718 H Street, Northwest. Their private correspondence reveals, as no formal memorandum or policy statement can, the wide circle of friends who staffed the subcabinets of the Wilson and Harding administrations. Chandler Anderson's diary and the private memoranda of Robert Lansing document the continuity of personnel and of policy from another, more critical point of view.

The papers of Charles Evans Hughes, in the Library of Congress, are as disappointing as they are extensive. The Biographical Notes, dictated when Hughes had retired from the Supreme Court, have a dry, official sound, although they constitute an invaluable source. They are to be edited for publication with an Introduction by Joseph S. Tulchin and David J. Danelski. The famous Beeritz memoranda are syntheses of obvious secondary materials and very little data from the private papers of the secretary of state. The papers themselves contain very little that sheds light on the personality of the man or his policies. The papers of Dwight W. Morrow, in Amherst College, are much richer than the larger collection of Hughes's papers. Morrow played a vital, if unofficial, role in United States policy toward Cuba from 1920 to 1925, by virtue of his close relationship with General Enoch Crowder, special representative of the president and then ambassador to Cuba. Morrow was a partner in J. P. Morgan and Company, which did most of Cuba's financing during the period Crowder was on the island. What Morrow's papers do not reveal about the banking world, they do tell about the formulation of a nonintervention policy with regard to Cuba. Criticisms of the Hughes policies can be found in the Barrett papers and in the papers of Samuel Guy Inman, in the Library of Congress.

II. MEMOIRS AND BIOGRAPHIES

Memoirs and biographies of statesmen, by and large, are not helpful. For the period of the war, one, Josephus Daniels, *The Wilson Era. Years of War and After 1917–1923* (Chapel Hill, N. C.: University of North Carolina Press, 1946), does touch on a number of relevant subjects. Daniels was a passionate Wilsonian, and as secretary of the navy he had a voice in the formulation of policy toward the Caribbean protectorates. Frank Freidel, *Frank D. Roosevelt,* 2 vols. (Boston: Little, Brown, 1952–54) gives a good picture of the navy during the war. Others which contain tidbits of information are William Phillips, *Ventures in Diplomacy* (privately printed, 1952); William G. McAdoo, *Crowded Years*

(Boston: Houghton Mifflin, 1931); and Bernard M. Baruch, *The Public Years* (New York: Holt, Rinehart and Winston, 1960). F. M. Huntington Wilson recounts the origins of dollar diplomacy in *Memoirs of an Ex-Diplomat* (Boston: Bruce Humphries, 1945). There is no first-rate biography of Robert Lansing. Julius W. Pratt, "Robert Lansing," in S. F. Bemis, ed., *The American Secretaries of State and Their Diplomacy,* 10 vols. (New York: Alfred A. Knopf, 1927–29) X, 47–175, is no more than a sketch; Daniel M. Smith, *Robert Lansing and American Neutrality, 1914–1917* (Berkeley: University of California Press, 1958), is better. For information on Woodrow Wilson, one must go to the work of Arthur S. Link. His *Wilson,* 5 vols. (Princeton, N. J.: Princeton University Press, 1947–   ) now reaches the neutrality period. Rather different views of Wilson are presented in John M. Blum, *Woodrow Wilson and the Politics of Morality* (Boston: Little, Brown, 1956); and Cary T. Grayson, *Woodrow Wilson: An Intimate Memoir* (New York: Holt, Rinehart and Winston, 1959). Grayson was Wilson's personal physician. The period immediately after the war is practically a blank. Everyone seems anxious to write about the league. An exception, Bainbridge Colby, *The Close of Woodrow Wilson's Administration and the Final Years* (New York: Mitchell Kennerly, 1930), is eulogistic. Such efforts as John Spargo, "Bainbridge Colby," in Bemis, ed., *The American Secretaries of State,* X, 179–218, and Katharine Crane, *Mr. Carr of State* (New York: St. Martin's Press, 1960), are of little value. Daniel M. Smith, "Aftermath of War: Bainbridge Colby and Wilsonian Diplomacy 1920–1921," *Memoirs of the American Philosophical Society,* 80 (May 1970) should help to fill the gap. There is a biography of Norman H. Davis, undersecretary of state in 1920, Harold B. Whiteman, Jr., "Norman H. Davis and the Search for International Peace and Security, 1917–1944," unpublished Ph.D. dissertation, Yale University, 1958.

The principles of Charles Evans Hughes's foreign policies are explained most clearly in the secretary's own public speeches. The most important of these are collected in *The Pathway of Peace* (New York: Harper and Brothers, 1925). Another important speech, "The Centenary of the Monroe Doctrine," is in *The Annals,* Supplement to vol. CXI (January 1924), 7–19. There are a number of biographies of Hughes, none of which really answers any questions about his Latin American policies. The most famous is Merlo J. Pusey, *Charles Evans Hughes,* 2 vols. (New York: Macmillan, 1951). This prize-winning biography is of very little help for this study. Dexter Perkins, *Charles Evans Hughes and American Democratic Statesmanship* (Boston: Little, Brown, 1956), is an interpretative work that does not quite prove its thesis that Hughes was a great statesman with exceptional abilities who worked within the confines of public opinion. The sketches by Charles Cheney Hyde, "Charles Evans Hughes," in S. F. Bemis, ed., *The American Secretaries of State and Their Diplomacy,* X, 221–401, and John Chalmers Vinson, "Charles Evans Hughes," in Norman Graebner, ed., *An Uncertain Tradition. American Secretaries of State in the Twentieth Century* (New York: McGraw-Hill, 1961), 128–48, are short and perceptive. The most controversial attempt to explain Hughes's policies is Betty Glad, *Charles Evans Hughes and the Illusion of Innocence* (Urbana, Ill.: University of Illinois Press, 1966), a systematic application of political science and psychological techniques to the analysis of Hughes's personality and his policies. Its greatest flaw is that it relies almost exclusively on the official Hughes—his Biographical Notes and his speeches—and pays too little attention to the State Department papers and the actual conduct of foreign relations. There was a wide gap between the two. Hughes's Biographical Notes are still more useful than any of the biographies.

Willard L. Beaulac, *Career Ambassador* (New York: Macmillan, 1951), is the anecdotal memoir of a diplomat who served many years in Latin America. David A. Lockmiller, *Enoch H. Crowder Soldier, Lawyer, and Statesman, 1859–1932,* University of Missouri Studies, vol. XXVII (Columbia, 1955), is a pedestrian biography of the man who was responsible for carrying out the policy of nonintervention in Cuba from 1920 to 1925. Hughes's successor, Frank B. Kellogg has one full dress official biography, David Bryn-Jones, *Frank B. Kellogg* (New York: G. Putnam and Sons, 1937), and a historian of his administration, L. Ethan Ellis, *Frank B. Kellogg and American Foreign Relations* (New Brunswick, N. J.: Rutgers University Press, 1961). Ellis' chapters on Latin America are quite good, and his chapters on the difficulties in communication between Washington and the field are very much to the point.

III. SECONDARY SOURCES

The best survey of the war period is Link, *Woodrow Wilson and the Progressive Era, 1910–1917* (New York: Harper and Brothers, 1954), which also contains an extensive bibliographical essay. Background for Wilson's foreign policies is given in Harley Notter, *The Origins of the Foreign Policy of Woodrow Wilson* (Baltimore: The Johns Hopkins Press, 1934); Link, *Wilson the Diplomatist* (Baltimore: The Johns Hopkins Press, 1957); and Edward H. Buehrig, ed., *Wilson's Foreign Policy in Perspective* (Bloomington, Ind.: Indiana University Press, 1957).

The most competent survey of United States policy toward Latin America is still Bemis, *The Latin American Policy of the United States* (New York: Harcourt, Brace, 1943). Bemis had no use for what he called Wilson's "moral" foreign policy and said as much in "Woodrow Wilson and Latin America," reprinted in *American Foreign Policy and the Blessings of Liberty and Other Essays* (New Haven: Yale University Press, 1962).

Every student of inter-American relations owes a debt to the careful research of Dana G. Munro. His *Intervention and Dollar Diplomacy in the Caribbean, 1900–1921* (Princeton, N. J.: Princeton University Press, 1964) is a monument of careful scholarship. However, Munro, like Bemis, devotes very little attention to the problems of the war. Still, for the period up to 1917, there is no source more reliable than Munro's book. Wilfrid Hardy Callcott, *The Caribbean Policy of the United States, 1890–1920* (Baltimore: Johns Hopkins University Press, 1942), is now completely superseded. Studies of special aspects of United States Latin American policy are: Selig Adler, "Bryan and Wilsonian Caribbean Penetration," *Hispanic American Historical Review*, XX (1940), 198–226; C. H. Carlisle, "Woodrow Wilson's Pan American Pact," *Proceedings of the South Carolina Historical Association*, XIX (1949), 3–15; William S. Coker, "Dollar Diplomacy versus Constitutional Legitimacy," *Southern Quarterly*, VI (1968), 428–37; and J. A. S. Grenville, "Diplomacy and War Plans in the United States, 1890–1917," *Royal Historical Society—Transactions*, Series V, II (1961), 1–21.

There are a number of studies of the war which throw light on United States relations with Latin America. The most extensive is Benedict Crowell and Robert Forrest Wilson, *How America Went to War*, 6 vols. (New Haven: Yale University Press, 1921). Others are: Thomas A. Bailey, "The United States and the Blacklist During the Great War," *The Journal of Modern History*, VI (1934), 14–35; Bailey, *The Policy of the United States toward the Neutrals, 1917–1918* (Baltimore: The Johns Hopkins Press, 1942); James R. Mock and Cedric Larsen, *Words That Won the War* (Princeton: Princeton University Press, 1939), a rather exaggerated description of the value of the Committee on Public Information; Mock, "The Creel Committee in Latin America," *Hispanic American Historical Review*, XXIII (1942), 262–79. Richard Van Alstyne, "Private American Loans to the Allies, 1914–1916," *Pacific Historical Review*, II (1933), 180–93, is still useful, although it has been amended by Link's research and by G. Gaddis Smith, *Britain's Clandestine Submarines, 1914–1915* (New Haven: Yale University Press, 1964). Of the earlier studies, the data in Alexander D. Noyes, *The War Period of*

American Finance, 1908–1925 (New York: G. Putnam and Sons, 1926), is still valuable.

The comments of contemporaries on the impact of the war tended to focus on economic affairs. Businessmen and government officials point out the new opportunities which the war offered to United States business, or underline the problems that blocked the rapid expansion of inter-American trade during the European crisis. *The Annals* devotes two numbers to these problems: vol. LX (1915), *America's Interests as Affected by the European War* and vol. LXI (1915), *America's Interests After the European War*. It is the consensus of the contributors to these volumes, and of F. C. Schwedtman, "Lending Our Financial Machinery to Latin America," *The American Political Science Review*, XI (1917), 239–51, that the United States should do everything possible to seize the advantage presented by the war, that Latin America was suffering from severe economic dislocation as a result of the war in Europe, and that the United States had an obligation to replace Europe in Latin American markets. Secretary of the Treasury William G. McAdoo, another advocate of strong inter-American ties, stresses many of the same points in "The International High Commission and Pan American Cooperation," *The American Journal of International Law*, XI (1917), 772–89. Typical of Latin America's response to America's role in the war are Octavio N. Brito, *O Monroismo e a Sua Nova Phase* (Rio de Janeiro: Jornal do Comercio, 1918); Enrique Gil, *Evolución del Pan Americanismo* (Buenos Aires: Casa Editora de Jesus Menendez, 1933); and articles by C. Castro-Ruiz and F. Alonzo Pézet in *The American Political Science Review*, XI (1917), 217–38.

Secondary works on the postwar period tend to begin with the Harding administration and give only perfunctory attention to the last years of the Wilson administration. Gene Smith had an excellent idea when he decided to write *When the Cheering Stopped* (New York: Morrow, 1964), a book about Wilson's last years, but his dramatic sense overcomes his scholarship. We will have to wait until Arthur Link reaches the postwar period. Wesley Marvin Bagby, *The Road to Normalcy; the Presidential Campaign and Election of 1920* (Baltimore: The Johns Hopkins Press, 1962), analyzes the political events of 1920; John D. Hicks, *Rehearsal for Disaster* (Gainesville, Fla.: University of Florida Press, 1961), and Everett E. Hagen and Paul A. Samuelson, *After the War, 1918–1920* (Washington, D. C.: National Resources Planning Board, 1943), do the same for the sharp boom and recession of 1920–21. The impact of war on the United States' position in the world economy is described with greatest success by George Soule, *Prosperity Decade: From War to Depression, 1917–1929*, vol. VIII of *The Economic History of the United States* (New York: Rinehart and Company, 1947) and Joseph Dorfman, *The Economic Mind in American Civilization*, vol. IV, 1918–1932 (New York: Viking Press, 1959). Herbert Feis has some interesting observations in *The Changing Pattern of International Economic Affairs* (New York: Harper and Brothers, 1940), and *Europe: The World's Banker: 1870–1914* (New Haven: Yale University Press, 1930). An invaluable source for trade statistics during this period is the Department of Commerce Bureau of Foreign and Domestic Commerce, *Statistical Abstract of the United States* (Washington, D. C.: 1918–27).

Wilson's Mexican policy after the war has not as yet been the subject of a special study. Charles C. Cumberland, "The Jenkins Case and Mexican American Relations," *Hispanic American Historical Review*, XXXI (1951), 586–607, covers only one phase of a crisis in Mexican–United States relations. Background information is in Arthur Link's biography of Wilson; Clarence C. Clendenen, *The United States and Pancho Villa: A Study in Unconventional Diplomacy* (Ithaca, N. Y.: Cornell University Press, 1961); Robert E. Quirk, *An Affair of Honor: Woodrow Wilson and the Occupation of Vera Cruz* (Lexington, Ky.: University of Kentucky Press, 1962); Peter Calvert, *The Mexican Revolution, 1910–1914: The Diplomacy of Anglo-American Conflict* (Cambridge: At the University Press, 1968); and Kenneth J. Grieb, *The United States and Huerta* (Lincoln, Neb.: University of Nebraska Press, 1969). The Mexican side of the story is in Isidro Fabela, *Historia Diplomática de la Revolución Mexicana*, 2 vols. (Mexico: Fondo de Cultura Económica, 1958); Luis G. Zorilla, *Historia de las Relaciones Entre Mexico y los Estados Unidos de America, 1800–1958*, 2 vols. (Mexico: Editorial Porrua, 1965); and Adolfo Manero Suárez and José Paniagua Arredondo, *Los Tratados de Bucareli*, 2 vols. (Mexico: n.p., 1958). M. S. Alperovich and B. T. Rudenko, *La Revolución Mexicana de 1910–1917 y la política de los Estados Unidos* (Mexico: Fondo de Cultura Popular, 1960), is a Soviet contribution to the discussion.

Herbert J. Spinden, "Shall the United States Intervene in Cuba?," *The World's Week* (March 1921), 465–83; Dana G. Munro, "Pan-Americanism and the War," *The North American Review*, CCVIII (1918), 710–21; and Mark McChesney, "Latin America and the Monroe Doctrine," *Unpopular Review*, IX (1919), 97–111, are contemporary summaries of the issues confronting the Wilson administration. George W. Baker, Jr., "Woodrow Wilson's Use of Non-Recognition Policy in Costa Rica," *The Americas*, XXII (1965), 3–21, misses the change in policy after the war. Daniel Smith, "Bainbridge Colby and the Good Neighbor Policy, 1920–1921," *Mississippi Valley Historical Review,* L (1963), 56–78, does Colby a service by underlining his role in the formulation of policy.

Watt Stewart, "The Ratification of the Thomson-Urrutia Treaty," *The Southwestern Political and Social Science Quarterly,* X (1930), 416–28, throws light on the role of oil in international relations as do E. Taylor Parks, *Colombia and the United States, 1765–1934* (Durham, N. C.: Duke University Press, 1935), and J. Fred Rippy, *The Capitalists and Colombia* (New York: The Vanguard Press, 1931). Oil has stimulated a flow of books, good and bad. John A. DeNovo has done the most careful, recent research. His article, "The Movement for an Aggressive American Oil Policy Abroad, 1918–1920," *American Historical Review,* LXI (1956), 854–76, is very good; his monograph *American Interests and Policies in the Middle East, 1900–1939* (Minneapolis: University of Minnesota Press, 1963) puts the struggle for petroleum into proper world perspective, as do Gerald D. Nash, *United States Oil Policy, 1890–1964* (Pittsburgh: University of Pittsburgh Press, 1968); Herbert Feis, "Petroleum and American Foreign Policy," *Commodity Policy Studies,* No. 3 (Stanford, Cal.: Food Research Institute of Stanford University, 1944) and *Seen From E. A.* (New York: Alfred A. Knopf, 1947); and Leonard M. Fanning, *American Oil Operations Abroad* (New York: McGraw-Hill Company, 1947). The industry point of view is expressed in George S. Gibb and Evelyn H. Knowlton, *The Resurgent Years, 1911–1927* (New York: Harper and Brothers, 1956), and Harold F. Williamson *et al., The American Petroleum Industry: The Age of Energy, 1899–1959* (Evanston, Ill.: Northwestern University Press, 1963). Charles W. Hamilton, *Americans and Oil in the Middle East* (Houston: Gulf Refining Company, 1962), is propaganda. A new book, Lorenzo Meyer, *México y Estados Unidos En el Conflicto Petrolero (1917–1942)* (Mexico: El Colegio de Mexico, 1968), includes material from Mexican archives.

There are a number of older books on petroleum which are still of interest to the scholar because they convey the intensity of Anglo-American competition for control of the petroleum resources of the world and American fears. In some cases the titles indicate the nature of the book: E. H. Davenport and Sidney Russell Cooke, *The Oil Trusts and Anglo-American Relations* (New York: The Macmillan Company, 1924); Ludwell Denny, *America Conquers Britain* (New York: Alfred A. Knopf, 1930); and *We Fight for Oil* (New York: Alfred A. Knopf, 1928); Louis Fischer, *Oil Imperialism* (New York: International Publishers, 1926); Anton Mohr, *The Oil War* (New York: Harcourt, Brace and Company, 1926); and John Ise, *The United States Oil Policy* (New Haven: Yale University Press, 1926). Rather different perspectives are offered in Camilo Barcia Trelles, *El Imperialismo del Petroleo y La Paz Mundial* (Valladolid: Universidad de Valladolid, 1925); and Pierre l'Espagnol de la Tramerye, *The World Struggle for Oil*, trans. C. Leonard Leese (New York: Alfred A. Knopf, 1924).

The economic moguls of the period have not been well served by biographers. Men whose accomplishments indicate exciting personalities, appear dull in their own memoirs, as in Sir Henri Deterding, *An International Oilman* (London: Ivor Nicholson and Watson, 1934), or in turgid official biographies, such as John Rowland and Basil, Second Baron Cadman, *Ambassador for Oil, the Life of John, First Baron Cadman* (London: Herbert Jenkins, 1960), and J. A. Spender, *Weetman Pearson, First Viscount Cowdray* (London: Cassell and Company, 1930). At the other extreme, they are made into inhuman monsters by muckrackers like Harvey O'Conner in *Mellon's Millions* (New York: Blue Ribbon Books, 1933); *The Guggenheims* (New York: Covici-Friede, 1937); or Glyn Roberts, *The Most Powerful Man in the World* (New York: Covici-Friede, 1938), a study of Deterding. Ralph Hewins, *Mr. Five Per Cent* (London: Hutchinson and Company, 1957), is a fascinating story of a fantastic individual, Calouste Gulbenkian, the man who engineered the formation of the Royal Dutch-Shell and the Iraq Petroleum consortium; but the book contains little information about Latin America. Harold Nicholson, *Dwight Morrow* (New York: Harcourt, Brace and Company, 1935), is a bad book by a good historian.

The general situation in submarine cables from the British point of view is in F. J. Brown, *The Cable and Wireless Communications of the World* (London: Sir Isaac Pitman and Sons, 1927). Brown was the chief British delegate to the preliminary communications conference in 1920. International conventions on all kinds of communications are summarized in Keith Clark, *International Communications—The American Attitude* (New York: Columbia University Press, 1931), which also attempts to describe the unusual split in the United States between private enterprise and government over responsibility in the field of international communications. The question of cables in the Pacific area is covered well by Leslie Bennett Tribolet, *The International Aspects of Electrical Communications in the Pacific Area* (Baltimore: The Johns Hopkins Press, 1929), which is more comprehensive than the title suggests, and by two memoranda published by the Institute of Pacific Relations, *Memorandum on Cable Communications in the Pacific*, No. 16 (September 1, 1932), and *Memorandum on Radio Communications in the Pacific*, No. 23 (December 15, 1932). The fight with Western Union is in United States Senate Subcommittee of the Committee on Interstate Commerce, Hearings on Cable-Landing Licenses, S. 4301, 66 Cong., 3rd Sess. (Washington, D. C.: Government Printing Office, 1921), and Department of Commerce, Bureau of Foreign and Domestic Commerce, *International Communications and the International Telegraph Convention* (Washington, D. C.: Government Printing Office, 1923).

There is little writing on the international organizations of this period that adds to our understanding of United States policy toward Latin America. Warren H. Kelchner, *Latin American Relations with the League of Nations* (Boston: World Peace Foundation, 1930), is a superficial examination. Ignacio Calderón, "The Pan American Union and the Monroe Doctrine," *Journal of International Relations,* X (1919), 133–37, is typical of Latin American comments on the Monroe Doctrine vis-à-vis the League of Nations Covenant. Two contemporary articles on the Inter-American High Commission never go beyond formal statement and superficial generalities: Percy Alvin Martin, "Notes and Comment: The Second Pan American Financial Conference," *Hispanic American Historical Review,* III (1920), 202–13; and John Bassett Moore, "The Pan American Financial Conferences and the Inter-American High Commission," *The American Journal of International Law,* XIV (1920), 343–55.

One of the most pressing questions at the end of the war was how the United States economy would fare. Most contemporary businessmen were optimistic. They urged the government to end its control over crucial sectors of the economy in order to release the energies for continued economic expansion. *The Annals* devotes an entire issue to this problem, *International Economics,* vol. LXXXIII (May 1919), with articles by William B. Colver, Burwell S. Cutler, Grosvenor M. Jones, L. F. Schmeckeiber, J. Russell Smith, and Edward D. Trowbridge. Within a year, businessmen had become more aggressive champions of international trade and investment. Nearly half of a special issue of *The Annals, Bonds and the Bond Market,* vol. LXXXVIII (March 1920), emphasizes the need to invest in foreign securities. The issue contains bullish articles by William S. Kies, Thomas W. Lamont, Hastings Lyon, Arthur J. Rosenthal, and James Sheldon. Lamont has another article on the same subject "Capital Needs of Foreign Trade," in an earlier issue of *The Annals, The New American Thrift,* vol. LXXXVII (January 1920), pp. 100–105. In 1921, yet another issue of *The Annals* is devoted to the problems facing the United States in international trade and to the need for government support, *The International Trade Situation,* vol. XCIV (March 1921). Henry R. Mussey, "The New Normal in Foreign Trade," *Political Science Quarterly,* XXXVII (1922), 369–88, is very perceptive. Frank O'Malley,

Our South American Trade and Its Financing (New York: The National City Bank, 1920), is a technical handbook for the prospective entrepreneur doing business in Latin America.

The views of the business community and the activities of United States companies abroad can be gleaned from the files of the *Wall Street Journal* and the New York *Journal of Commerce and Commercial Bulletin.* The business press kept a close watch on events in Mexico, particularly as they affected the petroleum industry. Industry journals convey the petroleum companies' attitude toward United States government policy and report their activities in foreign markets. The Tulsa *Oil and Gas Journal;* Standard Oil's *Bulletin;* and the *Petroleum Times* of London are the most useful.

The public press gave very little space to Latin America from 1917 to 1925. Aside from events in Mexico, nothing in Latin America held the public interest for any length of time. A congressional investigation in 1922 of the occupations of Haiti and the Dominican Republic, and the discussion of the disoccupation of Nicaragua, were the only political crises during the period that provoked much press comment. Samples of public opinion on these issues reveal apathy. A sampling of newspapers might include the *New York Times,* because of its complete coverage and its invaluable index; the *New York World,* which tried to be a spokesman for the Wilson administration; the *Chicago Tribune,* a vehicle for William Randolph Hearst's outspoken views on foreign policy; the *Washington Post* for its views of happenings within the government; and the *Boston Evening Transcript,* for its conservative internationalism. The *Atlanta Constitution, San Francisco Examiner,* and *St. Louis Post-Dispatch* offer opinion in different parts of the country. The *New York Tribune* and the *Christian Science Monitor* are good sources of international views, as are the *Literary Digest,* a weekly, and *Current Opinion,* a monthly.

Although the primary sources are best for a description of the situation in the Department of State during the transition between administrations, there are several secondary works which are helpful. Lawrence E. Gelfand, *The Inquiry* (New Haven: Yale University Press, 1963), deals with the department indirectly, but effectively. Four studies of the State Department and the Foreign Service cover longer periods and give a good deal of attention to the Rogers Act of 1924; William Barnes and John H. Morgan, *The Foreign Service of the United States* (Washington, D. C.: Bureau of Public Affairs, Department of State, 1961); Bertram D. Hulen, *Inside the Department of State* (New York: Whittlesey House, 1939); Warren Frederick Ilchman, *Professional Diplomacy in the United States, 1779–1939* (Chicago: University of Chicago Press, 1961); and Graham H. Stuart, *The Department of State* (New York: Macmillan, 1949). A contemporary study, Tracy Hollingsworth Lay, *The Foreign Service of the United States* (New York: Prentice Hall, 1925), is an unabashed argument in favor of the State Department in the struggle with the Commerce Department for control over the foreign relations of the United States. Dexter Perkins, "The Department of State and American Public Opinion," in Gordon Craig and Felix Gilbert, eds., *The Diplomats, 1919–1929* (Princeton, N. J.: Princeton University Press, 1953), 282–308, asserts that the State Department operated only within the strict limits set by American public opinion. The most detailed work on the "family" of diplomats and government officials is Waldo H. Heinrichs, Jr., "The Establishment of the American Foreign Service," an unpublished paper dated March 6, 1963, most of which is incorporated in his *American Ambassador; Joseph C. Grew and the Development of United States Diplomatic Traditions* (Boston: Little, Brown, 1966).

General surveys of the Harding administration and the 1920s rarely give Latin America and Latin American policy more than perfunctory attention. Three that try to fit Latin American policy into the broader framework of foreign policy during the 1920s are: John D. Hicks, *Republican Ascendancy, 1919–1933* (New York: Harper and Brothers, 1960); William E. Leuchtenburg, *The Perils of Prosperity, 1914–1932* (Chicago: University of Chicago Press, 1958); and L. Ethan Ellis, *Republican Foreign Policy, 1921–1933* (New Brunswick, N. J.: Rutgers University Press, 1968). Special studies which deal with aspects of Caribbean policy during this period are: Virginia L. Greer, "State Department Policy in Regard to the Nicaragua Election of 1924," *Hispanic American Historical Review*, XXXIV (1954), 445–67; "Charles Evans Hughes and Nicaragua, 1921–1925," unpublished Ph.D. dissertation, University of New Mexico, 1954; Marvin Goldwert, "The Constabulary in the Dominican Republic and Nicaragua," *Latin American Monographs*, 17 (Gainesville, Fla.: University of Florida School of Inter-American Studies, 1961); Robert Debs Heinl, Jr., *Soldiers of the Sea* (Annapolis: United States Naval Institute, 1962); Joseph Robert Juárez, "United States Withdrawal from Santo Domingo," *Hispanic American Historical Review*, XLII (1962), 152–90; James B. McKenna, "The Role of the United States Marine Corps in the Intervention and Occupation of Haiti, 1915–1934" (unpublished paper, 1962); and Walter H. Pesner, "American Marines in Haiti, 1915–1922," *The Americas*, XX (1964), 231–66. Heinl, McKenna, and Pesner discuss the military problems of the United States protectorates in the Caribbean and how those military problems led to political difficulties.

Of the broader studies of individual protectorates, those that have information on the postwar period include: William Kamman, *A Search for Stability. United States Diplomacy Toward Nicaragua, 1925–1933* (Notre Dame, Ind.: University of Notre Dame Press, 1968); Neill Macaulay, *The Sandino Affair* (Chicago: Quadrangle Books, 1967); Ludwell Lee Montague, *Haiti and the United States, 1714–1938* (Durham, N. C.: Duke University Press, 1940); Russell H. Fitzgibbon, *Cuba and the United States, 1900–1935* (Menasha, Wisc.: The Collegiate Press, 1935); *Leland H. Jenks, Our Cuban Colony* (New York: Vanguard Press, 1928); Robert F. Smith, *The United States and Cuba: Business and Diplomacy, 1917–1960* (New York: Bookman Associates, 1960). Considering the documents available when it was written, Jenks's book is remarkably sensitive to the changes in Cuban policy after the war and during the period of Crowder's mission in the early 1920s. Chester Lloyd Jones, "Loan Controls in the Caribbean," *Hispanic American Historical Review,* XIV (1934), 141–62, is an excellent summary of United States financial methods in the Caribbean Danger Zone; James C. Carey, *Peru and the United States, 1900–1962* (Notre Dame, Ind.: University of Notre Dame Press, 1964), is very spotty. Far more interesting is James Ferrer, Jr., "United States-Argentine Economic Relations," unpublished Ph.D. dissertation, University of California, Berkeley, 1964.

Latin American hostility to American imperialism is evident wherever one turns in contemporary journals and books. Cubans, Haitians, and Dominicans kept up a constant barrage of criticism published at home, in Spain, or in friendly journals around Latin America. Take as examples: Cosme de la Torriente, *Cuba y los Estados Unidos* (Havana: Rambla, Bouza y Cia, 1929); Tulio M. Cestero, *Estados Unidos y las Antillas* (Madrid: Compañía Ibero-Americana de Publicaciones, 1931); and articles by Enrique José Varona and Antonio Escobar published in the *Revista de Filosofía* (Buenos Aires), 14 (1921), 311–13, and 15 (1922), 472–76.

The literature on the economic activities of the period is much richer than the literature on formal diplomacy or international politics, and yet, it too, is still a subject about which we know very little. Most studies are only exploratory. Joseph Brandes, *Herbert Hoover and Economic Diplomacy* (Pittsburgh: University of Pittsburgh Press, 1962), merely whets the appetite for more information on Hoover. The secretary of commerce played such an important role in the international relations of the United States that it may take several scholars to mine the riches of the Department of Commerce Records and the Hoover papers, which were restricted when this study was written. Alexander DeConde,

Herbert Hoover's Latin American Policy (Stanford, Calif.: Stanford University Press, 1951), is official history devoted largely to Hoover's presidency. Dorfman, *Economic Mind,* and Soule, *Prosperity Decade,* are excellent introductions to the entire period. Oil and politics under Harding are discussed in the following: Edward Meade Earle, "Oil and American Policy," *The New Republic,* Aug. 20, 1924; Burl Noggle, *Teapot Dome: Oil and Politics in the 1920s* (Baton Rouge: Louisiana State University Press, 1962); and J. Fred Rippy, "The United States and Colombian Oil," *Foreign Policy Association Information Service,* vol. V (April 3, 1929).

Herbert Feis, *The Diplomacy of the Dollar-First Era, 1919–1932* (Baltimore: The Johns Hopkins Press, 1950), focuses on two different economic problems, the Statement on Loans of March 3, 1922, and the struggle for oil in the Near East, both of which were crucial in the formulation of foreign policy. Arthur P. Whitaker, "From Dollar Diplomacy to the Good Neighbor Policy," *Inter-American Economic Affairs,* IV (1950), 12–19, takes issue with Feis by emphasizing the similarities between diplomacy of the dollar and dollar diplomacy. Benjamin Gerig, *The Open Door and the Mandate System* (London: George Allen and Unwin, 1930), combines politics and economics. Two earlier studies which consider finance as a part of foreign policy are: James W. Angell, *Financial Foreign Policy of the United States* (New York: Council on Foreign Relations, 1933), and James W. Gantenbein, *Financial Questions in United States Foreign Policy* (New York: Columbia University Press, 1939). Ilse Mintz, *Deterioration in the Quality of Foreign Bonds Issued in the United States, 1920–1930* (New York: National Bureau of Economic Research, 1951), and Charles Cortez Abbott, *The New York Bond Market, 1920–1930* (Cambridge: Harvard University Press, 1937), are technical studies of great value. Max Winkler, *Foreign Bonds: An Autopsy* (Philadelphia: Roland Swain Company, 1933), is less objective but includes some useful case studies of loans to Latin American nations. Brown Brothers and Company, *Foreign Dollar Bonds* (New York: Brown Brothers and Company, 1928), is a listing of dollar bonds sold on the New York market.

Data on United States investments in Latin America have to be collected from various sources. Among the secondary works dealing with this controversial subject are: Robert W. Dunn, *American Foreign Investments* (New York: B. W. Huebsch and The Viking Press, 1926); Willy Feuerlain and Elizabeth Hannan, *Dollars in Latin America* (New York: Council on Foreign Relations, 1941); M. F. Jolliffe, *The United States as a Financial Centre, 1919–1933* (Cardiff: University of Wales Press Board,

1935); Cleona Lewis, *America's Stake in International Investments* (Washington, D. C.: The Brookings Institution, 1938); Clyde William Phelps, *The Foreign Expansion of American Banks* (New York: The Ronald Press Company, 1927); Dudley Maynard Phelps, *Migration of Industry to South America* (New York: McGraw-Hill, 1936); J. Fred Rippy, *British Investments in Latin America, 1822–1949* (Minneapolis: University of Minnesota Press, 1959); Benjamin H. Williams, *Economic Foreign Policy of the United States* (New York: McGraw-Hill, 1929); and Max Winkler, *Investments of United States Capital in Latin America* (Boston: World Peace Foundation, 1929). J. Fred Rippy, "Diplomatic Protection of American Investors Abroad," *Foreign Policy Association, Information Service,* vol. III (April 1927), discusses the extent to which the United States government was willing to defend private interests abroad. Some works on the United States economy contain bits of information on foreign trade and investment. They include: Charles C. Chapman, *The Development of American Business and Banking Thought, 1913–1936* (London: Longmans, Green, 1936); George Mygatt Fisk and Paul S. Peirce, *International Commercial Policy* (New York: Macmillan, 1923); William J. Kemnitzer, *Rebirth of Monopoly* (New York: Harper and Brothers, 1938); Harry W. Laidler, *Concentration of Control in American Industry* (New York: Thomas Y. Crowell Company, 1931); and H. Parker Willis and Jules I. Bogan, *Investment Banking,* rev. ed. (New York: Harper and Brothers, 1936). Margaret A. Marsh, *The Bankers in Bolivia* (New York: The Vanguard Press, 1928); and J. Fred Rippy, *The Capitalists and Colombia* (New York: The Vanguard Press, 1931) are studies of United States investment in individual countries in Latin America.

Contemporary comment on United States investment in Latin America was very critical of what it considered the aggressive stance of the United States government in defending private interests abroad. Examples of the critical literature are: Scott Nearing and Joseph Freeman, *Dollar Diplomacy* (New York: B. W. Huebsch and The Viking Press, 1925); Robert Morss Lovett, "American Foreign Policy: A Progressive View," *Foreign Affairs,* vol. III (September 1924); and David Y. Thomas, "Foreign Investments and the Attitude of the State Department," *The Southwestern Political and Social Science Quarterly,* VII (1926), 101–15. Naturally, the financial press encouraged government support of private enterprise, and government officials published statements defending the government. See, for example, Julius Klein, "Economic Rivalries in Latin America," *Foreign Affairs,* III (1924), 236–43, and *Frontiers of Trade* (New York: The Century Company, 1929). Klein was chief of the Bureau of Foreign and Do-

mestic Commerce when Hoover was secretary of commerce. Two
contemporary comments which are notable for their objectivity
and thoughtful suggestions are: Abraham Berglund, "The Tariff
Act of 1922," and Henry Bruère, "Constructive versus Dollar
Diplomacy," both in *The American Economic Review,* XIII
(1923), 14–33 and 68–76, respectively.

Index

273

DATE DUE